W9-AMP-558
Easy Homemade
Cookie Cookbook

# Easy Homemade Cookie COOKBOOK

Simple Recipes for the Best Chocolate Chip Cookies, Brownies, Christmas Treats, and Other American Favorites

MIRANDA COUSE

ROCKRIDGE PRESS

For general information on our other products and services or to obtain technical support, please contact our Customer Care Department within the United States at (866) 744-2665, or outside the United States at (510) 253-0500.

Rockridge Press publishes its books in a variety of electronic and print formats. Some content that appears in print may not be available in electronic books, and vice versa.



ISBN: Print 978-1-62315-979-5
eBook 978-1-62315-980-1

For my husband & son,
my two favorite
cookie monsters.

# CONTENTS

## New Classics 43

## Shortbread, Slice 'n' Bakes, and Cut-Out Cookies 75

## Sandwich Cookies, Whoopie Pies, Thumbprints, and Macaroons 121

## Christmas and Other Holiday Cookies 173

## 7 Brownies and Bars 225

# Introduction

### WHO DOESN'T LOVE COOKIES?

The heat from the oven warms the house and heart alike as the delicious smells drift from room to room to those with mouths watering and tummies rumbling in anticipation. As a little girl, it was this excitement that had me scrambling my words as I joyfully yelled for "chocolate cooked chippies." Okay, maybe it still happens from time to time.

Some of my favorite childhood memories, and what gave me my first real interest in taking this baking journey, were of helping my mom make cookies. Needless to say, as a working mother who was teaching her young daughter to bake, she wasn't using exotic recipes with several-hour prep times. Nope, these were simple and practical recipes that worked every time and always pleased.

When I became a stay-at-home mom, I found myself with a little extra time and a yearning for a creative outlet. Being a longtime Food Network binge watcher, a lifelong baker, and a generally creative sort, I felt confident enough to jump into the blogging world to share my recipes and build my own portfolio on my blog, *Cookie Dough and Oven Mitt*.

My blog-related cookie explorations have led me to put ingredients into recipes that I would never have dreamed of as a child (and that make my mom question my sanity). Writing the blog has taught not only me, but also my readers, many good lessons about baking. For instance, I've learned that more isn't always better. No matter how much you love an ingredient, or how pretty it is, if you go overboard with it you'll ruin your recipe. And sometimes a flavor that works great as a stand-alone, such as cotton candy or bubble gum, just doesn't translate well into a cookie.

As with any learning experience, especially in the baking world, there have been successes and failures—and some downright disasters. (Some members of my family might still be inebriated after a particular rum cake.) Choosing to become a dessert blogger and bake for a career has given me the opportunity and luxury to experiment and step out of my comfort zone, but as a busy mother myself, I still crave those simple, never-fail recipes that can be turned out with the basic items I always have in my pantry. Because, let it be known, my picky-eater husband and six-year-old son want—no, *need*—those warm, tasty cookies right now!

And that is where my baking really began, with my family. Like many other bakers before me, I thrive on family, friends, and even strangers enjoying my recipes. It gives me a feeling of satisfaction and accomplishment. What do my two guys like? Cookies, of course! I want to make them cookies that are unique and fun, but still within their flavor comfort zones. And the recipes have to be relatable to my loyal blog followers, too. I'm not afraid to take the idea of a classic dessert and turn it into a cookie. If I try out a new recipe and it gets both a thumbs-up from my husband and an "It's good, Mama!" from my son, I know I've done my job and that the recipe is blog-worthy.

In this book, you'll find more than 150 recipes for homemade cookies. I've made sure every recipe is easy and fun to make. The ingredients are common items that are affordable and easy to find in your local supermarket—and may already be in your pantry. I've kept prep times short, because I know how busy life can be. Finally, the recipes don't require any complicated or expensive equipment. If you've got a mixing bowl, a wooden spoon, and a cookie sheet or baking pan, you'll be able to make just about every recipe in this book. A few inexpensive items—like cookie cutters and cookie scoops—will give you the ability to make all sorts of fun cookies with ease.

Here you'll find traditional drop cookies like Old-Fashioned Chocolate Chip Cookies (page 21) and Snickerdoodles (page 19), but you'll also find unusual variations like Banana Bread Cookies (page 36) and Apple-Cinnamon Cookies (page 35), and "new classics" like Salted Caramel–Chocolate Chip Cookies (page 58), Creamsicle Drops (page 45), and Cookies and Cream Pudding Cookies (page 67).

Chapter 4, Shortbread, Slice 'n' Bakes, and Cut-Out Cookies, features standards like Classic Sugar Cookies (page 103) and Lemon Shortbread Cookies (page 86), along with creative offerings like Cinnamon Roll Slice 'n' Bake Cookies (page 98) and Sweet Tea Shortbread Cookies (page 82). Chapter 5, Sandwich Cookies, Whoopie Pies, Thumbprints, and Macaroons, features everything from homemade Chocolate Sandwich Cookies (page 122) with creamy white frosting in the middle, to Funfetti Whoopie Pies (page 144). There's also an entire chapter devoted to holiday-themed and decorated cookies that includes treats like Peppermint Candy Swirl Cookies (page 182) for Christmas and Creepy Eyeballs (page 206) for Halloween. And because sometimes you want something a bit more than a cookie, there's a whole chapter on other American favorites like Classic Brownies (page 228), Butterscotch Pudding Cookie Bars (page 241), and Piña Colada Bars (page 258).

I know this book will help you create some of your favorite cookies, and I hope you'll also discover some new favorites. But even more than that, I hope these easy recipes will show you what treasures can be made with simple ingredients. And I hope you get as much enjoyment from these cookie recipes as I do.

Classic Sugar Cookies, *page 103*

# Easy Essentials to Get Started

I'm going to show you how to step up your cookie game with unique flavor combinations that you can get from easily available ingredients. You'll learn how to turn regular butter into brown butter, fill cookies with surprises, and add pudding mixes to doughs for unique sweets. There are plenty of innovative ideas and cookie classics to please the most discerning cookie lovers.

As far as equipment goes, I'm setting aside my stand mixer and food processor because they're just not essential for these recipes. Get out your handheld electric mixer or even just a trusted wooden spoon, plus a cookie sheet—we won't need much of anything else!

# Simple Ingredients

Since these cookie recipes require just a few ingredients, it's important that you buy the best—like high-quality butter and pure vanilla extract. If you haven't used those tins or jars of spices within the last six months, replace them with fresh ones.

If you're a cookie baker like me, then keep the basic staples—flour, sugar, butter, flavorings, nuts, chocolate chips—in your pantry and your refrigerator or freezer so that you can make cookies whenever you want. That way you'll never have to panic when you suddenly realize that you need a sweet treat for your child's bake sale or a potluck lunch at work.

**FLOUR** Two types of flour are used in these cookies: all-purpose flour and cake flour. Bread flour, self-rising flour, and whole-wheat flour are not good substitutes for all-purpose and/or cake flour.

If you don't have commercial cake flour on hand, it's easy to make your own: Remove 2 tablespoons from a level cup of all-purpose flour and replace it with 2 tablespoons of cornstarch.

Flour adds stability and structure to cookies. What determines whether a cookie is a drop cookie or a cut-out cookie is the flour-to-wet-ingredients ratio. For example, if you want to make shortbread or cut-out cookies, you'll add more flour than wet ingredients, making a crumbly texture. For drop cookies, the flour-to-wet-ingredients ratio would be more or less equal depending on whether you want a chewy or crumbly cookie. Brownies require the least amount of flour, because the batter is very loose and is made up of mostly wet ingredients.

**BAKING SODA & BAKING POWDER** Baking soda and baking powder are leaveners, or rising agents. In other words, they're what make cookies and other baked goods puff up as they bake. Baking soda is most commonly used when an acid is already incorporated into the recipe. Buttermilk, lemon juice, honey, and vanilla are all acids that are commonly found in cookies. When the recipe doesn't contain any acidic ingredients, baking powder is used. That's because baking powder is simply baking soda with a dry acid incorporated into it.

**SALT** Salt is a flavor enhancer that turns a good cookie into an excellent cookie. Salt helps brings out the sweetness, cuts any bitterness, and balances the flavors in a cookie. I recommend table salt for most baking recipes because it is fine-grained and distributes throughout a batter well. If you are using salt to sprinkle on top of baked goods, as for a salted caramel cookie, coarse sea salt is a good choice because its larger grains will provide a nice salty crunch.

**BUTTER** Butter provides flavor and moisture and coats the proteins in flour to yield tender cookies. Butter has a lower melting point than vegetable shortening, so it makes a thinner, crispier cookie.

I use unsalted butter in my recipes, because I prefer to add salt to the dry ingredients. When a recipe calls for room-temperature butter, that means you should be able to leave an indentation in the butter by pressing on it lightly with your index finger. Remove the butter from the refrigerator and allow it to sit out for 30 minutes to an hour to come to room temperature. If the butter has been in the freezer, it will take 3 to 4 hours to come to room temperature.

**MILK** Milk is used to make frostings and icings, and in some dough or crust recipes. For the recipes in this book, any type of milk (whole, reduced-fat, low-fat, or nonfat) will work fine. The richer the milk, the richer the result, obviously, but in many cases, you are adding only a tablespoon or two, so it won't make a huge difference.

I also use buttermilk in many recipes. Commercially produced cultured buttermilk is cows' milk that has been homogenized and pasteurized and then inoculated with a culture that gives it the traditional sour flavor. If you don't have buttermilk, you can make your own by adding 1 tablespoon of lemon juice or white vinegar to 1 scant cup of milk and letting it sit for 5 to 10 minutes, until it thickens and curdles.

**SUGAR** While sugar provides sweetness, this essential ingredient also affects whether the cookies will be thin or thick, crispy or chewy.

Three kinds of sugar—granulated (white), brown (light and dark), and confectioners' (powdered)—are used in these recipes. The

## Fat Substitutions

**MARGARINE & SHORTENING** can sometimes be substituted for butter. Margarine is made from various types of vegetable oil, with water and other ingredients added, which means that its fat content varies. If you choose to use margarine, use one with a high fat percentage (preferably 80 percent or higher). Margarines that are lower in fat contain more water, which will result in more spreading of your cookies. Margarine provides fat, but it is not as flavorful as butter.

Shortening offers absolutely no flavor unless you buy the butter-flavored variety, but even that doesn't compare to real butter. I sometimes combine butter and shortening when making cookies. Why? Shortening is made from vegetable oil that is processed to be solid and contains no water. It has a higher melting point than either butter or margarine, which means that it won't melt as quickly as the cookie dough bakes, so you get cookies that hold their shape better. By combining the two, you get the textural advantages of shortening while still retaining the rich flavor of butter.

most common is granulated sugar. Using granulated sugar in a cookie recipe will yield flatter, crispier cookies.

Brown sugar is granulated sugar with molasses added. Light versus dark refers to the amount of molasses in the sugar. Using brown sugar in cookies makes them dense, moist, and chewy. It also gives the cookies a deep, round flavor.

Lastly, confectioners' sugar is simply granulated sugar that has been ground to a powder with some cornstarch added. The cornstarch prevents the cookies from spreading during baking, resulting in a softer, more tender cookie than you get by using granulated sugar.

**EGGS** Eggs are the glue that hold cookies together, providing structure and moisture. In recipes that require separated eggs, the yolks provide richness while the whites impart a dry, cakey texture. Large eggs are used in all my recipes.

**VANILLA EXTRACT AND OTHER FLAVORINGS** While alcohol-based vanilla extract adds its own uniqueness to cookies, it also enhances other flavors, like chocolate. Always use pure vanilla extract rather than imitation! Trust me, I grew up on imitation and once you get that pure extract, it will open your eyes to a flavorful new world. I use other extracts throughout the book, such as raspberry or orange, too.

I also use flavor emulsions, like red velvet emulsion, cream cheese emulsion, and butter vanilla emulsion. Unlike extracts, emulsions are water-based rather than alcohol-based. The intensity of the emulsion is the same as extracts, but is does not evaporate as quickly. I particularly like using the red velvet emulsion because it provides flavor as well as that intense red color.

**FOOD COLORING** There are many products available to color cookies, cakes, and icings. They range from water-based synthetic food coloring to dyes derived from natural ingredients, plus gels, pastes, and powders. The most common, and therefore the easiest to find, are synthetic liquid food coloring and gel paste food coloring, so those are what I use throughout these recipes.

Gel paste food coloring is a thick gel that usually comes in a little tub or pot. The gel is very thick and the color is intense. These are especially useful when you want to achieve deep, rich colors without adding a lot of liquid to your recipe. I prefer to use gel paste food coloring whenever possible. It can be found in some supermarkets, cake decorating or craft shops (such as Michaels), or ordered online. A toothpick is a great tool to use for mess-free application. Scoop up a small blob with the end of the toothpick and add it to your dough, batter, or icing. Start with a small amount, since you can always add more as needed.

I call for gel paste food coloring in the recipes that use food coloring, but you can always substitute the liquid if you can't find the gel paste. Liquid food coloring is widely available—you can get it in any grocery store—but the color is less intense, and if you use too much, it can change the texture.

## Fresh-Baked Cookies on Demand

**NEED A COOKIE FIX**, but don't want an entire batch tempting you from the counter? Scoop out the dough and place the scoops onto a parchment or wax paper-lined cookie sheet (they can be close together, but not touching) and place in the freezer for several hours. Once frozen, transfer the frozen balls of dough to a freezer-safe plastic bag and store in the freezer for up to 3 months. You can bake the cookies straight from the freezer according to the original baking instructions, but they may need an additional minute or two of baking.

Liquid food coloring usually comes in small squeeze bottles. To use, simply squeeze a few drops into your batter, dough, or icing.

**CHOCOLATE** There are so many forms of chocolate—chips, bars, and cocoa powder—that can be used in cookies. Let's start with chocolate chips, which are made with chocolate and stabilizers and are designed not to melt. (Have you noticed that even when they're soft and gooey, they still hold their shape?) The most common chocolate chip is semisweet, but there are also bittersweet, milk chocolate, white, butterscotch, and peanut butter flavors.

Baking chocolate bars come in unsweetened, bittersweet, and semisweet varieties. Bars can be melted for use in dense, fudgy cookies, or chopped and folded into dough in place of chocolate chips.

Unsweetened cocoa powder gives cookies a rich chocolate flavor. It's easily mixed into the dough with the dry ingredients. My go-to brand is Hershey's.

**NUTS** Nuts can be hit or miss in cookies and brownies for people—some people love them, while others either can't stand them or are allergic to them. Nuts are optional in all of the recipes here except for those, like Peanut Butter Cookies (page 30) or Pecan Pie Bars (page 240), where nuts are central to the recipe.

Peanuts, pecans, walnuts, almonds, and macadamia nuts are the most common nuts used in cookies. Pistachios may be used occasionally as well. Whenever possible, purchase nuts still in their shells to ensure freshness. The next best option is to buy whole, shelled nuts and chop them yourself. I do buy nuts already chopped or sliced, either for a shortcut or because they suit the recipe better, as in my Monster Cookie Sandwiches (page 200), where sliced almonds make the perfect "teeth."

Always store nuts in an airtight container because they can pick up other odors, which makes them taste unpleasant or rancid. Keep them in a cool, dark place in the cupboard for up to 6 months, in the refrigerator for up to 9 months, or in the freezer for a year or more.

# Basic Equipment

One of the reasons cookies are my favorite go-to baked goods is that they don't require a lot of equipment. All you need to make the cookies in this book are the following items.

## MUST HAVES

**COOKIE SHEETS** Rimless cookie sheets make it easy to slide the cookies right off without having to maneuver around hot sides with a spatula. Cookie sheets also help circulate air in the oven for even baking. I use 14-by-18-inch cookie sheets, but a 13-by-18-inch rimmed half-sheet pan is a good substitute. To help preserve your cookie sheets, and for easy cleanup, line the cookie sheets with parchment paper before baking.

When baking cookies, I recommend using two cookie sheets, but only baking one sheet at a time. This way you can set up the next batch on one sheet while the first is in the oven. The first sheet will then have time to cool by the time the second sheet comes out. By baking them one sheet at a time, they will bake evenly without having to be moved around during baking.

**BAKING PANS** Deep-sided 11-by-7-inch and 9-by-13-inch baking pans are used for bar cookies. I line them with parchment paper and leave overhangs on two sides of the pan to use as "handles" to pull out the bars to be cut once they are cooled. Parchment paper also makes for easy cleanup and prevents knives or metal spatulas from scratching your pans.

**BROWNIE PAN** I use an 8-inch square baking pan for my brownie recipes. I use the same parchment paper trick as above to line the pans, which makes it easy to pull out the brownies before slicing them.

**MEASURING CUPS & SPOONS** Since baking is based on accurate measurements, measuring cups and spoons are absolutely essential. Please don't try to just eyeball the ingredients! You will need two types of measuring cups. First, a 1- or 2-cup liquid measuring cup that is made of glass or plastic with graduated lines along the side. Second, a set of dry measuring cups (¼ cup, ⅓ cup, ½ cup, and 1 cup) designed to be filled to the rim with dry ingredients and leveled off. Additionally, you'll need a set of measuring spoons (⅛ teaspoon, ¼ teaspoon, ½ teaspoon, 1 teaspoon, and 1 tablespoon).

When measuring dry ingredients such as flour, spoon the ingredient into the measuring cup so that it is heaped and then use the back of a butter knife to scrape off the excess. This provides a more accurate measurement than pouring and then using your hand to remove the excess, which can compact extra flour in the cup.

**WIRE COOLING RACKS** A wire rack allows air to circulate so that all sides of your cookies cool at the same rate. Transfer cookies from the cookie sheet to a wire rack about 5 minutes after they come out of the oven to prevent further baking and to accelerate cooling.

## NICE-TO-HAVES

**SIFTER** A sifter is handy for sifting flour and other dry ingredients together after measuring them to ensure that they are well blended and lump free. If you don't have a sifter, you can use a fine-mesh sieve instead. Combine the dry ingredients in the sieve over a mixing bowl and gently tap the side of the sieve until all the powder has fallen through into the bowl. You can also use a wire whisk to give the dry ingredients a good whisking in the bowl before adding them to the wet ingredients.

**HANDHELD ELECTRIC MIXER** Many of the recipes in this book can be made without an electric mixer, using just a wooden spoon, but a simple handheld electric mixer certainly makes the job easier. For most recipes, I've given instructions for either an electric mixer or a wooden spoon.

**STAND MIXER** A stand mixer is a wonderful tool that makes mixing up cookie dough easy, but it is by no means essential. It can be used to cream butter and sugar even when the butter is cold, and it makes easy work of large batches of cookie dough. It's also great for making things like meringue or buttercream frosting that require long beating times, since you can set the machine and use your hands for other tasks.

**ROLLING PIN** There are two common types of rolling pins. The French rolling pin is tapered on either end, while the traditional American rolling pin is a long cylinder with two handles. The French rolling pin is light and has more pressure control. It's great for rolling out pie crust and pastry.

The traditional American rolling pin is probably the most familiar to all of us and considered an all-purpose rolling pin. It's commonly made of hardwood and is heavier than a French rolling pin, which means you need to use less pressure and do less work to roll out cookies. In a pinch, you can use another heavy cylindrical object, such as a wine bottle, as a rolling pin.

**COOKIE CUTTERS** Choose simple cookie cutters that don't have a lot of grooves and tight spaces for the dough to get caught in; overly fancy cutters can also be difficult to use, especially for children. With a set of holiday-themed cutters and a 2-inch round cutter, you'll be set for just about any occasion. If you need a bigger or smaller round cutter, you can usually use an object from your kitchen, such as a glass or bowl, as a cutting guide.

**COOKIE SCOOPS** Cookie scoops are great for making uniformly sized cookies, which will bake more evenly than free-form cookies. You can buy scoops in three different sizes. A small scoop is 1 tablespoon, medium is 1½ tablespoons, and large is 3 tablespoons. The medium size is the one you'll use most often, but if you bake cookies frequently, a complete set of cookie scoops is worth the small investment.

### A 3-TIERED WIRE COOLING RACK

If you bake cookies as much as I do, a stackable 3-tier cooling rack is a great space saver.

## The Baker's Dozen

Isn't it funny how the "baker's dozen" is 13 and not 12? I've read several different explanations, but I'm going to stick with what my grandma used to say: "The 13th was for the baker to have." Here are my baker's dozen of tips to keep in mind when baking cookies.

1. **Read the recipe in its entirety before starting.** You don't want to start baking and then realize halfway through that you don't have all the ingredients on hand or that the dough needs to chill for 2 hours before the cookies can be formed and baked.

2. **Adjust the rack in the oven before preheating.** Cookies are best baked when the rack is in the middle, where the temperature is not too hot or too cold and the heat circulates effectively. Baking cookies in the middle means they are less likely to burn.

3. **Preheat the oven.** Even after the oven is up to temperature, wait another 5 minutes to make sure it is fully preheated. If your oven doesn't beep when it's preheated, wait 15 minutes after setting the temperature to make sure it's ready, or use an oven thermometer.

### Gifts

**WHO DOESN'T LOVE** receiving a gift of homemade cookies? There are several ways you can wrap your goodies for gift giving. Stack cookies in a cellophane bag and tie with some ribbon. Or stack the cookies in a reusable wide-mouth canning jar. Place a square of festive fabric on the mouth, then seal with the lid. Line a small gift box with brown wax paper. Arrange the cookies slightly overlapping each other. Fold the wax paper over top of the cookies before closing the box and tying on a ribbon. No matter how you wrap your cookies, add a gift tag and perhaps an index card with the recipe.

4. **Bring all refrigerated ingredients to room temperature before using in cookie dough.** This will enable them to be incorporated into the dough properly. Allow butter, eggs, and milk to sit at room temperature for 30 minutes to 1 hour. Doing so also helps trap air in the dough for a lighter texture.

5. **Use the appropriate measuring cups for liquid versus dry ingredients.** Use clear plastic or glass graduated measuring cups with lines for liquids, such as milk, oil, honey, and molasses. Use dry measuring cups for flour, sugar, and other dry ingredients. If you try to use a dry measuring cup

for liquids, you would need to pour in the liquid to the very top for an accurate measurement, which would lead to spillage. And it's nearly impossible to get an accurate measurement when using a liquid measuring cup for dry ingredients.

6. **Sift or whisk flour and other dry ingredients together before adding them to the wet ingredients.** This removes lumps and blends the ingredients together. When you are just using flour, sifting or whisking isn't crucial, but if the flour is combined with baking soda or powder, cornstarch, salt, spices, and/or cocoa powder, sifting or whisking ensures that the ingredients are well distributed. A sifter is the best tool to accomplish this, but if you don't have one, you can use a fine-mesh sieve or a wire whisk.

7. **Mix the dry ingredients and wet ingredients separately.** Mixing all the dry ingredients together before adding them to the wet ones allows the baking soda, baking powder, salt, cocoa powder, and other dry ingredients to be evenly distributed in the flour.

8. **Don't overwork the dough when adding the dry ingredients to the wet ingredients.** After adding the dry ingredients to the wet ingredients, mix the dough just until it holds together unless stated otherwise in the recipe. The more the dough is mixed, the more the gluten in the flour will be activated, resulting in tough, hard cookies.

9. **Line two cookie sheets with parchment paper.** Cookies can stick even to a nonstick pan, and cooking sprays are not recommended for use on nonstick pans. While buttering the sheet works, parchment paper prevents sticking and makes for easy cleanup. By using two parchment-lined pans, you can save time while baking. I recommend baking only one sheet at a time, but you can set up the second sheet of cookies while the first one is in the oven. Then the first sheet can cool while the second one is cooking, and it will be ready if you need to bake a third batch.

10. **Use a timer and check for doneness at the minimum time.** It's easy to forget when you put your cookies in the oven if you're multitasking, so get a good timer and use it every time. Cookies can burn in a minute, so it's best to check the cookies at the earliest time possible. The cooking time will determine whether a cookie is soft and chewy, or hard and crunchy. (I prefer an underbaked cookie to an overbaked one any day.)

11. **Let the cookies cool.** I always let my cookies cool on the hot cookie sheet or in the baking pan for 5 minutes before transferring them to a wire rack. Cookies are still gooey when they come out of the oven, but 5 minutes allows them enough time to firm up so they can be transferred to the cooling rack. Brownies need to be fully cooled in their baking pan before removal. Allow them to cool for an hour or two before lifting them out of the pan and cutting them into squares.

12. **Store cookies properly.** After going through the work to make the best cookies, you'll want to store them properly. Once cooled completely, place them in an airtight container or resealable plastic bag and store them at room temperature for up to 5 days.

13. **Freeze your cookies.** Cookies will keep in the freezer for up to several months. Let the cookies cool completely after baking them and then set them in the freezer on a parchment-lined cookie sheet. You can layer the cookies with parchment in between the layers. Let them freeze completely and then transfer them to resealable plastic bags or airtight containers. To thaw them, remove them from the container and set them out on the countertop for 15 to 20 minutes. You can also put them in a 275°F oven for 10 or 15 minutes to warm them up. They'll taste just like fresh baked!

Oatmeal-Raisin Cookies, *page 14*

# Favorite Drop Cookies

# Oatmeal-Raisin Cookies

**MAKES ABOUT 44 COOKIES**
Prep: 15 minutes
Chill: 30 to 60 minutes
Bake: 12 to 13 minutes
Shelf Life: 4 to 5 days

- 2 cups all-purpose flour
- 1 teaspoon baking soda
- 1 teaspoon ground cinnamon
- ½ teaspoon table salt
- 1 cup (2 sticks) unsalted butter, at room temperature
- 1 cup packed light brown sugar
- ½ cup granulated sugar
- 2 large eggs
- 2 tablespoons molasses
- 2 teaspoons pure vanilla extract
- 2½ cups old-fashioned rolled oats
- 1 cup raisins

These are a must-make for any oatmeal-raisin cookie lover! They have been raved about by friends and family. They're filled with plenty of oats and plump raisins, the edges have a slight crunch, and the center is perfectly chewy thanks to the addition of a bit of molasses.

1. In a medium mixing bowl, sift or whisk together the flour, baking soda, cinnamon, and salt.
2. In a large mixing bowl, using an electric mixer on medium speed or a wooden spoon, beat together the butter and both sugars until light and creamy. This will take about 3 minutes if using an electric mixer or 5 to 6 minutes if creaming by hand. Add the eggs, molasses, and vanilla, and beat until combined. Add the dry ingredients and beat on low speed or by hand until the dough comes together. Using a rubber spatula, fold in the oats and raisins.
3. Form the cookie dough into a large ball and flatten it slightly into a disk. Wrap in plastic wrap and refrigerate until firm, 30 to 60 minutes.
4. Preheat the oven to 350°F. Line a cookie sheet with parchment paper.
5. Using a medium (1½-tablespoon) cookie scoop, scoop the dough into balls and drop them 2 inches apart on the prepared cookie sheet.
6. Bake for 12 to 13 minutes, until the edges are golden brown.
7. Let the cookies rest on the cookie sheets for 5 minutes before transferring them to wire racks to cool completely.

When measuring sticky ingredients like molasses, spray the inside of the measuring spoon or cup with cooking spray for easy release.

# Chocolate-Walnut Oatmeal Cookies

**MAKES ABOUT 48 COOKIES**
Prep: 20 minutes
Bake: 12 to 13 minutes
Shelf Life: 4 to 5 days

1 3/4 cups all-purpose flour
1 teaspoon ground cinnamon
1/2 teaspoon baking soda
1/2 teaspoon baking powder
1/2 teaspoon table salt
1 cup (2 sticks) unsalted butter, at room temperature
1 cup packed light brown sugar
1/2 cup granulated sugar
2 large eggs
1 tablespoon pure vanilla extract
2 1/2 cups old-fashioned rolled oats
2 cups semisweet chocolate chips
1 cup walnuts (optional)

Oatmeal cookies can be bland at times, but there's nothing to worry about with this recipe. These cookies are dense, chewy, and incredibly soft. You'll also find hints of cinnamon in every bite. The walnuts are optional, but they provide a nice texture and buttery flavor.

1. Preheat the oven to 350°F. Line a cookie sheet with parchment paper.
2. In a medium mixing bowl, sift or whisk together the flour, cinnamon, baking soda, baking powder, and salt.
3. In a large mixing bowl, using an electric mixer on medium speed or a wooden spoon, beat together the butter and both sugars until light and creamy. This will take about 3 minutes if using an electric mixer or 5 to 6 minutes if creaming by hand. Add the eggs and vanilla, and beat until combined. Add the dry ingredients and beat on low speed or by hand until the dough comes together. Using a rubber spatula, fold in the oats, chocolate chips, and walnuts (if using).
4. Using a medium (1½-tablespoon) cookie scoop, scoop the dough into balls and drop them 2 inches apart on the prepared cookie sheet.
5. Bake for 12 to 13 minutes, until the edges are golden brown and the centers are set.
6. Let the cookies rest on the cookie sheets for 5 minutes before transferring them to wire racks to cool completely.

Instant or quick-cooking oats can't be used as a substitution for old-fashioned oats. They absorb liquid too quickly, resulting in dry cookies.

# Oatmeal Lace Cookies

**MAKES ABOUT 22 COOKIES**
Prep: 15 minutes
Bake: 12 to 13 minutes
Shelf Life: 4 to 5 days

½ cup (1 stick) unsalted butter

1 cup packed light brown sugar

1 ½ tablespoons all-purpose flour

¼ teaspoon table salt

1 large egg

1 teaspoon pure vanilla extract

1 ¼ cups old-fashioned rolled oats

Staying true to a lace cookie, these are nearly transparent in some spots and may also have small holes from bubbling, giving the appearance of lace. They will be golden brown and paper-thin. They're crispy on the outer edges and chewy in the centers.

1. Preheat the oven to 350°F. Line a cookie sheet with parchment paper.
2. Combine the butter and sugar in a saucepan and heat over medium heat, stirring, until the butter is melted and the mixture is smooth. Remove from the heat and whisk in the flour and salt.
3. Whisk in the egg and vanilla extract until incorporated. Stir in the oats.
4. Using a small (1-tablespoon) cookie scoop, scoop the dough into balls and drop them 2½ inches apart on the prepared cookie sheet.
5. Bake for 12 to 13 minutes, until golden brown.
6. Let the cookies rest on the cookie sheets for 10 minutes before transferring them to wire racks to cool completely.

The cookies should easily peel off the parchment paper. If they don't, let them cool for a bit longer.

# Peanut Butter-Oatmeal Cookies

**MAKES ABOUT 24 COOKIES**
Prep: 15 minutes
Bake: 12 to 13 minutes
Shelf Life: 4 to 5 days

1 cup all-purpose flour
½ teaspoon baking powder
½ teaspoon table salt
½ cup (1 stick) unsalted butter, at room temperature
¾ cup packed light brown sugar
¼ teaspoon granulated sugar
½ cup creamy peanut butter
1 large egg
2 teaspoons pure vanilla extract
1 cup old-fashioned rolled oats

These may sound similar to my No-Bake Chocolate Peanut Butter–Oatmeal Cookies (page 32), but they are quite different. These are chewy from the oats and packed full of peanut butter. They were inspired by my favorite oatmeal.

1. Preheat the oven to 350°F. Line a cookie sheet with parchment paper.
2. In a medium mixing bowl, sift or whisk together flour, baking powder, and salt.
3. In a large mixing bowl, using an electric mixer on medium speed or a wooden spoon, beat together the butter, both sugars, and peanut butter until light and creamy. This will take about 3 minutes if using an electric mixer or 5 to 6 minutes if creaming by hand. Add the egg and vanilla, and beat until combined. Using a rubber spatula, fold in the oats.
4. Using a medium (1½-tablespoon) cookie scoop, scoop the dough into balls and drop them 2 inches apart on the prepared cookie sheet.
5. Bake for 12 to 13 minutes, until the edges are golden brown.
6. Let the cookies rest on the cookie sheets for 5 minutes before transferring them to wire racks to cool completely.

If you love the combination of chocolate and peanut butter, add 1 cup semisweet chocolate chips to the dough, folding them in along with the oats.

# Drop Sugar Cookies

**MAKES ABOUT 24 COOKIES**
Prep: 20 minutes
Bake: 11 to 12 minutes
Shelf Life: 4 to 5 days

- 2 cups cake flour
- 1 teaspoon cream of tartar
- 1 teaspoon baking powder
- ½ teaspoon baking soda
- ½ teaspoon table salt
- ¾ cup (1 ½ sticks) unsalted butter, at room temperature
- ½ cup granulated sugar
- ½ cup confectioners' sugar
- 2 large eggs
- 2 teaspoons pure vanilla extract

These drop sugar cookies are thick, soft, and almost cakelike. Add some sprinkles before baking to give the cookies a little contrast. I like to make these when I'm not feeling up to making frosting to slather on top since they're sweet enough on their own.

1. Preheat the oven to 350°F. Line a cookie sheet with parchment paper.
2. In a medium mixing bowl, sift or whisk together the flour, cream of tartar, baking powder, baking soda, and salt.
3. In a large mixing bowl, using an electric mixer on medium speed or a wooden spoon, beat together the butter and both sugars until light and creamy. This will take about 3 minutes if using an electric mixer or 5 to 6 minutes if creaming by hand. Add the eggs and vanilla, and beat until combined. Add the dry ingredients and beat on low speed or by hand until the dough comes together.
4. Using a medium (1½-tablespoon) cookie scoop, scoop the dough into balls and drop them 2 inches apart on the prepared cookie sheets.
5. Bake for 11 to 12 minutes, until the center is set and the edges are firm to the touch.
6. Let the cookies rest on the cookie sheets for 5 minutes before transferring them to wire racks to cool completely.

If you like a flatter cookie, use your palm to flatten the cookies out before baking. You can also dip your fork in sugar to prevent the dough from sticking, and add crisscross marks with the fork tines on the top of each cookie.

# Snickerdoodles

**MAKES ABOUT 36 COOKIES**
Prep: 20 minutes
Bake: 12 to 13 minutes
Shelf Life: 4 to 5 days

2 3/4 cups cake flour
2 teaspoons cream of tartar
1 1/2 teaspoons baking soda
1/2 teaspoon table salt
1/2 cup (1 stick) unsalted butter, at room temperature
1/2 cup vegetable shortening
1 1/2 cups granulated sugar, divided
1/2 cup packed light brown sugar
2 large eggs
2 teaspoons pure vanilla extract
2 teaspoons ground cinnamon

I've had so many cakey snickerdoodles, I decided I wanted mine to be different. My snickerdoodles are thin and tender. They have the beautiful cracked top from being rolled in the cinnamon-sugar prior to baking. They taste great with a cup of warm coffee.

1. Preheat the oven to 350°F. Line a cookie sheet with parchment paper.

2. In a medium mixing bowl, sift or whisk together the cake flour, cream of tartar, baking soda, and salt.

3. In a large mixing bowl, using an electric mixer on medium speed or a wooden spoon, beat the butter, shortening, 1 cup of granulated sugar, and brown sugar until light and creamy. This will take about 3 minutes if using an electric mixer or 5 to 6 minutes if creaming by hand. Add the eggs and vanilla, and beat until combined. Add the dry ingredients and beat on low speed or by hand until the dough comes together.

4. In a shallow bowl, mix the remaining ½ cup of granulated sugar and cinnamon for rolling.

5. Using a medium (1½-tablespoon) cookie scoop, scoop the dough into balls, drop each ball into the bowl of cinnamon-sugar, and roll to coat evenly. Place the balls 2 inches apart on the prepared cookie sheet.

6. Bake for 12 to 13 minutes, until the edges are golden brown.

7. Let the cookies rest on the cookie sheets for 5 minutes before transferring them to wire racks to cool completely.

For more rich, buttery flavor, use butter-flavored shortening in this recipe.

# Old-Fashioned Chocolate Chip Cookies

**MAKES ABOUT 36 COOKIES**
Prep: 20 minutes
Bake: 10 to 11 minutes
Shelf Life: 4 to 5 days

- 2½ cups all-purpose flour
- 1 teaspoon baking soda
- ½ teaspoon table salt
- 1 cup (2 sticks) unsalted butter, at room temperature
- 1 cup packed light brown sugar
- ½ cup granulated sugar
- 2 large eggs
- 2 teaspoons pure vanilla extract
- 2 cups semisweet chocolate chips

These are my son's all-time favorite cookies. They're soft, thin, and loaded up with chocolate chips. They are quick to mix up, too! What we love the most about these is that you can guarantee that every bite has at least a couple of chocolate chips in it.

1. Preheat the oven to 350°F. Line a cookie sheet with parchment paper.
2. In a medium mixing bowl, sift or whisk together the flour, baking soda, and salt.
3. In a large mixing bowl, using an electric mixer on medium speed or a wooden spoon, beat together the butter and both sugars until light and creamy. This will take about 3 minutes if using an electric mixer or 5 to 6 minutes if creaming by hand. Add the eggs and vanilla, and beat until combined. Add the dry ingredients and beat on low speed or by hand until the dough comes together. Using a rubber spatula, fold the chocolate chips into the dough.
4. Using a medium (1½-tablespoon) cookie scoop, scoop the dough into balls and drop them 2 inches apart on the prepared cookie sheet.
5. Bake for 10 to 11 minutes, until the edges are golden brown.
6. Let the cookies rest on the cookie sheets for 5 minutes before transferring them to wire racks to cool completely.

To intensify the flavor of these cookies, before baking them, cover the dough balls with plastic wrap and refrigerate for 24 hours. This will let the flavors deepen.

# The Perfect Chocolate Chip Cookie

Some people prefer their chocolate chip cookies soft, while others like them crisp. Here are some tips on how to adjust the ingredients and baking times for various results to please every chocolate chip cookie lover:

For an ooey-gooey cookie, add 1¼ cups of extra flour to the recipe. The outside will set long before the inside, making for a gooey center.

For a cookie with a golden brown, crispy edge and a soft center, decrease the baking soda to ¼ teaspoon and add ¼ teaspoon baking powder. These cookies will spread more.

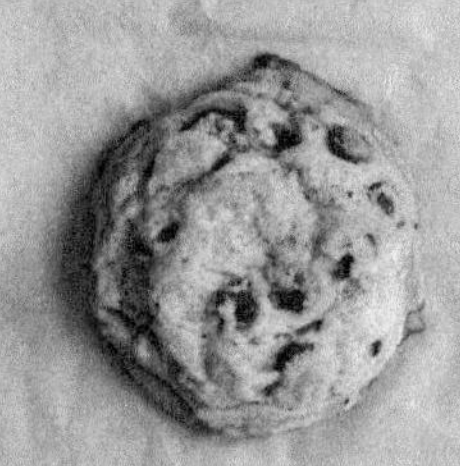

For a chewier cookie, replace the all-purpose flour with an equal amount of bread flour.

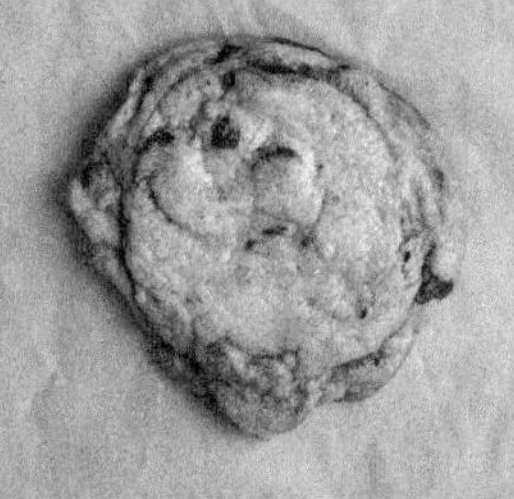

For a thicker cookie, place the bowl of dough in the freezer for 30 to 60 minutes before scooping the cookies. The butter will solidify and prevent the cookie from spreading.

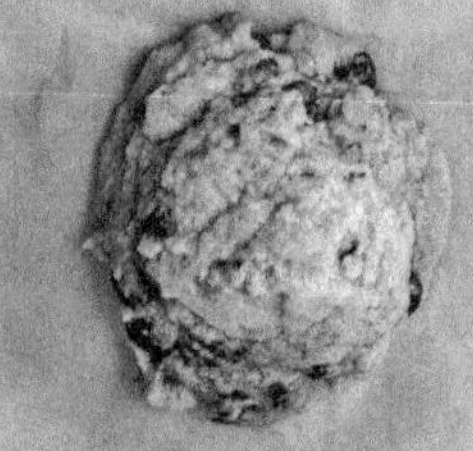

For a cakey cookie, omit the baking soda, but add ½ teaspoon baking powder to the dry ingredients.

# Double Chocolate Chip Cookies

**MAKES ABOUT 36 COOKIES**
Prep: 25 minutes
Bake: 10 to 11 minutes
Shelf Life: 4 to 5 days

1 ½ cups all-purpose flour
⅓ cup unsweetened cocoa powder
½ teaspoon baking soda
½ teaspoon baking powder
½ teaspoon table salt
¾ cup (1 ½ sticks) unsalted butter, at room temperature
¾ cup packed light brown sugar
½ cup granulated sugar
2 large eggs
2 teaspoons pure vanilla extract
2 cups semisweet chocolate chips

Sometimes you just need an over-the-top chocolate cookie, and this recipe is it. The chocolate chips and cocoa powder give these thick, chewy, fudgy cookies a double dose of chocolate. If you're thinking these would be great with a glass of milk, you are correct!

1. Preheat the oven to 350°F. Line a cookie sheet with parchment paper.

2. In a medium mixing bowl, sift or whisk together the flour, cocoa powder, baking soda, baking powder, and salt.

3. In a large mixing bowl, using an electric mixer on medium speed or a wooden spoon, beat together the butter and both sugars until light and creamy. This will take about 3 minutes if using an electric mixer or 5 to 6 minutes if creaming by hand. Add the eggs and vanilla, and beat until combined. Add the dry ingredients and beat on low speed or by hand until the dough comes together. Using a rubber spatula, fold in the chocolate chips.

4. Using a medium (1½-tablespoon) cookie scoop, scoop the dough into balls and drop them 2 inches apart on the prepared cookie sheet.

5. Bake for 10 to 11 minutes, until the cookies are set.

6. Let the cookies rest on the cookie sheets for 5 minutes before transferring them to wire racks to cool completely.

For prettier cookies, stick the chocolate chips into the cookies right when they come out of the oven.

# Molasses Cookies

**MAKES ABOUT 52 COOKIES**
Prep: 15 minutes
Chill: 30 to 60 minutes
Bake: 13 to 14 minutes
Shelf Life: 4 to 5 days

- 4 ½ cups all-purpose flour
- 2 teaspoons baking soda
- 1 ¼ teaspoons ground ginger
- 1 teaspoon ground cinnamon
- ½ teaspoon table salt
- ½ cup (1 stick) unsalted butter, at room temperature
- ½ cup vegetable shortening
- 1 ¼ cups granulated sugar
- 1 cup molasses
- ½ cup milk
- 1 large egg
- 2 teaspoons pure vanilla extract

Soft, yet dense, and with a nice balance of molasses and spice, these drop cookies are perfect for the holidays, but I like to make them any time of year. Molasses is the key flavor here, so be sure to choose a high-quality, full-flavored molasses.

1. In a medium mixing bowl, sift or whisk together the flour, baking soda, ginger, cinnamon, and salt.
2. In a large mixing bowl, using an electric mixer on medium speed or a wooden spoon, beat the butter, shortening, and sugar until light and creamy. This will take about 3 minutes if using an electric mixer or 5 to 6 minutes if creaming by hand. Add the molasses, milk, egg, and vanilla, and beat until combined. Add the dry ingredients and beat on low speed or by hand until the dough comes together.
3. Form the dough into a large ball and flatten it slightly into a disk. Wrap in plastic wrap and refrigerate until firm, 30 to 60 minutes.
4. Preheat the oven to 350°F. Line a cookie sheet with parchment paper.
5. Using a medium (1½-tablespoon) cookie scoop, scoop the dough into balls and drop them 2 inches apart on the prepared cookie sheet.
6. Bake for 13 to 14 minutes, until the center is set and the edges are firm to the touch.
7. Let the cookies rest on the cookie sheets for 5 minutes before transferring them to wire racks to cool completely.

Use a full-flavored molasses rather than blackstrap molasses for this recipe. Blackstrap molasses will overpower all the other flavors in the cookie.

# Chewy Ginger Cookies

**MAKES ABOUT 28 COOKIES**
Prep: 15 minutes
Bake: 12 to 13 minutes
Shelf Life: 4 to 5 days

- 2 cups all-purpose flour
- 1 teaspoon baking soda
- ½ teaspoon salt
- 1 teaspoon ground cinnamon
- 1 teaspoon ground ginger
- ¼ teaspoon ground cloves
- ½ cup vegetable oil
- ¾ cup packed light brown sugar
- ½ cup granulated sugar, divided
- ⅓ cup molasses
- 1 large egg
- 1 teaspoon pure vanilla extract

With a crinkly top, chewy interior, and a kick of ginger, these cookies go well with a cup of hot chocolate. I want to say this about every cookie, but this is one of my favorites. I love how the spice from the ginger wakes up my taste buds with every bite!

1. Preheat the oven to 350°F. Line a cookie sheet with parchment paper.
2. In a medium mixing bowl, sift or whisk together the flour, baking soda, salt, cinnamon, ginger, and cloves.
3. In a large mixing bowl, using an electric mixer on medium speed or a wooden spoon, beat together the oil, brown sugar, and ¼ cup of the granulated sugar until light and creamy. This will take about 3 minutes if using an electric mixer or 5 to 6 minutes if creaming by hand. Add the molasses, egg, and vanilla, and beat until combined. Add the dry ingredients and beat on low speed or by hand until the dough comes together.
4. Put the remaining ¼ cup of granulated sugar in a shallow bowl for rolling.
5. Using a medium (1½-tablespoon) cookie scoop, scoop the dough into balls, drop them into the bowl of sugar, and roll to coat. Place the balls 2 inches apart on the prepared cookie sheet.
6. Bake for 12 to 13 minutes, until the center is set and the edges are firm to the touch.
7. Let the cookies cool on the cookie sheet for 5 minutes before transferring them to wire racks to cool completely.

Use the same graduated measuring cup to measure the molasses as you did the vegetable oil to prevent the molasses from sticking to the cup.

# Butter Wafers

**MAKES ABOUT 18 COOKIES**
Prep: 10 minutes
Bake: 14 to 15 minutes
Shelf Life: 4 to 5 days

- ¾ cup all-purpose flour
- ¼ teaspoon table salt
- ½ cup (1 stick) unsalted butter, at room temperature
- ½ cup granulated sugar
- 1 teaspoon pure vanilla extract

Buttery, thin, and crisp with a hint of vanilla, these cookies go well with a cup of coffee or tea. If you're an after-dinner coffee drinker, this would be the perfect dessert. You can also dip the wafers in the coffee glaze recipe on page 93 for your coffee fix.

1. Preheat the oven to 350°F. Line a cookie sheet with parchment paper.
2. In a medium mixing bowl, sift or whisk together the flour and salt.
3. In a large mixing bowl, using an electric mixer on medium speed or a wooden spoon, beat together the butter and sugar until light and creamy. This will take about 3 minutes if using an electric mixer or 5 to 6 minutes if creaming by hand. Add the vanilla and mix to combine. Add the dry ingredients and beat on low speed or by hand until the dough comes together.
4. Using a small (1-tablespoon) cookie scoop, scoop the dough into balls and drop them 2 inches apart on the prepared cookie sheet.
5. Bake for 14 to 15 minutes, until the cookies are flat and the edges are golden brown.
6. Let the cookies rest on the cookie sheets for 5 minutes before transferring them to wire rack to cool completely.

Want a little extra butter flavor in your wafers? Substitute ¼ teaspoon of butter extract for the same amount of vanilla to enhance the buttery flavor.

# Brown Sugar Cookies

**MAKES ABOUT 30 COOKIES**
Prep: 23 minutes
Bake: 13 to 14 minutes
Shelf Life: 4 to 5 days

- 2 ¼ cups all-purpose flour
- 2 teaspoons cornstarch
- ½ teaspoon baking powder
- ½ teaspoon table salt
- 1 cup (2 sticks) unsalted butter, at room temperature
- 1 ½ cups packed dark brown sugar
- 1 large egg
- 2 teaspoons pure vanilla extract

These soft, buttery cookies are a favorite with everyone who has tried them. The dark brown sugar is what makes them dense, and adds an extra molasses flavor. Just looking at them, you wouldn't think that they were anything special, but they are a hidden treasure.

1. Preheat the oven to 350°F. Line a cookie sheet with parchment paper.
2. In a medium mixing bowl, sift or whisk together the flour, cornstarch, baking powder, and salt.
3. In a large mixing bowl, using an electric mixer on medium speed or a wooden spoon, beat together the butter and brown sugar until light and creamy. This will take about 3 minutes if using an electric mixer or 5 to 6 minutes if creaming by hand. Add the egg and vanilla, and beat until combined. Add the dry ingredients and beat on low speed or by hand until the dough comes together.
4. Using a medium (1½-tablespoon) cookie scoop, scoop the dough into balls and drop them 2 inches apart on the prepared cookie sheet.
5. Bake for 13 to 14 minutes, until the edges are golden brown.
6. Let the cookies rest on the cookie sheets for 5 minutes before transferring them to wire racks to cool completely.

You can replace the dark brown sugar with light brown sugar, but the flavor will be much less intense.

# Honey Drops

**MAKES ABOUT 28 COOKIES**
Prep: 10 minutes
Bake: 12 to 13 minutes
Shelf Life: 4 to 5 days

2 ½ cups all-purpose flour
½ teaspoon table salt
½ teaspoon baking soda
¼ teaspoon baking powder
¼ cup (½ stick) unsalted butter, at room temperature
¾ cup granulated sugar
½ cup vegetable oil
½ cup honey
1 large egg
2 teaspoons pure vanilla extract

Have you ever had a honey cookie? They are a real treat! The honey gives them intense flavor and a lovely golden color. The cookie itself is soft, thick, and puffy. I guarantee that your family will find this cookie unique and want to share.

1. Preheat the oven to 350°F. Line a cookie sheet with parchment paper.

2. In a medium mixing bowl, sift or whisk together the flour, salt, baking soda, and baking powder.

3. In a large mixing bowl, using an electric mixer on medium speed or a wooden spoon, beat together the butter and sugar until light and creamy. This will take about 3 minutes if using an electric mixer or 5 to 6 minutes if creaming by hand. Add the oil, honey, egg, and vanilla, and beat until combined. Add the dry ingredients and beat on low speed or by hand until the dough comes together.

4. Using a medium (1½-tablespoon) cookie scoop, scoop the dough into balls and drop them 2 inches apart on the prepared cookie sheet.

5. Bake for 12 to 13 minutes, until the edges are golden brown.

6. Let the cookies rest on the cookie sheets for 5 minutes before transferring them to wire racks to cool completely.

Use the same graduated measuring cup to measure the honey as you did the vegetable oil. The residual oil will help prevent the honey from sticking to the inside of the cup.

# Maple-Spice Cookies

**MAKES ABOUT 28 COOKIES**
Prep: 15 minutes
Bake: 12 to 13 minutes
Shelf Life: 4 to 5 days

2 1/4 cups all-purpose flour
1 teaspoon baking soda
1/2 teaspoon table salt
1/2 teaspoon ground cinnamon
1/4 teaspoon ground ginger
1/4 teaspoon ground nutmeg
1/8 teaspoon ground cloves
1/2 cup (1 stick) unsalted butter, at room temperature
1 cup packed light brown sugar
1/2 cup granulated sugar
2 large eggs
2 teaspoons maple extract
1 teaspoon pure vanilla extract

The maple and spice in these cookies make the perfect flavor combination. The flavors remind me of everything I love about fall and would make the perfect back-to-school sweet for the kids, especially if you're running short on time. The cookies are soft, thin, and have a cracked top.

1. Preheat the oven to 350°F. Line a cookie sheet with parchment paper.

2. In a medium mixing bowl, sift or whisk together the flour, baking soda, salt, cinnamon, ginger, nutmeg, and cloves.

3. In a large mixing bowl, using an electric mixer on medium speed or a wooden spoon, beat together the butter and both sugars until light and creamy. This will take about 3 minutes if using an electric mixer or 5 to 6 minutes if creaming by hand. Add the eggs, maple extract, and vanilla, and beat until combined. Add the dry ingredients and beat on low speed or by hand until the dough comes together.

4. Using a medium (1½-tablespoon) cookie scoop, scoop the dough into balls and drop them 2 inches apart on the prepared cookie sheet.

5. Bake for 12 to 13 minutes, until the edges are golden brown.

6. Let the cookies rest on the cookie sheets for 5 minutes before transferring them to wire racks to cool completely.

Do you love the combination of pecans and maple? Fold ½ cup chopped pecans into the dough.

# Peanut Butter Cookies

**MAKES ABOUT 36 COOKIES**
Prep: 10 minutes
Bake: 12 to 13 minutes
Shelf Life: 4 to 5 days

1 3/4 cups all-purpose flour
1/2 teaspoon baking soda
1/2 teaspoon baking powder
1/2 teaspoon table salt
3/4 cup (1 1/2 sticks) unsalted butter, at room temperature
1 cup creamy peanut butter
1 cup granulated sugar, divided
3/4 cup packed light brown sugar
1 large egg
2 teaspoons pure vanilla extract

Peanut butter cookies are a weakness of both my husband's and mine. They're also a favorite to take to bake sales since they're always the first to sell! The cookies are rolled in sugar before baking to give them a crisp crust. Underneath that crispy sugar crust is a soft, tender cookie that's irresistible!

1. Preheat the oven to 350°F. Line a cookie sheet with parchment paper.
2. In a medium mixing bowl, sift or whisk together the flour, baking soda, baking powder, and salt.
3. In a large mixing bowl, using an electric mixer on medium speed or a wooden spoon, beat together the butter, peanut butter, ¾ cup of granulated sugar, and brown sugar. This will take about 3 minutes if using an electric mixer or 5 to 6 minutes if creaming by hand. Add the egg and vanilla, and beat until combined. Add the dry ingredients and beat on low speed or by hand until the dough comes together.
4. Put the remaining ¼ cup of granulated sugar in a shallow bowl for rolling.
5. Using a medium (1½-tablespoon) cookie scoop, scoop the dough into balls, drop them into the bowl of sugar, and roll to coat. Place the balls 2 inches apart on the prepared cookie sheet. Using a fork, make crisscross marks on the top of each dough ball.
6. Bake for 12 to 13 minutes, until the edges are golden brown.
7. Let the cookies rest on the cookie sheets for 5 minutes before transferring them to wire racks to cool completely.

You can substitute chunky peanut butter for the creamy peanut butter in this recipe.

# No-Bake Chocolate–Peanut Butter Cookies

**MAKES ABOUT 18 COOKIES**
Prep: 15 minutes
Shelf Life: 4 to 5 days

½ cup (1 stick) unsalted butter, at room temperature

2 cups granulated sugar

½ cup milk

3 tablespoons unsweetened cocoa powder

½ cup creamy or chunky peanut butter

2¾ cups quick-cooking oats

1 teaspoon pure vanilla extract

½ teaspoon table salt

There's no need to turn on the oven to make these classics. These fudgy cookies are a childhood favorite. They have a great chocolate–peanut butter flavor and oatmeal for a nice texture. This is a recipe that my mom passed down to me, and I make it regularly for my family.

1. Lay out a sheet of parchment paper on a clean countertop.
2. Combine the butter, sugar, milk, and cocoa powder in a saucepan and bring to a rolling boil over medium heat. Let it boil for 2 minutes, reducing the heat as needed to prevent the mixture from burning or boiling over.
3. Remove the pan from the heat and stir in the peanut butter, oats, vanilla, and salt until incorporated.
4. Using a medium (1½-tablespoon) cookie scoop, scoop the dough into balls and drop them 1 inch apart on the parchment paper.
5. Let cool for 30 minutes until firm.

Not a fan of peanut butter? Substitute any other nut butter for the peanut butter in this recipe.

# Hermits

**MAKES ABOUT 24 COOKIES**
Prep: 20 minutes
Bake: 12 to 13 minutes
Shelf Life: 4 to 5 days

2 cups all-purpose flour
1 teaspoon ground cinnamon
½ teaspoon ground nutmeg
¼ teaspoon ground cloves
½ teaspoon baking powder
½ teaspoon table salt
½ cup (1 stick) unsalted butter, at room temperature
1 cup packed light brown sugar
1 large egg
¼ cup buttermilk
2 tablespoons molasses
1 teaspoon pure vanilla extract
1 cup raisins
1 cup chopped walnuts or pecans (optional)

Hermits date way back to the 19th century. I put a spin on this classic but stayed true to what makes a hermit a hermit. They are rich cookies, with spices, chopped fruit, and nuts added to them. My son, a huge raisin fan, can't stop eating these.

1. Preheat the oven to 350°F. Line a cookie sheet with parchment paper.
2. In a medium mixing bowl, sift or whisk together the flour, cinnamon, nutmeg, cloves, baking powder, and salt.
3. In a large mixing bowl, using an electric mixer on medium speed or a wooden spoon, beat together the butter and sugar until light and creamy. This will take about 3 minutes if using an electric mixer or 5 to 6 minutes if creaming by hand. Add the egg, buttermilk, molasses, and vanilla, and beat until combined. Add the dry ingredients and beat on low speed or by hand until the dough comes together. Using a rubber spatula, fold in the raisins and chopped nuts (if using).
4. Using a medium (1½-tablespoon) cookie scoop, scoop the dough into balls and drop them 2 inches apart on the prepared cookie sheet.
5. Bake for 12 to 13 minutes, until the cookies are set.
6. Let the cookies rest on the cookie sheets for 5 minutes before transferring them to wire racks to cool completely.

For a chunkier cookie, add an additional ½ cup dried fruit of your preference or chopped walnuts.

# Pumpkin Cookies

**MAKES ABOUT 30 COOKIES**
Prep: 15 minutes
Bake: 10 to 11 minutes
Shelf Life: 4 to 5 days

- 1 3/4 cups all-purpose flour
- 1/2 teaspoon baking powder
- 1/2 teaspoon baking soda
- 1/2 teaspoon table salt
- 1 teaspoon ground cinnamon
- 1/4 teaspoon ground ginger
- 1/4 teaspoon ground nutmeg
- 1/4 teaspoon ground cloves
- 3/4 cup (1 1/2 sticks) unsalted butter, at room temperature
- 3/4 cup packed light brown sugar
- 1/2 cup granulated sugar
- 2 large eggs
- 1/2 cup canned pumpkin purée (not pumpkin pie filling)
- 2 teaspoons pure vanilla extract
- 1 cup chopped pecans (optional)

These pumpkin cookies are soft and cake-like. They taste just like a piece of pumpkin pie, but in cookie form, making them a perfect addition to a Thanksgiving cookie platter. Be sure to use pure pumpkin purée, not pumpkin pie filling.

1. Preheat the oven to 350°F. Line a cookie sheet with parchment paper.
2. In a medium mixing bowl, sift or whisk together the flour, baking powder, baking soda, salt, cinnamon, ginger, nutmeg, and cloves.
3. In a large mixing bowl, using an electric mixer on medium speed or a wooden spoon, beat together the butter and both sugars until light and creamy. This will take about 3 minutes if using an electric mixer or 5 to 6 minutes if creaming by hand. Add the eggs, pumpkin, and vanilla, and beat until combined. Add the dry ingredients and beat on low speed or by hand until the dough comes together. Using a rubber spatula, fold in the pecans (if using).
4. Using a medium (1½-tablespoon) cookie scoop, scoop the dough into balls and drop them 2 inches apart on the prepared cookie sheet.
5. Bake for 10 to 11 minutes, until the edges are golden brown.
6. Let the cookies rest on the cookie sheets for 5 minutes before transferring them to wire racks to cool completely.

Dress up these cookies by folding in ¾ cup semisweet chocolate chips or cinnamon chips along with the pecans. Or make them into cookie sandwiches with a thin layer of Nutella or the cream cheese glaze from the Red Velvet Cut-Out Cookies (page 114) in the center.

# Apple-Cinnamon Cookies

**MAKES ABOUT 24 COOKIES**
Prep: 20 minutes
Bake: 13 to 14 minutes
Shelf Life: 4 to 5 days

2 cups all-purpose flour
1 teaspoon ground cinnamon
½ teaspoon baking powder
½ teaspoon salt
½ cup (1 stick) unsalted butter, at room temperature
¾ cup granulated sugar
½ cup packed light brown sugar
1 large egg
2 teaspoons pure vanilla extract
1 cup shredded apple

Hello, delicious fall cookie! I couldn't make an apple cookie without cinnamon, since they just belong together. These cookies are similar to apple bread, except the apples are shredded instead of cubed.

1. Preheat the oven to 350°F. Line a cookie sheet with parchment paper.
2. In a medium mixing bowl, sift or whisk together the flour, baking powder, cinnamon, and salt.
3. In a large mixing bowl, using an electric mixer on medium speed or a wooden spoon, beat together the butter and both sugars until light and creamy. This will take about 3 minutes if using an electric mixer or 5 to 6 minutes if creaming by hand. Add the egg and vanilla, and beat to combine. Add the dry ingredients and beat on low speed or by hand until the dough comes together. Using a rubber spatula, fold in the apples.
4. Using a medium (1½-tablespoon) cookie scoop, scoop the dough into balls and drop them 2 inches apart on the prepared cookie sheet.
5. Bake for 13 to 14 minutes, until the edges are golden brown and the top is set.
6. Let the cookies rest for 5 minutes on the cookie sheets before transferring them to wire racks to cool completely.

Tart apples such as Granny Smiths make the best apple-cinnamon cookies, but just about any sweet apples can be substituted.

# Banana Bread Cookies

**MAKES ABOUT 28 COOKIES**
Prep: 10 minutes
Bake: 12 to 13 minutes
Shelf Life: 4 to 5 days

- 2 cups all-purpose flour
- 2 teaspoons cornstarch
- ½ teaspoon baking powder
- ½ teaspoon table salt
- 1 cup (2 sticks) unsalted butter, at room temperature
- 1 cup packed dark brown sugar
- ½ cup granulated sugar
- 1 large egg
- 2 teaspoons pure vanilla extract
- 2 ripe bananas, mashed

The flavors of banana bread—ripe bananas and plenty of vanilla—are packed into these sweet, super-soft cookies. This recipe is a great way to use up the overripe bananas that you have sitting on your counter. The riper the banana, the sweeter the cookie!

1. Preheat the oven to 350°F. Line a cookie sheet with parchment paper.
2. In a medium mixing bowl, sift or whisk together the flour, cornstarch, baking powder, and salt.
3. In a large mixing bowl, using an electric mixer on medium speed or a wooden spoon, beat together the butter and both sugars until light and creamy. This will take about 3 minutes if using an electric mixer or 5 to 6 minutes if creaming by hand. Add the egg, vanilla, and bananas and beat until combined. Add the dry ingredients and beat on low speed or by hand until the dough comes together.
4. Using a medium (1½-tablespoon) cookie scoop, scoop the dough into balls and drop them 2 inches apart on the prepared cookie sheet.
5. Bake for 12 to 13 minutes, until the center no longer looks gooey.
6. Let the cookies rest for 5 minutes on the cookie sheets before transferring them to wire racks to cool completely.

If you're not ready to bake when your bananas start getting overripe, simply peel them and store them in small resealable plastic bags in the freezer. Then just thaw them out before using.

# Orange Cookies

**MAKES ABOUT 30 COOKIES**
Prep: 20 minutes
Bake: 12 to 13 minutes
Shelf Life: 4 to 5 days

- 2½ cups all-purpose flour
- 1 teaspoon baking soda
- ½ teaspoon table salt
- ½ cup (1 stick) unsalted butter, at room temperature
- 1 cup granulated sugar
- ½ cup packed light brown sugar
- 2 large eggs
- 1 teaspoon pure vanilla extract
- 1 teaspoon orange extract
- 1 tablespoon grated orange zest
- 1 teaspoon grated lemon zest

Orange cookies are for people like me who can't get enough of that fruity flavor. The orange extract and the zest of both orange and lemon give these cookies a refreshing citrusy flavor. You won't taste the lemon zest as much, but it gives the cookies a bright flavor.

1. Preheat the oven to 350°F. Line a cookie sheet with parchment paper.
2. In a medium mixing bowl, sift or whisk together the flour, baking soda, and salt.
3. In a large mixing bowl, using an electric mixer on medium speed or a wooden spoon, beat together the butter and both sugars until light and creamy. This will take about 3 minutes if using an electric mixer or 5 to 6 minutes if creaming by hand. Add the eggs, extracts, and zests and beat until combined. Add the dry ingredients and beat on low speed or by hand until the dough comes together.
4. Using a medium (1½-tablespoon) cookie scoop, scoop the dough into balls and drop them 2 inches apart on the prepared cookie sheet.
5. Bake for 12 to 13 minutes, until the edges are golden brown.
6. Let the cookies rest on the cookie sheets for 5 minutes before transferring them to wire racks to cool completely.

Replace the orange zest and orange extract with additional lemon zest and lemon extract for lemon drop cookies.

# Half-Moons

**MAKES ABOUT 24 COOKIES**
Prep: 20 minutes
Bake: 14 to 15 minutes
Shelf Life: 4 to 5 days

**FOR THE COOKIES**

2 cups all-purpose flour

¾ cup unsweetened cocoa powder

1 teaspoon baking powder

½ teaspoon baking soda

½ teaspoon table salt

¾ cup vegetable shortening

1 cup packed light brown sugar

½ cup granulated sugar

2 teaspoons pure vanilla extract

3 large eggs

1 cup buttermilk

These half-moons are large, cake-like chocolate cookies that are covered half-and-half with chocolate and vanilla frosting. Don't confuse these with black and white cookies—these are much tastier! They originated in New York state near where I live and can be found in most grocery stores.

**TO MAKE THE COOKIES**

1. Preheat the oven to 350°F. Line a cookie sheet with parchment paper.
2. In a medium mixing bowl, sift or whisk together the flour, cocoa powder, baking powder, baking soda, and salt.
3. In a large mixing bowl, using an electric mixer on medium speed or a wooden spoon, beat together the shortening and both sugars until light and creamy. This will take about 3 minutes if using an electric mixer or 5 to 6 minutes if creaming by hand. Add the vanilla and then the eggs, one at a time, beating after each addition until combined.
4. Alternately add the dry ingredients and buttermilk to the shortening mixture, starting and ending with the flour, and beat to combine after each addition.
5. Using a large (3-tablespoon) cookie scoop, scoop the dough into balls and drop them about 2 inches apart on the prepared cookie sheet.
6. Bake for 14 to 15 minutes, until the cookies are domed and set.
7. Let the cookies rest for 5 minutes on the cookie sheets before transferring to wire racks to cool completely.

**FOR THE CHOCOLATE FROSTING**

- 1/4 cup (1/2 stick) unsalted butter, at room temperature
- 2 cups confectioners' sugar
- 2 tablespoons unsweetened cocoa powder
- 2 tablespoons milk
- 1 teaspoon pure vanilla extract

**FOR THE VANILLA FROSTING**

- 6 tablespoons (3/4 stick) unsalted butter, at room temperature
- 3 cups confectioners' sugar
- 2 tablespoons milk
- 2 teaspoons pure vanilla extract

**TO MAKE THE CHOCOLATE FROSTING**

In a large bowl, using an electric mixer on medium speed or a wooden spoon, beat together the butter, confectioners' sugar, cocoa powder, milk, and vanilla until smooth.

**TO MAKE THE VANILLA FROSTING**

In a large bowl, using an electric mixer on medium speed or a wooden spoon, beat together the butter, confectioners' sugar, milk, and vanilla until smooth. Once smooth, beat for 1 minute to whip the frosting.

**TO FROST THE COOKIES**

Turn the cooled cookies over so they are resting on their domed tops. Cover one side of the bottom of the cookie with a layer of chocolate frosting. Cover the other side with the vanilla frosting, making it slightly higher than the chocolate frosting.

If you don't have buttermilk on hand, you can make your own by adding 1 tablespoon of lemon juice or white vinegar to 1 scant cup of milk, then let it sit for 5 to 10 minutes, until it thickens and curdles.

# Butterscotch Haystacks

**MAKES ABOUT 16 COOKIES**
Prep: 10 minutes
Shelf Life: 4 to 5 days

1 1/2 cups butterscotch chips
1/2 cup creamy peanut butter
1/2 cup salted peanuts
4 cups uncooked chow mein noodles

Kids love making these no-bake cookies because they look just like haystacks in cartoons. The chow mein noodles provide the best crunch! Peanut butter and butterscotch aren't a pairing that I would normally put together, but it really works here.

1. Lay out a sheet of wax paper or parchment paper.
2. In a double boiler, melt the butterscotch chips and peanut butter over medium heat, stirring frequently. Once melted, remove from the heat. Using a rubber spatula, fold in the peanuts and chow mein noodles.
3. Using a small (1-tablespoon) cookie scoop, scoop the dough into balls and drop them 2 inches apart on the paper.
4. Let cool for 2 to 3 hours, until the butterscotch is set and the haystacks easily pull away from the paper.

If you don't have a double boiler, fill a small saucepan with about an inch of water. Place a heatproof bowl on top of the saucepan, making sure that the bottom doesn't touch the water in the saucepan.

# Ranger Cookies

**MAKES ABOUT 32 COOKIES**
Prep: 15 minutes
Bake: 13 to 14 minutes
Shelf Life: 4 to 5 days

1 cup all-purpose flour
½ teaspoon baking soda
½ teaspoon baking powder
½ teaspoon table salt
½ cup vegetable shortening
½ cup packed light brown sugar
½ cup granulated sugar
2 large eggs
2 teaspoons pure vanilla extract
1 cup crushed corn flakes
1 cup old-fashioned rolled oats
1 cup semisweet chocolate chips
¾ cup sweetened coconut flakes

Here's another cookie with a mystery name. The common belief is that these cookies originated in Texas and were originally called Texas Ranger Cookies or Lone Ranger Cookies. All I know is that they are chunky and full of some shockingly tasty ingredients. These are a must-share with family and friends!

1. Preheat the oven to 350°F. Line a cookie sheet with parchment paper.
2. In a medium mixing bowl, sift or whisk together the flour, baking soda, baking powder, and salt.
3. In a large mixing bowl, using an electric mixer on medium speed or a wooden spoon, beat together the shortening and both sugars until light and creamy. This will take about 3 minutes if using an electric mixer or 5 to 6 minutes if creaming by hand. Add the eggs and vanilla, and beat until combined. Add the dry ingredients and beat on low speed or by hand until the dough comes together. Using a rubber spatula, fold in the corn flakes, oats, chocolate chips, and coconut flakes.
4. Using a medium (1½-tablespoon) cookie scoop, scoop the dough into balls and drop them 2 inches apart on the prepared cookie sheet.
5. Bake for 13 to 14 minutes, until the edges are golden brown.
6. Let the cookies rest for 5 minutes on the cookie sheets before transferring them to wire racks to cool completely.

Substitute raisins or chopped dried cranberries for the chocolate chips.

Chocolate Crinkle Cookies, *page 70*

# New Classics

# Coconut-Lime Cookies

**MAKES ABOUT 30 COOKIES**
Prep: 15 minutes
Bake: 12 to 13 minutes
Shelf Life: 4 to 5 days

- 2 cups all-purpose flour
- ½ teaspoon baking powder
- ½ teaspoon baking soda
- ½ teaspoon table salt
- ½ cup (1 stick) unsalted butter, melted
- 1 ¼ cups granulated sugar
- 1 large egg
- 1 teaspoon pure vanilla extract
- Grated zest and juice of 2 limes
- ½ teaspoon coconut extract
- 1 cup sweetened coconut flakes

Let's all sing it together now: "She put the lime in the coconut. . ."! Dense and chewy in texture with a citrus zing, these cookies should be served at all summer events. The combination of lime and coconut brings a tropical touch to any party.

1. Preheat the oven to 350°F. Line a cookie sheet with parchment paper.
2. In a medium mixing bowl, sift or whisk together the flour, baking powder, baking soda, and salt.
3. In a large mixing bowl, using an electric mixer on medium speed or a wooden spoon, beat together the butter and sugar until light and creamy. Add the egg, vanilla, lime zest, lime juice, and coconut extract, and beat until combined. Add the dry ingredients and coconut flakes and beat on low speed or by hand until the dough comes together.
4. Using a medium (1½-tablespoon) cookie scoop, scoop the dough into balls and drop them 2 inches apart on the prepared cookie sheet.
5. Bake for 12 to 13 minutes, until the edges are golden brown.
6. Let the cookies rest on the cookie sheets for 5 minutes before transferring them to wire racks to cool completely.

Fold ¾ cup white chocolate chips into the cookie dough to turn these into coconut lime chocolate chip cookies.

# Creamsicle Drops

**MAKES ABOUT 30 COOKIES**
Prep: 10 minutes
Bake: 12 to 13 minutes
Shelf Life: 4 to 5 days

1 3/4 cups all-purpose flour

1 teaspoon baking powder

1/2 teaspoon table salt

1/2 cup (1 stick) unsalted butter, at room temperature

1 1/4 cups granulated sugar

1 large egg

1 teaspoon pure vanilla extract

1 teaspoon orange extract

1 or 2 drops orange gel paste food coloring (optional)

1 1/2 cups white chocolate chips

These cookies are tinted light orange and studded with white chocolate chips. They are soft and have the perfect ratio of cookie to white chocolate chips. I kid you not, these taste just like a Creamsicle! They've been so popular, I've had people asking to buy some from me.

1. Preheat the oven to 350°F. Line a cookie sheet with parchment paper.

2. In a medium mixing bowl, sift or whisk together the flour, baking powder, and salt.

3. In a large mixing bowl, using an electric mixer on medium speed or a wooden spoon, beat together the butter and sugar until light and creamy. This will take about 3 minutes if using an electric mixer or 5 to 6 minutes if creaming by hand. Add the egg, vanilla, orange extract, and orange food coloring (if using), and beat until combined. Add the dry ingredients and beat on low speed or by hand just until incorporated, about 1 minute.

4. Using a rubber spatula, fold in the white chocolate chips until evenly distributed.

5. Using a medium (1½-tablespoon) cookie scoop, scoop the dough into balls and place them 2 inches apart on the prepared cookie sheet.

6. Bake for 12 to 13 minutes, until the edges are golden brown.

7. Let the cookies rest on the cookie sheets for 5 minutes before transferring them to wire racks to cool completely.

Orange gel paste food color can be found in the cake decorating aisle of your supermarket.

# Lemon Crinkle Cookies

**MAKES ABOUT 24 COOKIES**
Prep: 15 minutes
Bake: 11 to 12 minutes
Shelf Life: 4 to 5 days

- 2 cups all-purpose flour
- 2 teaspoons baking powder
- ½ teaspoon table salt
- ½ cup (1 stick) unsalted butter, at room temperature
- 1 cup granulated sugar
- 2 large eggs
- 1 ½ teaspoons grated lemon zest (from 2 lemons)
- 2 tablespoons freshly squeezed lemon juice
- ¼ teaspoon lemon extract
- 1 or 2 drops lemon yellow gel paste food coloring (optional)
- ½ cup confectioners' sugar

These soft, tangy cookies are loaded with a triple dose of lemon flavor from lemon juice, lemon zest, and lemon extract. Before baking, the cookies are rolled in confectioners' sugar to create the gorgeous crinkle effect. These cookies remind me of spring and Easter with their bright, fresh flavors and color.

1. Preheat the oven to 350°F. Line a cookie sheet with parchment paper.
2. In a medium mixing bowl, sift or whisk together the flour, baking powder, and salt.
3. In a large mixing bowl, using an electric mixer on medium speed or a wooden spoon, beat together the butter and sugar until light and creamy. This will take about 3 minutes if using an electric mixer or 5 to 6 minutes if creaming by hand. Add the eggs, lemon zest, lemon juice, lemon extract, and food coloring (if using), and beat until combined. Add the dry ingredients and beat on low speed or by hand until the dough comes together.
4. Using a medium (1½-tablespoon) cookie scoop, scoop the dough into balls and drop them 2 inches apart on the prepared cookie sheets.
5. Bake for 11 to 12 minutes, until the center is set and the edges are firm to the touch..
6. Let the cookies rest on the cookie sheets for 5 minutes before transferring them to wire racks to cool completely.

Make these into orange crinkle cookies by substituting orange zest, juice, and extract for the lemon.

# Brown Butter–Sugar Cookies

**MAKES ABOUT 24 COOKIES**
Prep: 20 minutes
Bake: 12 to 13 minutes
Shelf Life: 4 to 5 days

- 2 cups all-purpose flour
- 2 teaspoons cornstarch
- ½ teaspoon baking powder
- ½ teaspoon baking soda
- ½ teaspoon table salt
- ½ cup (1 stick) unsalted butter
- 1 cup granulated sugar
- ¼ cup packed light brown sugar
- 2 large eggs
- 2 teaspoons pure vanilla extract

These cookies are dense and chewy. The nutty, toasted flavor of browned butter really takes these sugar cookies to the next level. Keep in mind that the melted butter can go from brown to burnt in seconds, so keep a close eye on it!

1. Preheat the oven to 350°F. Line a cookie sheet with parchment paper.
2. In a medium mixing bowl, sift or whisk together the flour, cornstarch, baking powder, baking soda, and salt.
3. In a small saucepan, melt the butter over medium heat. Cook the butter, swirling occasionally, until it begins to brown, 10 to 12 minutes. Remove from the heat.
4. In a large mixing bowl, whisk together the browned butter and both sugars. Add the eggs and vanilla, and beat by hand until combined. Add the dry ingredients and beat by hand to combine.
5. Using a medium (1½-tablespoon) cookie scoop, scoop the dough into balls and drop them 2 inches apart on the prepared cookie sheet.
6. Bake for 12 to 13 minutes, until the edges are golden brown.
7. Let the cookies rest on the cookie sheets for 5 minutes before transferring them to wire racks to cool completely.

Want to spice things up? Roll the scooped cookie dough in cinnamon sugar before baking.

# Brown Butter–Toffee Cookies

**MAKES ABOUT 24 COOKIES**
Prep: 20 minutes
Bake: 10 to 11 minutes
Shelf Life: 4 to 5 days

- 1 ¾ cups all-purpose flour
- ½ teaspoon baking powder
- ½ teaspoon baking soda
- ½ teaspoon table salt
- ½ cup (1 stick) unsalted butter
- 1 cup packed light brown sugar
- ¼ cup granulated sugar
- 1 large egg
- 2 teaspoons pure vanilla extract
- 1 cup toffee bits

These cookies have the most enticing aroma! The brown butter gives them a nutty, toasted flavor that goes great with the toffee bits. The toffee bits provide a rich English toffee flavor as well as a nice crunch.

1. Preheat the oven to 350°F. Line a cookie sheet with parchment paper.
2. In a medium mixing bowl, sift or whisk together the flour, baking powder, baking soda, and salt.
3. In a small saucepan, melt the butter over medium heat. Cook the butter, swirling occasionally, until it begins to brown, 10 to 12 minutes. Remove from the heat.
4. In a large mixing bowl, beat or whisk together the browned butter and both sugars until smooth. Add the egg and vanilla, and whisk to combine. Add the dry ingredients and beat by hand just until incorporated, about 1 minute. Using a rubber spatula, fold in the toffee bits until evenly distributed.
5. Using a medium (1½-tablespoon) cookie scoop, scoop the dough into balls and drop them 2 inches apart on the prepared cookie sheet.
6. Bake for 10 to 11 minutes, until the edges are golden brown.
7. Let the cookies rest on the cookie sheets for 5 minutes before transferring them to wire racks to cool completely.

I enjoy a little chocolate with my toffee and you might, too. Fold ½ cup mini chocolate chips into the dough for small pockets of chocolate in your cookies.

# Brown Sugar–Rolo Cookies

**MAKES ABOUT 22 COOKIES**
Prep: 15 minutes
Bake: 11 to 12 minutes
Shelf Life: 2 to 3 days

- 2 cups all-purpose flour
- ½ teaspoon baking powder
- ½ teaspoon baking soda
- ½ teaspoon table salt
- ½ cup (1 stick) unsalted butter, melted
- ¾ cup packed light brown sugar
- ½ cup packed dark brown sugar
- ¼ cup granulated sugar
- 1 large egg
- 2 teaspoons pure vanilla extract
- 22 Rolo candies

These soft, chewy brown sugar cookies have gooey chocolate caramel centers thanks to the Rolo candies stuffed inside of them. Everyone loves a cookie that has been stuffed with a candy from their childhood, especially if it's one of their favorites. This one is for you, Aunt Ann!

1. Preheat the oven to 350°F. Line a cookie sheet with parchment paper.
2. In a medium mixing bowl, sift or whisk together the flour, baking powder, baking soda, and salt.
3. In a large bowl, stir together the melted butter and all three sugars until combined. Add the egg and vanilla, and beat by hand until smooth. Add the dry ingredients and stir just until the flour is incorporated, about 1 minute.
4. Using a medium (1½-tablespoon) cookie scoop, scoop the dough into balls. Using your finger, create a hole in the center of each ball and push a Rolo candy into it. Cover the opening with dough. Place the filled balls 2 inches apart on the prepared cookie sheet.
5. Bake for 11 to 12 minutes, until the edges are golden brown.
6. Let the cookies rest on the cookie sheet for 5 minutes before transferring them to wire racks to cool completely.

In a pinch, you can use all dark brown sugar or all light brown sugar, depending on what you have on hand.

# Cream Cheese Cookies

**MAKES ABOUT 30 COOKIES**
Prep: 10 minutes
Bake: 17 to 18 minutes
Shelf Life: 2 to 3 days

- 1 ¾ cups all-purpose flour
- ½ teaspoon baking powder
- ½ teaspoon table salt
- ½ cup (1 stick) unsalted butter, at room temperature
- 8 ounces cream cheese, at room temperature
- 1 ¼ cups granulated sugar
- ½ cup confectioners' sugar
- 1 large egg
- 2 teaspoons pure vanilla extract

These cream cheese cookies are soft and cake-like. They have a smooth cream cheese flavor and aren't overly sweet. The addition of cream cheese can make a cookie gummy, so I remade these over and over again, testing different proportions, until I was sure I had gotten it right. Now they have the perfect texture every time.

1. Preheat the oven to 350°F. Line a cookie sheet with parchment paper.
2. In a medium mixing bowl, sift or whisk together the flour, baking powder, and salt.
3. In a large mixing bowl, using an electric mixer on medium speed or a wooden spoon, beat together the butter, cream cheese, and both sugars until light and creamy. This will take about 3 minutes if using an electric mixer or 5 to 6 minutes if creaming by hand. Add the egg and vanilla, and beat until combined. Add the dry ingredients and beat on low speed or by hand until the dough comes together.
4. Using a medium (1½-tablespoon) cookie scoop, scoop the dough into balls and drop them 2 inches apart on the prepared cookie sheet.
5. Bake for 17 to 18 minutes, until the edges are golden brown.
6. Let the cookies rest on the cookie sheets for 5 minutes before transferring them to wire racks to cool completely.

Dust confectioners' sugar onto the cooled cookies for extra sweetness and to help cover up any imperfections.

# White Chocolate–Macadamia Cookies

**MAKES ABOUT 36 COOKIES**

Prep: 15 minutes

Bake: 12 to 13 minutes

Shelf Life: 4 to 5 days

- 2 ¼ cups all-purpose flour
- 1 teaspoon baking soda
- ½ teaspoon table salt
- ½ cup (1 stick) unsalted butter, at room temperature
- 1 cup packed light brown sugar
- ½ cup granulated sugar
- 2 large eggs
- 2 teaspoons pure vanilla extract
- ¾ cup white chocolate chips
- ¾ cup chopped macadamia nuts

Soft and tender, these cookies are studded with white chocolate chips and macadamia nuts. My friend and faithful taste-tester fell in love with these. She mentioned them several times even after taste-testing almost every one of the recipes in this book, which means they stood out.

1. Preheat the oven to 350°F. Line a cookie sheet with parchment paper.
2. In a bowl, sift or whisk together in the flour, baking soda, and salt.
3. In a large mixing bowl, using an electric mixer on medium speed or a wooden spoon, beat together the butter and both sugars until light and creamy. This will take about 3 minutes if using an electric mixer or 5 to 6 minutes if creaming by hand. Add the eggs and vanilla, and beat until combined. Add the dry ingredients and beat on low speed or by hand until the dough comes together. Using a rubber spatula, fold in the white chocolate chips and macadamia nuts.
4. Using a medium (1½-tablespoon) cookie scoop, scoop the dough into balls and drop them 2 inches apart on the prepared cookie sheet.
5. Bake for 12 to 13 minutes, until the edges are golden brown.
6. Let the cookies rest on the cookie sheets for 5 minutes before transferring them to wire racks to cool completely.

Want a chunkier cookie? Add another ¼ cup each white chocolate chips and macadamia nuts (or ½ cup of either one).

# White Chocolate–Cranberry Cookies

**MAKES ABOUT 36 COOKIES**
Prep: 15 minutes
Bake: 11 to 12 minutes
Shelf Life: 4 to 5 days

- 2 ¼ cups all-purpose flour
- 1 teaspoon baking soda
- ½ teaspoon table salt
- ½ cup (1 stick) unsalted butter, at room temperature
- 1 cup packed light brown sugar
- ½ cup granulated sugar
- 2 large eggs
- 2 teaspoons pure vanilla extract
- ¾ cup white chocolate chips
- ¾ cup dried cranberries

I think Christmas when I think about these chewy cookies. In fact, I would recommend leaving some of these cookies and a glass of milk for Santa on Christmas Eve. The dried cranberries help cut the sweetness of the white chocolate and provide great flavor.

1. Preheat the oven to 350°F. Line a cookie sheet with parchment paper.
2. In a medium mixing bowl, sift or whisk together the flour, baking soda, and salt.
3. In a large mixing bowl, using an electric mixer on medium speed or a wooden spoon, beat together the butter and both sugars until light and creamy. This will take about 3 minutes if using an electric mixer or 5 to 6 minutes if creaming by hand. Add the eggs and vanilla, and beat to combine. Add the dry ingredients and beat on low speed or by hand just until incorporated, about 1 minute. Using a rubber spatula, fold in the white chocolate chips and cranberries until evenly distributed.
4. Using a medium (1½-tablespoon) cookie scoop, scoop the dough into balls and place them 2 inches apart on the prepared cookie sheet.
5. Bake for 11 to 12 minutes, until the edges are golden brown.
6. Let the cookies rest on the cookie sheets for 5 minutes before transferring them to wire racks to cool completely.

Turn this cookie into a chocolate chip–raisin cookie by replacing the cranberries with raisins and the white chocolate chips with semisweet chocolate chips.

# Milk Chocolate–Macadamia Cookies

**MAKES ABOUT 36 COOKIES**
Prep: 25 minutes
Bake: 11 to 12 minutes
Shelf Life: 4 to 5 days

3 ¼ cups all-purpose flour

1 teaspoon baking soda

½ teaspoon table salt

¾ cup (1 ½ sticks) unsalted butter, at room temperature

1 cup packed light brown sugar

½ cup granulated sugar

2 large eggs

2 teaspoons pure vanilla extract

¾ cup milk chocolate chips

1 cup chopped macadamia nuts

These simple cookies have a nice crunch from the bits of macadamia nuts. They're thin, soft, and chewy. The milk chocolate chips have a sweeter chocolate flavor than the semisweet chocolate chips most recipes call for.

1. Preheat the oven to 350°F. Line a cookie sheet with parchment paper.
2. In a medium mixing bowl, sift or whisk together the flour, baking soda, and salt.
3. In a large mixing bowl, using an electric mixer on medium speed or a wooden spoon, beat together the butter and both sugars until light and creamy. This will take about 3 minutes if using an electric mixer or 5 to 6 minutes if creaming by hand. Add the eggs and vanilla, and beat until combined. Add the dry ingredients and beat on low speed or by hand until the dough comes together. Using a rubber spatula, fold in the milk chocolate chips and macadamia nuts.
4. Using a medium (1½-tablespoon) cookie scoop, scoop the dough into balls and drop them 2 inches apart on the prepared cookie sheet.
5. Bake for 11 to 12 minutes, until the edges are golden brown.
6. Let the cookies rest on the cookie sheets for 5 minutes before transferring them to wire racks to cool completely.

For a double-chocolate macadamia nut cookie, substitute ½ cup unsweetened cocoa powder for ½ cup of the flour, sifting or whisking it in with the rest of the dry ingredients.

# White Chocolate Chip–Peanut Butter Cookies

**MAKES ABOUT 40 COOKIES**
Prep: 20 minutes
Bake: 12 to 13 minutes
Shelf Life: 4 to 5 days

- 2 cups all-purpose flour
- ½ teaspoon baking powder
- ½ teaspoon baking soda
- ½ teaspoon table salt
- ½ cup (1 stick) unsalted butter, at room temperature
- ¾ cup creamy peanut butter
- 1 cup packed light brown sugar
- ½ cup granulated sugar
- 2 large eggs
- 2 teaspoons pure vanilla extract
- 1 ½ cups white chocolate chips

I love white chocolate peanut butter cups, so I decided to combine those same flavors in these cookies. I started out with a peanut butter cookie, because the more peanut butter, the better. To mimic the white chocolate in the peanut butter cups, I went the easy route and used white chocolate chips.

1. Preheat the oven to 350°F. Line a cookie sheet with parchment paper.
2. In a medium bowl, sift together the flour, baking powder, baking soda, and salt.
3. In a large mixing bowl, using an electric mixer on medium speed or a wooden spoon, beat together the butter, peanut butter, and both sugars until creamy. This will take about 3 minutes if using an electric mixer or 5 to 6 minutes if creaming by hand. Add the eggs and vanilla, and beat until smooth. Add the dry ingredients and beat on low speed or by hand just until incorporated, about 1 minute. Using a rubber spatula, fold in the white chocolate chips.
4. Using a medium (1½-tablespoon) cookie scoop, scoop the dough into balls and place them 2 inches apart on the prepared cookie sheet.
5. Bake for 12 to 13 minutes, until the edges of the cookies are golden brown.
6. Let the cookies rest on the cookie sheets for 5 minutes before transferring them to wire racks to cool completely.

Cut up about ¼ cup of white chocolate peanut butter cups and mix them into the cookies with the white chocolate chips for an extra chunky cookie.

# Peanut Butter Cup–Stuffed Brownie Cookies

**MAKES ABOUT 30 COOKIES**
Prep: 20 minutes
Bake: 12 to 13 minutes
Shelf Life: 4 to 5 days

- ¾ cup all-purpose flour
- ¼ cup unsweetened cocoa powder
- ½ teaspoon baking powder
- ½ teaspoon table salt
- ½ cup (1 stick) unsalted butter, melted
- 8 ounces semisweet baking chocolate, coarsely chopped
- ¾ cup packed light brown sugar
- ¾ cup granulated sugar
- 3 large eggs
- 2 teaspoons pure vanilla extract
- 8 peanut butter cups, quartered

These shiny, crinkle-topped cookies have rich, fudgy insides. In the center of these brownie cookies is a piece of a peanut butter cup. It's a pleasant surprise for us chocolate–peanut butter lovers. My local taste-testers went a little berserk for these.

1. Preheat the oven to 350°F. Line a cookie sheet with parchment paper.
2. In a medium mixing bowl, sift or whisk together the flour, cocoa powder, baking powder, and salt.
3. Combine the melted butter and baking chocolate in a large microwave-safe bowl. Heat at 30-second intervals, stirring in between, until the chocolate is completely melted and the mixture is smooth. Add both sugars and beat, using an electric mixer on medium speed or a wooden spoon, until creamy. This will take about 3 minutes if using an electric mixer or 5 to 6 minutes if creaming by hand. Add the eggs and vanilla, and beat until combined. Add the dry ingredients and beat on low, or by hand, just until incorporated.
4. Using a medium (1½-tablespoon) cookie scoop, scoop the dough into balls. Push one quarter of a peanut butter cup into the center of each ball and cover the opening with additional dough. Place the balls 2 inches apart on the prepared cookie sheet.
5. Bake for 12 to 13 minutes, until the center is set and the edges are firm to the touch.
6. Let the cookies rest on the cookie sheets for 5 minutes before transferring them to wire racks to cool completely.

Instead of a microwave, you can melt the chocolate with the butter in a double boiler on the stove top.

# Almond Joy Cookies

**MAKES ABOUT 38 COOKIES**
Prep: 15 minutes
Bake: About 15 minutes
Shelf Life: 4 to 5 days

- 2 cups all-purpose flour
- ½ teaspoon baking soda
- ½ teaspoon table salt
- ½ cup (1 stick) unsalted butter, melted
- ¾ cup packed light brown sugar
- ¾ cup granulated sugar
- 2 large eggs, room temperature
- 2 teaspoons pure vanilla extract
- ½ teaspoon coconut extract
- 1 cup sweetened coconut flakes
- ¾ cup chopped almonds
- 1 ½ cups semisweet chocolate chips

The familiar flavors of the classic candy bar—coconut, almond, and chocolate—are packed into these cookies. They are the perfect soft-and-chewy cookies. As soon as they came out of the oven, I knew immediately that I had to make these for my mom, who is an Almond Joy fanatic.

1. Preheat the oven to 350°F. Line a cookie sheet with parchment paper.
2. In a medium mixing bowl, sift or whisk together the flour, baking soda, and salt.
3. In a large mixing bowl, using an electric mixer on medium speed or a wooden spoon, beat together the melted butter and both sugars until well combined. Add the eggs, vanilla, and coconut extract, and beat to combine. Add the dry ingredients and coconut flakes, and beat or stir for about 1 minute, until just combined. Using a rubber spatula, fold in the chopped almonds and chocolate chips.
4. Using a medium (1½-tablespoon) cookie scoop, scoop the dough into balls and drop them 2 inches apart on the prepared cookie sheet.
5. Bake for about 15 minutes, until the edges are golden brown.
6. Let the cookies rest for 5 minutes on the cookie sheets before transferring them to wire racks to cool completely.

You can leave the chocolate chips out of the cookie and use them to make a chocolate coating for the cookies instead. Put the chocolate chips in a microwave-safe bowl and heat in the microwave on 50 percent power in 30-second intervals, stirring in between, until the chocolate is completely melted and smooth. Dip the cooled cookies in the chocolate and place on parchment paper to dry.

# Salted Caramel–Chocolate Chip Cookies

**MAKES ABOUT 36 COOKIES**
Prep: 20 minutes
Bake: 12 to 13 minutes
Shelf Life: 4 to 5 days

2 ¼ cups all-purpose flour
1 teaspoon baking soda
½ teaspoon table salt
½ cup (1 stick) unsalted butter, at room temperature
1 cup packed light brown sugar
½ cup granulated sugar
2 large eggs
2 teaspoons pure vanilla extract
1 cup semisweet chocolate chips
20 caramel squares, quartered
1 ½ teaspoons coarse sea salt

These are my favorite kind of chocolate chip cookies. The coarse sea salt brings out the sweetness of the melted caramel candies in these chewy cookies. They tend to be sticky, so I store them on wax paper, which easily peels away.

1. Preheat the oven to 350°F. Line a cookie sheet with parchment paper.
2. In a medium mixing bowl, sift or whisk together the flour, baking soda, and salt.
3. In a large mixing bowl, using an electric mixer on medium speed or a wooden spoon, beat together the butter and both sugars until light and creamy. This will take about 3 minutes if using an electric mixer or 5 to 6 minutes if creaming by hand. Add the eggs and vanilla, and beat until combined. Add the dry ingredients and beat on low speed or by hand until the dough comes together. Using a rubber spatula, fold in the chocolate chips and caramel pieces.
4. Using a medium (1½-tablespoon) cookie scoop, scoop the dough into balls and drop them 2 inches apart on the prepared cookie sheet. Sprinkle a bit of coarse sea salt on the top of each dough ball.
5. Bake for 12 to 13 minutes, until the edges are golden brown.
6. Let the cookies rest on the cookie sheets for 5 minutes before transferring them to wire racks to cool completely.

If you're unable to find caramel squares, the caramel bits that are sold in the baking aisle are a great substitute.

# Red Velvet–Chocolate Chunk Cookies

**MAKES ABOUT 30 COOKIES**
Prep: 10 minutes
Chill: 1 hour
Bake: 14 to 15 minutes
Shelf Life: 4 to 5 days

- 1 3/4 cups all-purpose flour
- 1/4 cup unsweetened cocoa powder
- 1 teaspoon baking soda
- 1/2 teaspoon table salt
- 1/2 cup (1 stick) unsalted butter, at room temperature
- 1 cup packed light brown sugar
- 1/2 cup granulated sugar
- 1 large egg
- 2 teaspoons pure vanilla extract
- 1 tablespoon red velvet emulsion or red gel paste food coloring
- 1 1/2 cups semisweet chocolate chunks

Like the classic cake, these cookies have a light chocolate flavor and a gorgeous red color. I love to use red velvet emulsion for all my red velvet desserts because it provides both flavor and color in one shot. You can find this emulsion at a cake decorating store or on Amazon. If you don't have it, you can substitute red gel paste food coloring.

1. In a medium mixing bowl, sift or whisk together the flour, cocoa powder, baking soda, and salt.
2. In a large mixing bowl, using an electric mixer on medium speed or a wooden spoon, beat together the butter and both sugars until light and creamy. This will take about 3 minutes if using an electric mixer or 5 to 6 minutes if creaming by hand. Add the egg, vanilla, and emulsion or food coloring, and beat until combined. Add the dry ingredients and beat on low speed or by hand until just incorporated. Using a rubber spatula, fold in the chocolate chunks. Cover the dough with plastic wrap and chill for at least 1 hour.
3. Preheat the oven to 350°F. Line a cookie sheet with parchment paper.
4. Using a medium (1½-tablespoon) cookie scoop, scoop the dough into balls and drop them 2 inches apart on the prepared cookie sheet.
5. Bake for 14 to 15 minutes, until the centers are set and the edges are firm to the touch.
6. Let the cookies rest on the cookie sheets for 5 minutes before transferring them to wire racks to cool completely.

You can replace the semisweet chunks with any flavor chocolate chips.

# Chocolate Chip, Pumpkin, and Cream Cheese Cookies

**MAKES ABOUT 46 COOKIES**
Prep: 20 minutes
Bake: 13 to 14 minutes
Shelf Life: 4 to 5 days

2 ½ cups all-purpose flour
½ teaspoon baking powder
½ teaspoon baking soda
½ teaspoon table salt
1 teaspoon ground cinnamon
¼ teaspoon ground ginger
¼ teaspoon ground nutmeg
¼ teaspoon ground cloves
½ cup (1 stick) unsalted butter, at room temperature
4 ounces cream cheese, at room temperature
1 ¼ cups packed light brown sugar
½ cup granulated sugar
2 large eggs
2 teaspoons pure vanilla extract
1 cup canned pumpkin purée (not pumpkin pie filling)
1 cup semisweet chocolate chips

These thick, cakey cookies are super-soft and filled with pumpkin, spices, and chocolate chips. The addition of cream cheese gives them a creamy, smooth texture. If you haven't tried chocolate and pumpkin together, you need to try it as soon as possible! It's life changing.

1. Preheat the oven to 350°F. Line a cookie sheet with parchment paper.
2. In a medium mixing bowl, sift or whisk together the flour, baking powder, baking soda, salt, cinnamon, ginger, nutmeg, and cloves.
3. In a large mixing bowl, using an electric mixer on medium speed or a wooden spoon, beat together the butter, cream cheese, and both sugars until light and creamy. This will take about 3 minutes if using an electric mixer or 5 to 6 minutes if creaming by hand. Add the eggs, vanilla, and pumpkin, and beat until smooth. Add the dry ingredients and beat until incorporated. Using a rubber spatula, fold in the chocolate chips until evenly distributed.
4. Using a medium (1½-tablespoon) cookie scoop, scoop the dough into balls and drop them 2 inches apart on the prepared cookie sheet.
5. Bake for 13 to 14 minutes, until the tops of the cookies are set.
6. Let the cookies rest on the cookie sheets for 5 minutes before transferring them to wire racks to cool completely.

You can replace the semisweet chocolate chips with any kind of chocolate chips.

# Nutella-Stuffed Cookies

**MAKES ABOUT 24 COOKIES**
Prep: 20 minutes
Chill: 1 to 2 hours
Bake: 10 to 11 minutes
Shelf Life: 4 to 5 days

1 1/4 cups all-purpose flour

1/2 cup unsweetened cocoa powder

1/2 teaspoon baking soda

1/2 teaspoon table salt

1/2 cup (1 stick) unsalted butter, at room temperature

3/4 cup packed light brown sugar

3/4 cup granulated sugar

1 large egg

2 teaspoons pure vanilla extract

1/2 cup Nutella, chilled

Not a fan of chocolate-hazelnut spread? Use Hershey's chocolate spread or Reese's peanut butter chocolate spread instead.

These chocolate cookies have a pleasing outer crunch and a gooey Nutella filling. For those you don't know, Nutella is a chocolate-hazelnut spread that is all the rage. I love to break these cookies in half while they're still slightly warm and get the full gooey effect.

1. Preheat the oven to 350°F. Line a cookie sheet with parchment paper.

2. In a medium mixing bowl, sift or whisk together the flour, cocoa powder, baking soda, and salt.

3. In a large mixing bowl, using an electric mixer on medium speed or a wooden spoon, beat together the butter and both sugars until light and creamy. This will take about 3 minutes if using an electric mixer or 5 to 6 minutes if creaming by hand. Add the egg and vanilla, and beat to combine. Add the dry ingredients and beat on low speed or by hand just until incorporated, about 1 minute.

4. Form the dough into a ball, wrap in plastic wrap, and chill for 1 to 2 hours. Chill the Nutella at the same time.

5. Using a medium (1½-tablespoon) cookie scoop, scoop the dough into balls. Using a finger, create a hole in the center of each dough ball. Using a teaspoon, scoop out a ball of Nutella and press it into the well. Cover the opening with cookie dough. Roll the dough ball between your palms to make it smooth, then place it on the prepared cookie sheet, leaving about 2 inches of space between balls.

6. Bake for 10 to 11 minutes, until the outsides of the cookies are shiny.

7. Let the cookies rest for 5 minutes on the cookie sheets before transferring to wire racks to cool completely.

# Monster Cookies

**MAKES ABOUT 46 COOKIES**
Prep: 20 minutes
Bake: 11 to 12 minutes
Shelf Life: 4 to 5 days

- 1 1/4 cups all-purpose flour
- 1/2 teaspoon baking powder
- 1/2 teaspoon baking soda
- 1/2 teaspoon table salt
- 1/2 cup (1 stick) unsalted butter, at room temperature
- 3/4 cup creamy peanut butter
- 3/4 cup packed light brown sugar
- 3/4 cup granulated sugar
- 2 large eggs
- 2 teaspoons pure vanilla extract
- 2 cups old-fashioned rolled oats
- 3/4 cup semisweet chocolate chips
- 3/4 cup plain M&Ms

These cookies are soft, chewy, and quite chunky. They are packed full of flavors from the peanut butter, oatmeal, chocolate chips and M&Ms. I'm not exactly sure why they're called monster cookies, but I'm going to go with the fact that they have a monster list of ingredients. Also, this recipe makes a monster batch of cookies.

1. Preheat the oven to 350°F. Line a cookie sheet with parchment paper.
2. In a medium mixing bowl, sift or whisk together the flour, baking powder, baking soda, and salt.
3. In a large mixing bowl, using an electric mixer on medium speed or a wooden spoon, beat together the butter, peanut butter, and both sugars until creamy. This will take about 3 minutes if using an electric mixer or 5 to 6 minutes if creaming by hand. Add the eggs and vanilla, and beat until combined. Add the dry ingredients and beat on low speed or by hand just until incorporated. Using a rubber spatula, fold in the oats, chocolate chips, and M&Ms.
4. Using a medium (1½-tablespoon) cookie scoop, scoop the dough into balls and drop them 2 inches apart on the prepared cookie sheet.
5. Bake for 11 to 12 minutes, until golden brown.
6. Let the cookies rest on the cookie sheets for 5 minutes before transferring them to wire racks to cool completely.

I sometimes like to replace ¼ cup of the plain M&Ms with ¼ cup of mini M&Ms (they can found in the baking aisle next to the chocolate chips). It gives the cookies a fun appearance and even more contrast.

# Malted Milk Chocolate Cookies

**MAKES ABOUT 28 COOKIES**
Prep: 25 minutes
Bake: 10 to 11 minutes
Shelf Life: 2 to 3 days

1 3/4 cups all-purpose flour

3/4 cup malted milk powder

3 tablespoons unsweetened cocoa powder

2 teaspoons cornstarch

1 teaspoon baking powder

1/2 teaspoon table salt

1/4 cup (1/2 stick) unsalted butter, at room temperature

1/2 cup vegetable shortening

3/4 cup packed light brown sugar

1/2 cup granulated sugar

1 large egg

2 teaspoons pure vanilla extract

3/4 cup chopped malted milk balls (optional)

Malted milk desserts tend to get a lot of attention on my blog, so I thought I would make a cookie version to add to my cookie cookbook. You get a double-dose of malted milk in this cookie with the malted milk powder and malted candy balls.

1. Preheat the oven to 350°F. Line a cookie sheet with parchment paper.

2. In a medium mixing bowl, sift or whisk together the flour, malted milk powder, cocoa powder, cornstarch, baking powder, and salt.

3. In a large mixing bowl, using an electric mixer on medium speed or a wooden spoon, beat together the butter, shortening, and both sugars until light and creamy. This will take about 3 minutes if using an electric mixer or 5 to 6 minutes if creaming by hand. Add the egg and vanilla, and beat to combine. Add the dry ingredients and beat on low speed or by hand just until incorporated, about 1 minute. Using a rubber spatula, fold in the malted milk balls (if using).

4. Using a medium (1½-tablespoon) cookie scoop, scoop the dough into balls and place them 2 inches apart on the prepared cookie sheet.

5. Bake for 10 to 11 minutes, until the center is set and the edges are firm to the touch.

6. Let the cookies rest for 5 minutes on the cookie sheets before transferring them to wire racks to cool completely.

Malted milk powder can usually be found in the coffee aisle and/or juice aisle of your local supermarket.

# Inside-Out Sprinkle Sugar Cookies

**MAKES ABOUT 20 COOKIES**
Prep: 20 minutes
Bake: 13 to 14 minutes
Shelf Life: 4 to 5 days

**FOR THE FROSTING**

¼ cup vegetable shortening

2 cups confectioners' sugar

1½ tablespoons milk

1 teaspoon butter vanilla emulsion

**FOR THE COOKIES**

1¾ cups all-purpose flour

1 teaspoon baking powder

½ teaspoon table salt

½ cup (1 stick) unsalted butter, at room temperature

½ cup granulated sugar

1 large egg

2 teaspoons pure vanilla extract

¾ cup sprinkles

These treats are sugar cookies stuffed with frosting, rolled in some bright sprinkles, and then baked. They are a little time consuming to prepare, but the results are worth it. This is a great cookie to make with your kids! Butter vanilla emulsion can be found in the cake decorating aisle of your supermarket.

**TO MAKE THE FROSTING**

In a medium mixing bowl, using an electric mixer on medium speed or a wooden spoon, beat together the shortening, confectioners' sugar, milk, and butter vanilla emulsion until it comes together into a ball. Using a teaspoon, scoop out the frosting and roll into about 20 small balls. Set aside.

**TO MAKE THE COOKIES**

1. Preheat the oven to 350°F. Line a cookie sheet with parchment paper.

2. In a medium mixing bowl, sift or whisk together the flour, baking powder, and salt.

3. In a large mixing bowl, using an electric mixer on medium speed or a wooden spoon, beat together the butter and sugar until light and creamy. This will take about 3 minutes if using an electric mixer or 5 to 6 minutes if creaming by hand. Add the egg and vanilla, and beat to combine. Add the dry ingredients and beat on low speed or by hand just until incorporated, about 1 minute.

## Inside-Out Sprinkle Sugar Cookies *continued*

4. Using a medium (1½-tablespoon) cookie scoop, scoop the dough into balls. Make a hole in the center of each cookie dough ball with your finger. Press one ball of frosting into each ball of dough and cover the opening with cookie dough.

5. Put the sprinkles in a shallow bowl. Roll each ball of dough in the sprinkles to coat. Place the balls 2 inches apart on the prepared cookie sheet.

6. Bake for 13 to 14 minutes, until the edges are golden brown.

7. Let the cookies rest for 5 minutes on the cookie sheets before transferring them to wire racks to cool completely.

If you can't find butter vanilla emulsion in the cake section of your supermarket, substitute vanilla extract.

# Cookies and Cream Pudding Cookies

**MAKES ABOUT 40 COOKIES**
Prep: 15 minutes
Bake: 10 to 11 minutes
Shelf Life: 4 to 5 days

2 1/4 cups all-purpose flour

1 (4.2-ounce) package cookies and crème pudding mix

1/2 teaspoon baking powder

1/2 teaspoon baking soda

1/4 teaspoon table salt

1 cup (2 sticks) unsalted butter, at room temperature

1 cup granulated sugar

2 large eggs

2 teaspoons pure vanilla extract

2 cups crushed chocolate sandwich cookies (from about 26 cookies)

These cookies are soft and tender, and they taste just like cookies and cream ice cream. But don't worry—these cookies won't melt like the ice cream! They're loaded with crushed cookies that have been folded in and become soft. These are a hit with all the neighborhood kids!

1. Preheat the oven to 350°F. Line a cookie sheet with parchment paper.

2. In a medium mixing bowl, sift or whisk together the flour, dry pudding mix, baking powder, baking soda, and salt.

3. In a large mixing bowl, using an electric mixer on medium speed or a wooden spoon, beat together the butter and sugar until light and creamy. This will take about 3 minutes if using an electric mixer or 5 to 6 minutes if creaming by hand. Add the eggs and vanilla, and beat until combined. Add the dry ingredients and beat on low or by hand, just until the flour is incorporated. Using a rubber spatula, fold the crushed cookies into the dough until evenly distributed.

4. Using a medium (1½-tablespoon) cookie scoop, scoop the dough into balls and drop them 2 inches apart on the prepared cookie sheet.

5. Bake for 10 to 11 minutes, until the edges are golden brown.

6. Let the cookies rest on the cookie sheets for 5 minutes before transferring them to wire racks to cool completely.

For a decadent cookie, melt ½ cup white chocolate candy melts, which can be found in the baking aisle, and dip half of each cookie in the melted chocolate. Or you can put the melted white chocolate in a resealable plastic bag and snip off one corner of the bag. Lay the cookies on a sheet of parchment paper and drizzle each cookie with the melted white chocolate.

# Peanut Butter, Chocolate Chip, and Banana Cookies

**MAKES ABOUT 40 COOKIES**
Prep: 20 minutes
Bake: 12 to 13 minutes
Shelf Life: 4 to 5 days

2 ¼ cups all-purpose flour
½ teaspoon baking powder
½ teaspoon baking soda
½ teaspoon table salt
½ cup (1 stick) unsalted butter, at room temperature
¾ cup creamy peanut butter
¾ cup packed light brown sugar
¾ cup granulated sugar
2 large eggs
2 teaspoons pure vanilla extract
2 ripe bananas, mashed
1 ½ cups semisweet chocolate chips

These cookies are for those times that you can't decide whether you want peanut butter or chocolate with your banana cookies. Combine all three flavors and see what a sweet treat you will get. The cookies are so soft and satisfying you won't regret it!

1. Preheat the oven to 350°F. Line a cookie sheet with parchment paper.
2. In a medium mixing bowl, sift or whisk together the flour, baking powder, baking soda, and salt.
3. In a large mixing bowl, using an electric mixer on medium speed or a wooden spoon, beat together the butter, peanut butter, and both sugars until creamy. This will take about 3 minutes if using an electric mixer or 5 to 6 minutes if creaming by hand. Mix in the eggs, vanilla, and mashed bananas until incorporated. Add the dry ingredients and beat on low or by hand, just until incorporated. Using a rubber spatula, fold in the chocolate chips.
4. Using a medium (1½-tablespoon) cookie scoop, scoop the dough into balls and drop them 2 inches apart on the prepared cookie sheet.
5. Bake for 12 to 13 minutes, until the edges are golden brown.
6. Let the cookies rest for 5 minutes on the cookie sheets before transferring them to wire racks to cool completely.

For more texture, use chunky peanut butter in place of creamy. You can also substitute peanut butter chips for half of the chocolate chips for more intense peanut flavor.

# Potato Chip Cookies

**MAKES ABOUT 30 COOKIES**
Prep: 15 minutes
Bake: 12 to 13 minutes
Shelf Life: 4 to 5 days

2 cups all-purpose flour

1 teaspoon baking soda

½ teaspoon table salt

¾ cup (1 ½ sticks) unsalted butter, at room temperature

1 cup granulated sugar

½ cup light packed brown sugar

1 large egg

1 teaspoon pure vanilla extract

2 cups crushed plain potato chips

1 ½ teaspoons coarse sea salt (optional)

Potato chips in cookies? You bet. The chips add a salty flavor and a crunchy texture. This is another unique recipe that will have people questioning what's in them. There's one thing that I know for sure: people have a hard time putting these down.

1. Preheat the oven to 350°F. Line a cookie sheet with parchment paper.

2. In a medium mixing bowl, sift or whisk together the flour, baking soda, and table salt.

3. In a large mixing bowl, using an electric mixer on medium speed or a wooden spoon, beat together the butter and both sugars until light and creamy. This will take about 3 minutes if using an electric mixer or 5 to 6 minutes if creaming by hand. Add the egg and vanilla, and beat until combined. Add the dry ingredients and beat on low speed or by hand until the dough comes together. Using a rubber spatula, fold in the crushed potato chips.

4. Using a medium (1½-tablespoon) cookie scoop, scoop the dough into balls and drop them 2 inches apart on the prepared cookie sheet. Sprinkle the coarse sea salt on top.

5. Bake for 12 to 13 minutes, until the edges are golden brown.

6. Let the cookies rest on the cookie sheets for 5 minutes before transferring them to wire racks to cool completely.

To crush the potato chips, put them in a resealable plastic bag and crush them with a rolling pin or meat tenderizer.

# Chocolate Crinkle Cookies

**MAKES ABOUT 34 COOKIES**
Prep: 20 minutes
Bake: 12 to 13 minutes
Shelf Life: 4 to 5 days

2 cups all-purpose flour

¾ cup unsweetened cocoa powder

2 teaspoons baking powder

½ teaspoon table salt

¼ cup (½ stick) unsalted butter, at room temperature

¼ cup vegetable oil

1 ½ cups granulated sugar

½ cup packed light brown sugar

3 large eggs

2 teaspoons pure vanilla extract

½ cup confectioners' sugar

These sugar-coated chocolate cookies have a crunchy outside and a rich, fudgy inside. You see these most often during Christmas, but I'm okay with them year-round. I'm always in awe when I see these cookies come out of the oven. (That could just be my passion showing through!)

1. Preheat the oven to 350°F. Line a cookie sheet with parchment paper.

2. In a medium mixing bowl, sift or whisk together the flour, cocoa powder, baking powder, and salt.

3. In a large mixing bowl, using an electric mixer on medium speed or a wooden spoon, beat together the butter, oil, and both sugars until light and creamy. This will take about 3 minutes if using an electric mixer or 5 to 6 minutes if creaming by hand. Add the eggs and vanilla, and beat until combined. Add the dry ingredients and beat on low speed or by hand until the dough comes together.

4. Put the confectioners' sugar in a shallow bowl for rolling.

5. Using a medium (1½-tablespoon) cookie scoop, scoop the dough into balls, drop them into the confectioners' sugar, and roll to coat. Place the balls 2 inches apart on the prepared cookie sheet.

6. Bake for 12 to 13 minutes, until the cookies are cracked on top.

7. Let the cookies rest on the cookie sheets for 5 minutes before transferring them to wire racks to cool completely.

You can roll the cookie dough first in granulated sugar and then in the confectioners' sugar. This will help dry out the dough, giving your cookies even more of a cracked effect.

# Rum-Raisin Cookies

**MAKES ABOUT 22 COOKIES**
Prep: 15 minutes
Bake: 11 to 12 minutes
Shelf Life: 4 to 5 days

- 1 ½ cups all-purpose flour
- 1 teaspoon baking soda
- ½ teaspoon table salt
- ½ cup (1 stick) unsalted butter, at room temperature
- ¾ cup packed light brown sugar
- ¼ teaspoon granulated sugar
- 1 large egg
- 1 teaspoon pure vanilla extract
- 1 teaspoon rum extract
- 1 cup raisins

If you think rum-raisin ice cream is tasty, these cookies will knock your socks off. At first glance, they may look like basic chocolate chip cookies, but bite into one and you'll be surprised to find that they're actually filled with raisins and flavored with rum extract.

1. Preheat the oven to 350°F. Line a cookie sheet with parchment paper.
2. In a medium mixing bowl, sift or whisk together the flour, baking soda, and salt.
3. In a large mixing bowl, using an electric mixer on medium speed or a wooden spoon, beat together the butter and both sugars until creamy. This will take about 3 minutes if using an electric mixer or 5 to 6 minutes if creaming by hand. Add the egg, vanilla, and rum extract, and beat to combine. Add the dry ingredients and beat on low or by hand just until incorporated, about 1 minute. Using a rubber spatula, fold in the raisins.
4. Using a medium (1½-tablespoon) cookie scoop, scoop the dough into balls and drop them 2 inches apart on the prepared cookie sheet.
5. Bake for 11 to 12 minutes, until the edges are golden brown.
6. Let the cookies rest on the cookie sheets for 5 minutes before transferring them to wire racks to cool completely.

For an extra-boozy rum flavor, soak the raisins in rum before adding them to the cookies. Simply put the raisins in a Mason jar and cover them completely with rum, then let them soak for at least 3 hours, or preferably overnight.

# Bananas Foster Pudding Cookies

**MAKES ABOUT 36 COOKIES**
Prep: 20 minutes
Bake: 11 to 12 minutes
Shelf Life: 2 to 3 days

2¼ cups all-purpose flour
1 (3.4-ounce) package banana cream pudding mix
½ teaspoon baking powder
½ teaspoon baking soda
½ teaspoon table salt
1 cup (2 sticks) unsalted butter, at room temperature
½ cup packed light brown sugar
½ cup packed dark brown sugar
2 large eggs
1¼ teaspoons rum extract
1 teaspoon pure vanilla extract
20 caramel squares, quartered

These unique cookies are banana pudding cookies with a hint of rum flavoring and bits of caramel throughout it. They tend to be thin, soft, and slightly sticky. They're inspired by the well-known New Orleans dessert, Bananas Foster. The dessert is made with bananas, vanilla ice cream, and a sauce made from butter, brown sugar, cinnamon, rum, and banana liqueur.

1. Preheat the oven to 350°F. Line a cookie sheet with parchment paper.
2. In a medium mixing bowl, sift or whisk together the flour, dry pudding mix, baking powder, baking soda, and salt.
3. In a large mixing bowl, using an electric mixer on medium speed or a wooden spoon, beat together the butter and both sugars until creamy. This will take about 3 minutes if using an electric mixer or 5 to 6 minutes if creaming by hand. Add the eggs, rum extract, and vanilla, and beat to combine. Add the dry ingredients and beat on low or by hand until just incorporated, about 1 minute. Using a rubber spatula, fold the caramel pieces into the dough.
4. Using a medium (1½-tablespoon) cookie scoop, scoop the dough into balls and place them 2 inches apart on the prepared cookie sheet.
5. Bake for 11 to 12 minutes, until the center is set and the edges are golden brown.
6. Let the cookies rest on the cookie sheets for 5 minutes before transferring them to wire racks to cool completely.

If you're unable to find the caramel squares, use the caramel bits that can be found in the baking aisle next to the chocolate chips.

Neapolitan Slice 'n' Bake Cookies, page 96

# Shortbread, Slice 'n' Bakes, and Cut-Out Cookies

# Chocolate-Dipped Shortbread Cookies

**MAKES ABOUT 12 COOKIES**
Prep: 20 minutes
Bake: 13 to 14 minutes
Shelf Life: 4 to 5 days

**FOR THE COOKIES**

½ cup (1 stick) unsalted butter, at room temperature

⅓ cup confectioners' sugar

2 tablespoons granulated sugar

1 teaspoon pure vanilla extract

1 cup all-purpose flour

¼ teaspoon table salt

**FOR THE CHOCOLATE GANACHE**

4 ounces semisweet baking chocolate, chopped

¼ cup heavy cream

These shortbread cookies are rich, buttery, and slightly crumbly. Once baked and cooled, they are dipped in chocolate ganache. Shortbread cookies are usually made with all confectioners' sugar, but I love to add a little granulated sugar because I think it improves the flavor. Use a 2- or 2½-inch round cookie cutter for these.

**TO MAKE THE COOKIES**

1. Preheat the oven to 350°F. Line a cookie sheet with parchment paper.

2. In a large mixing bowl, using an electric mixer on medium speed or a wooden spoon, beat together the butter, both sugars, and vanilla until smooth, about 45 seconds. Add the flour and salt and beat on low speed or by hand until just incorporated, about 1 minute.

3. Place the dough between two sheets of wax paper or parchment paper. Using a rolling pin, roll out the dough to an even ½-inch thickness.

4. Using a 2- or 2½-inch round cookie cutter, cut out the cookies and place them 2 inches apart on the prepared cookie sheet.

5. Bake for 13 to 14 minutes, until the edges are golden brown.

6. Let the cookies rest on the cookie sheets for 5 minutes before transferring them to wire racks to cool completely.

**TO MAKE THE GANACHE**

1. In a microwave-safe bowl, combine the chopped chocolate and cream and heat on high for 45 seconds. Stir, then continue microwaving in 45-second intervals and stirring, until the chocolate is completely melted and the mixture is smooth.

2. Once the cookies have cooled completely, dip half of each in the ganache, allowing the excess to drip back into the bowl. Return the cookies to the wire rack to dry.

If you don't have 2- or 2½-inch round cookie cutter, check your cabinet for a juice glass with a 2- or 2½-inch opening. Dip the glass in flour and cut out the cookies with it.

# Maple-Pecan Shortbread Cookies

**MAKES ABOUT 12 COOKIES**
Prep: 15 minutes
Bake: 13 to 14 minutes
Shelf Life: 4 to 5 days

- ½ cup (1 stick) unsalted butter, at room temperature
- ⅓ cup confectioners' sugar
- 2 tablespoons granulated sugar
- 1 teaspoon pure vanilla extract
- ¼ teaspoon maple extract
- 1 cup all-purpose flour
- ¼ teaspoon table salt
- ¼ cup pecans, chopped

Maple and pecan go together so well, it only seems right to pair them in a cookie. These rich, crumbly shortbread cookies have a light maple flavor that complements the chopped pecans and butter flavor. You will love these crumbled on top of a bowl of maple-pecan ice cream.

1. Preheat the oven to 350°F. Line a cookie sheet with parchment paper.
2. In a large bowl, beat together the butter, both sugars, vanilla, and maple extract for about 45 seconds. Add the flour, salt, and pecans, and beat or mix by hand until just incorporated, about 1 minute.
3. Place the dough between two sheets of wax paper or parchment paper. Using a rolling pin, roll out the dough to an even ½-inch thickness.
4. Using a 2- or 2½-inch round cookie cutter, cut out the cookies and place them 2 inches apart on the prepared cookie sheet.
5. Bake for 13 to 14 minutes, until the edges are golden brown.
6. Let the cookies rest on the cookie sheets for 5 minutes before transferring them to wire racks to cool completely.

Substitute butter pecan extract for the maple extract.

## Rolling Dough

**I find that the best way to roll out cookie dough is between two sheets of wax paper or parchment paper. If you prefer, you can sprinkle a bit of flour on the work surface and the rolling pin before rolling out the dough, but that will result in additional flour being added to the dough.**

Whichever method you prefer, press the dough down to flatten it. Using a rolling pin and even pressure, roll out the dough to an even ¼- to ½-inch thickness, depending on what the recipe calls for.

If the dough becomes warm and sticky, refrigerate it for 15 to 30 minutes for easier rolling.

# Almond Shortbread Cookies

**MAKES ABOUT 12 COOKIES**
Prep: 15 minutes
Bake: 13 to 14 minutes
Shelf Life: 4 to 5 days

½ cup (1 stick) unsalted butter, at room temperature

⅓ cup confectioners' sugar

2 tablespoons granulated sugar

1 teaspoon pure vanilla extract

½ teaspoon almond extract

1 cup all-purpose flour

¼ teaspoon table salt

¼ cup sliced almonds, finely chopped

What better way to make an almond shortbread cookie than to have a double-dose of almond flavor? These shortbread cookies are speckled with bits of chopped almonds and flavored more with almond extract. The shortbread has a soft, crumbly texture with a bit of crunch from the almonds.

1. Preheat the oven to 350°F. Line a cookie sheet with parchment paper.

2. In a large mixing bowl, using an electric mixer on medium speed or a wooden spoon, beat together the butter, both sugars, vanilla, and almond extract until light and creamy. This will take about 3 minutes if using an electric mixer or 5 to 6 minutes if creaming by hand. Add the flour, salt, and almonds, and beat on low speed or by hand until the dough comes together, about 1 minute.

3. Place the dough between two sheets of wax paper or parchment paper. Using a rolling pin, roll out the dough to an even ½-inch thickness.

4. Using a 2-inch round cookie cutter, cut out the cookies and place them 2 inches apart on the prepared cookie sheet.

5. Bake for 13 to 14 minutes, until the edges are golden brown.

6. Let the cookies rest on the cookie sheets for 5 minutes before transferring them to wire racks to cool completely.

In a pinch, you can use any kind of almonds. Just chop them as finely as possible to avoid large chunks in the cookies.

# Pumpkin Spice Shortbread Cookies

**MAKES ABOUT 12 COOKIES**
Prep: 15 minutes
Chill: 30 minutes
Bake: 14 to 15 minutes
Shelf Life: 4 to 5 days

- 1 cup all-purpose flour
- ½ teaspoon pumpkin pie spice
- ¼ teaspoon table salt
- ½ cup (1 stick) unsalted butter, at room temperature
- 7 tablespoons confectioners' sugar
- 3 tablespoons packed light brown sugar
- 1 large egg
- 2 tablespoons canned pumpkin purée (not pumpkin pie filling)
- 1 teaspoon pure vanilla extract

This recipe is for my husband, who loves shortbread and pumpkin pie. These are classic shortbread cookies loaded with all the delectable flavors of pumpkin pie. They are, of course, perfect for a holiday cookie platter, but they'll be happily devoured any time of year.

1. In a medium mixing bowl, sift or whisk together the flour, pumpkin pie spice, and salt.
2. In a large mixing bowl, using an electric mixer on medium speed or a wooden spoon, beat together the butter and both sugars until light and creamy. This will take about 3 minutes if using an electric mixer or 5 to 6 minutes if creaming by hand. Add the egg, pumpkin purée, and vanilla, and beat to combine. Add the dry ingredients and beat on low speed or by hand until the dough comes together, about 1 minute.
3. Place the dough between two sheets of wax paper or parchment paper. Using a rolling pin, roll out the dough to an even ½-inch thickness. Wrap the dough in the paper and refrigerate until firm, about 30 minutes.
4. Preheat the oven to 350°F. Line a cookie sheet with parchment paper.
5. Using a 2-inch round cookie cutter, cut out the cookies and place them 2 inches apart on the prepared cookie sheet.
6. Bake for 14 to 15 minutes, until the edges are golden brown.
7. Let the cookies rest on the cookie sheets for 5 minutes before transferring them to wire racks to cool completely.

These cookies call for a very small amount of canned pumpkin purée, so it's best to freeze the rest of the pumpkin in ice cube trays or muffin tins and store in a resealable plastic bag. It will keep for several months.

# Sweet Tea Shortbread Cookies

MAKES ABOUT 12 COOKIES
Prep: 10 minutes
Chill: 30 minutes
Bake: 14 to 15 minutes
Shelf Life: 4 to 5 days

**FOR THE COOKIES**

½ cup (1 stick) unsalted butter, at room temperature

⅓ cup confectioners' sugar

2 tablespoons granulated sugar

1 teaspoon pure vanilla extract

2 tea bags

1 cup all-purpose flour

¼ teaspoon table salt

**FOR THE GLAZE**

1 tea bag

3 tablespoons water

1 cup confectioners' sugar

Sweet tea doesn't just come in drink form anymore. I was never a huge fan of unsweetened iced tea, but it turns out that I am a pretty big fan of sweet tea, and it is especially delicious in dessert form. These tea cookies are topped with a sweet tea glaze.

**TO MAKE THE COOKIES**

1. In a large mixing bowl, using an electric mixer on medium speed or a wooden spoon, beat together the butter and both sugars until light and creamy. This will take about 3 minutes if using an electric mixer or 5 to 6 minutes if creaming by hand. Add the vanilla and the contents of the tea bags, and beat to combine. Add the flour and salt and beat on low speed or by hand until the dough comes together, about 1 minute.

2. Place the dough between two sheets of wax paper or parchment paper. Using a rolling pin, roll out the dough to an even ½-inch thickness. Wrap the dough in the paper and refrigerate until firm, about 30 minutes.

3. Preheat the oven to 350°F. Line a cookie sheet with parchment paper.

4. Using a 2-inch round cookie cutter, cut out the cookies and place them 2 inches apart on the prepared cookie sheet.

5. Bake for 14 to 15 minutes, until the edges are golden brown.

6. Let the cookies rest on the cookie sheets for 5 minutes before transferring them to wire racks to cool completely.

**TO MAKE THE GLAZE**

1. While the cookies are cooling, put the tea bag and the water in a small microwave-safe bowl and microwave on high for 30 seconds. Let the tea steep for 2 to 3 minutes, then remove and discard the tea bag.

2. Add the confectioners' sugar to the tea and whisk until smooth.

3. When the cookies are completely cooled, dip the tops into the glaze and let the excess drip off. Place the cookies on a piece of wax paper to dry for 1 to 2 hours.

Wondering what kind of tea to use? I like either Earl Grey or chai for this recipe, but any strong black tea will work well.

# Cranberry-Pistachio Shortbread

**MAKES ABOUT 12 COOKIES**
Prep: 15 minutes
Chill: 30 minutes
Bake: 14 to 15 minutes
Shelf Life: 4 to 5 days

½ cup (1 stick) unsalted butter, at room temperature

⅓ cup confectioners' sugar

2 tablespoons granulated sugar

1 teaspoon pure vanilla extract

1 cup all-purpose flour

¼ teaspoon table salt

¼ cup chopped dried cranberries

¼ cup chopped pistachios

2 ounces white baking chocolate, chopped

Here's another cookie that belongs on your holiday cookie platter. Not only do the flavors scream Christmas, but the colors do, too. The cranberries provide a concentrated flavor while the pistachios add crunch as well as a nutty flavor. Surprisingly, they are pretty easy to cut with a cookie cutter.

1. In a large mixing bowl, using an electric mixer on medium speed or a wooden spoon, beat together the butter and both sugars until light and creamy. This will take about 3 minutes if using an electric mixer or 5 to 6 minutes if creaming by hand. Add the vanilla and beat to combine. Add the flour and salt, and beat on low speed or by hand until the dough comes together, about 1 minute. Using a rubber spatula, fold in the dried cranberries and pistachios until evenly distributed.

2. Place the dough between two sheets of wax paper or parchment paper. Using a rolling pin, roll out the dough to an even ½-inch thickness. Wrap the dough in the paper and refrigerate until firm, about 30 minutes.

3. Preheat the oven to 350°F. Line a cookie sheet with parchment paper.

4. Using a 2-inch round cookie cutter, cut out the cookies and place them 2 inches apart on the prepared cookie sheet.

5. Bake for 14 to 15 minutes, until the edges are golden brown.

6. Let the cookies rest on the cookie sheets for 5 minutes before transferring them to wire racks to cool completely.

7. To make the topping, put the white chocolate in a small microwave-safe bowl and heat in 30-second intervals, stirring in between, until the chocolate is completely melted and smooth. Transfer the melted white chocolate to a resealable plastic bag and snip off one of the corners. Drizzle the white chocolate over each cookie.

Not a white chocolate fan? Substitute semisweet baking chocolate.

# Lemon Shortbread Cookies

**MAKES ABOUT 10 COOKIES**
Prep: 15 minutes
Bake: 13 to 14 minutes
Shelf Life: 4 to 5 days

**FOR THE COOKIES**

½ cup (1 stick) unsalted butter, at room temperature

½ cup confectioners' sugar

2 teaspoons grated lemon zest

1 ½ tablespoons freshly squeezed lemon juice

1 cup all-purpose flour

¼ teaspoon table salt

**FOR THE GLAZE**

2 tablespoons freshly squeezed lemon juice

1 ¼ cups confectioners' sugar

To get the tangy lemon flavor, these rich, buttery lemon cookies are full of lemon zest and lemon juice. The best part to these cookies is the lemon glaze, so don't forget to add it! It takes the cookie from being a good lemon cookie to a standout lemon cookie.

**TO MAKE THE COOKIES**

1. Preheat the oven to 350°F. Line a cookie sheet with parchment paper.
2. In a large mixing bowl, using an electric mixer on medium speed or a wooden spoon, beat together the butter, confectioners' sugar, lemon zest, and lemon juice until light and creamy. This will take about 3 minutes if using an electric mixer or 5 to 6 minutes if creaming by hand. Add the flour and salt, and beat on low speed or by hand until just incorporated, about 1 minute.
3. Place the dough between two sheets of wax paper or parchment paper. Using a rolling pin, roll out the dough to an even ½-inch thickness.
4. Using a 2-inch round cookie cutter, cut out the cookies and place them 2 inches apart on the prepared cookie sheet.
5. Bake for 13 to 14 minutes, until the edges are golden brown.
6. Let the cookies rest on the cookie sheets for 5 minutes before transferring them to wire racks to cool completely.

### TO MAKE THE GLAZE

1. In a small bowl, whisk together the lemon juice and confectioners' sugar until smooth.

2. When the cookies are completely cooled, dip the tops into the glaze. Place the dipped cookies on a piece of wax paper or parchment paper to dry for 1 to 2 hours.

Add 1 teaspoon of grated lemon zest to the glaze to add extra lemon flavor and a bit of textural contrast.

# Blueberry-Lemon Shortbread Cookies

**MAKES ABOUT 12 COOKIES**
Prep: 15 minutes
Chill: 30 minutes
Bake: 14 to 15 minutes
Shelf Life: 4 to 5 days

½ cup (1 stick) unsalted butter, at room temperature

7 tablespoons confectioners' sugar

2 tablespoons granulated sugar

2 teaspoons grated lemon zest

1 ½ tablespoons freshly squeezed lemon juice

1 cup all-purpose flour

¼ teaspoon table salt

¼ cup chopped dried blueberries

Blueberries immediately make me think of summer, but the beauty of this recipe is that by using dried blueberries, you can make these cookies any time of the year. I like using dried blueberries here because their flavor is concentrated, making them pair especially well with the lemon zest to give these cookies intense fruity flavor.

1. In a large mixing bowl, using an electric mixer on medium speed or a wooden spoon, beat together the butter and both sugars until light and creamy. This will take about 3 minutes if using an electric mixer or 5 to 6 minutes if creaming by hand. Add the lemon zest and lemon juice and beat to combine. Add the flour and salt, and beat on low speed or by hand until the dough comes together, about 1 minute. Using a rubber spatula, fold in the blueberries until incorporated.

2. Place the dough between two sheets of wax paper or parchment paper. Using a rolling pin, roll out the dough to an even ½-inch thickness. Wrap the dough in the paper and refrigerate until firm, about 30 minutes.

3. Preheat the oven to 350°F. Line a cookie sheet with parchment paper.

4. Using a 2-inch round cookie cutter, cut out the cookies and place them 2 inches apart on the prepared cookie sheet.

5. Bake for 14 to 15 minutes, until the edges are golden brown.

6. Let the cookies rest on the cookie sheet for 5 minutes before transferring them to wire racks to cool completely.

You can substitute any other dried fruit you like for the dried blueberries in this recipe.

# Chocolate Chip Shortbread Cookies

**MAKES ABOUT 12 COOKIES**
Prep: 15 minutes
Bake: 13 to 14 minutes
Shelf Life: 4 to 5 days

½ cup (1 stick) unsalted butter, at room temperature

½ cup confectioners' sugar

1 teaspoon pure vanilla extract

1 cup all-purpose flour

¼ teaspoon table salt

½ cup mini semisweet chocolate chips

Of course you can add chocolate chips to shortbread! I love how mini chocolate chips speckled throughout these buttery cookies create a nice contrast. Using mini chocolate chips instead of regular-size chips also allows the cookies to be rolled thinner, making them easier to cut.

1. Preheat the oven to 350°F. Line a cookie sheet with parchment paper.

2. In a large mixing bowl, using an electric mixer on medium speed or a wooden spoon, beat together the butter and confectioners' sugar until light and creamy. This will take about 3 minutes if using an electric mixer or 5 to 6 minutes if creaming by hand. Add the vanilla, flour, salt, and chocolate chips, and beat on low speed or by hand until the dough comes together, about 1 minute.

3. Place the dough between two sheets of wax paper or parchment paper. Using a rolling pin, roll out the dough to an even ½-inch thickness.

4. Using a 2-inch round cookie cutter, cut out the cookies and place them 2 inches apart on the prepared cookie sheet.

5. Bake for 13 to 14 minutes, until the edges are golden brown.

6. Let the cookies rest on the cookie sheets for 5 minutes before transferring them to wire racks to cool completely.

Do you love cinnamon and chocolate together? Add ½ teaspoon ground cinnamon to the dry ingredients when making the dough.

# Cherry–Chocolate Chip Shortbread

**MAKES ABOUT 12 COOKIES**
Prep: 20 minutes
Chill: 30 minutes
Bake: 14 to 15 minutes
Shelf Life: 4 to 5 days

- ½ cup (1 stick) unsalted butter, at room temperature
- ⅓ cup confectioners' sugar
- 2 tablespoons granulated sugar
- 1 teaspoon maraschino cherry juice
- 1 cup all-purpose flour
- ¼ teaspoon table salt
- ¼ cup chopped maraschino cherries
- ¼ cup mini semisweet chocolate chips

This pink-hued shortbread is one of my favorites. The bits of maraschino cherries and mini chocolate chips make the cookie taste like a chocolate-covered cherry with a hint of buttery goodness. Make sure to drain the maraschino cherries well before adding them to the dough.

1. In a large mixing bowl, using an electric mixer on medium speed or a wooden spoon, beat together the butter and both sugars until light and creamy. This will take about 3 minutes if using an electric mixer or 5 to 6 minutes if creaming by hand. Add the maraschino cherry juice and beat to combine. Add the flour and salt, and beat on low speed or by hand until the dough comes together, about 1 minute. Using a rubber spatula, fold in the chopped cherries and mini chocolate chips until evenly distributed.
2. Place the dough between two sheets of wax paper or parchment paper. Using a rolling pin, roll out the dough to an even ½-inch thickness. Wrap the dough in the paper and refrigerate until firm, about 30 minutes.
3. Preheat the oven to 350°F. Line a cookie sheet with parchment paper.
4. Using a 2-inch round cookie cutter, cut out the cookies and place them 2 inches apart on the prepared cookie sheet.
5. Bake for 14 to 15 minutes, until the edges are golden brown.
6. Let the cookies rest on the cookie sheets for 5 minutes before transferring them to wire racks to cool completely.

The maraschino cherry juice can be left out, or you can use cherry extract instead.

# Coffee Shortbread Cookies

**MAKES ABOUT 12 COOKIES**
Prep: 15 minutes
Chill: 30 minutes
Bake: 14 to 15 minutes
Shelf Life: 4 to 5 days

**FOR THE COOKIES**

½ cup (1 stick) unsalted butter, at room temperature

⅓ cup confectioners' sugar

2 tablespoons granulated sugar

1 teaspoon pure vanilla extract

1 teaspoon instant coffee granules

1 cup all-purpose flour

¼ teaspoon table salt

**FOR THE GLAZE**

1 teaspoon instant coffee granules

2 teaspoons warm water

1 tablespoon milk

1 ¼ cups confectioners' sugar

I love coffee-flavored desserts and was pretty eager to make these. These rich, crumbly shortbread cookies were passed around town. Again, I took a good coffee cookie and made it a great one with the finishing touch of a strong coffee glaze. Serve them, of course, with fresh brewed coffee.

**TO MAKE THE COOKIES**

1. In a large mixing bowl, using an electric mixer on medium speed or a wooden spoon, beat together the butter and both sugars until light and creamy. This will take about 3 minutes if using an electric mixer or 5 to 6 minutes if creaming by hand. Add the vanilla and coffee and beat to combine. Add the flour and salt, and beat on low speed or by hand until the dough comes together, about 1 minute.

2. Place the dough between two sheets of wax paper or parchment paper. Using a rolling pin, roll out the dough to an even ½-inch thickness. Wrap the dough in the paper and refrigerate until firm, about 30 minutes.

3. Preheat the oven to 350°F. Line a cookie sheet with parchment paper.

4. Using a 2-inch round cookie cutter, cut out the cookies and place them 2 inches apart on the prepared cookie sheet.

5. Bake for 14 to 15 minutes, until the edges are golden brown.

6. Let the cookies rest on the cookie sheets for 5 minutes before transferring them to wire racks to cool completely.

**TO MAKE THE GLAZE**

1. While the cookies are cooling, in a small bowl, whisk together the coffee, warm water, milk, and confectioners' sugar until smooth.

2. Once the cookies have cooled completely, dip the tops into the glaze and let the excess drip off. Place on a piece of wax paper and let dry for 1 to 2 hours.

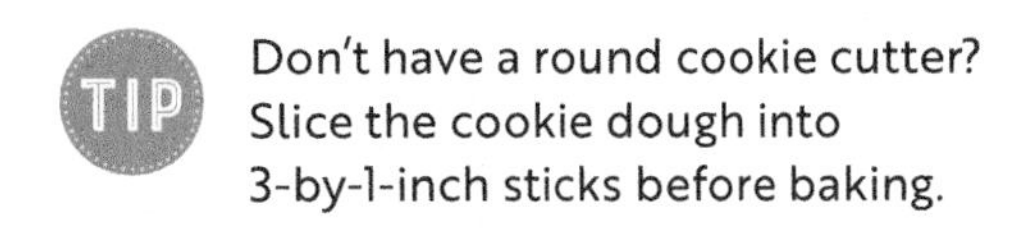

Don't have a round cookie cutter? Slice the cookie dough into 3-by-1-inch sticks before baking.

# Pretzel–Chocolate Chip Shortbread Cookies

**MAKES ABOUT 12 COOKIES**
Prep: 15 minutes
Chill: 30 minutes
Bake: 14 to 15 minutes
Shelf Life: 4 to 5 days

**½ cup (1 stick) unsalted butter, at room temperature**

**⅓ cup confectioners' sugar**

**2 tablespoons granulated sugar**

**1 teaspoon pure vanilla extract**

**1 cup all-purpose flour**

**¼ teaspoon table salt**

**¼ cup mini semisweet chocolate chips**

**⅓ cup chopped salted pretzels**

Add more flavor by melting ½ cup caramel squares with 1½ teaspoons milk in the microwave. Let it set up for about 10 minutes, and then spread it on top of the cookies. Sprinkle the cookies with coarse sea salt.

This is the perfect cookie for people who love sweet and salty (like yours truly). Like chocolate-covered pretzels, these cookies are sweet from the chocolate chips and salty from the pretzel bits. I like that there are pieces of pretzel and mini chocolate chips in every bite.

1. In a large mixing bowl, using an electric mixer on medium speed or a wooden spoon, beat together the butter and both sugars until light and creamy. This will take about 3 minutes if using an electric mixer or 5 to 6 minutes if creaming by hand. Add the vanilla and beat to combine. Add the flour and salt, and beat on low speed or by hand until the dough comes together, about 1 minute. Using a rubber spatula, fold in the mini chocolate chips and chopped pretzels until evenly distributed.
2. Place the dough between two sheets of wax paper or parchment paper. Using a rolling pin, roll out the dough to an even ½-inch thickness. Wrap the dough in the paper and refrigerate until firm, about 30 minutes.
3. Preheat the oven to 350°F. Line a cookie sheet with parchment paper.
4. Using a 2-inch round cookie cutter, cut out the cookies and place them 2 inches apart on the prepared cookie sheet.
5. Bake for 14 to 15 minutes, until the edges are golden brown.
6. Let the cookies rest on the cookie sheets for 5 minutes before transferring them to wire racks to cool completely.

# Homemade Graham Crackers

**MAKES ABOUT 22 COOKIES**
Prep: 20 minutes
Chill: 2 hours
Bake: 12 to 13 minutes
Shelf Life: 4 to 5 days

- 1 ¼ cups all-purpose flour
- 1 cup graham flour
- 1 teaspoon ground cinnamon
- ½ teaspoon baking soda
- ½ teaspoon table salt
- ¾ cup (1 ½ sticks) unsalted butter, at room temperature
- ¾ cup packed dark brown sugar
- 3 tablespoons honey
- 1 tablespoon pure vanilla extract

Can't find graham flour? Use whole-wheat flour instead.

These thin, crunchy cookies are filled with the flavors of honey and cinnamon. Just like whole-wheat flour, graham flour is made from whole grains, but it is not sifted during milling. Look for graham flour in the health foods or baking sections of your supermarket.

1. In a medium mixing bowl, sift or whisk together both flours, the cinnamon, baking soda, and salt.
2. In a large mixing bowl, using an electric mixer on medium speed or a wooden spoon, beat together the butter and sugar until light and creamy. This will take about 3 minutes if using an electric mixer or 5 to 6 minutes if creaming by hand. Add the honey and vanilla, and beat to combine. Add the dry ingredients and beat on low speed or by hand until the dough comes together, about 1 minute.
3. Place the dough between two sheets of wax paper or parchment paper. Using a rolling pin, roll it out to an even ⅛-inch thickness. Wrap the dough in the paper and refrigerate until firm, at least 2 hours.
4. Preheat the oven to 350°F. Line a cookie sheet with parchment paper.
5. Using a 2- or 2½-inch square cookie cutter, cut out the cookies and place them 2 inches apart on the prepared cookie sheet. With a skewer or other pointy object, draw a line down the center of each cookie and add 4 rows of 2 dots on either side of the line.
6. Bake for 12 to 13 minutes, until the edges are golden brown.
7. Let the cookies rest for 10 to 15 minutes on the cookie sheets before transferring them to wire racks to cool completely.

# Neapolitan Slice 'n' Bake Cookies

**MAKES ABOUT 24 COOKIES**
Prep: 35 minutes
Chill: 2 hours
Bake: 18 to 19 minutes
Shelf Life: 4 to 5 days

3½ cups all-purpose flour

½ teaspoon baking powder

½ teaspoon table salt

1½ cups (1 stick) unsalted butter, at room temperature

1½ cups granulated sugar

1 large egg

1 tablespoon pure vanilla extract

1½ teaspoons strawberry extract

1 or 2 drops pink gel paste food coloring

3 tablespoons unsweetened cocoa powder

Do you like Neapolitan ice cream? These cookies are for you! They're soft cookies with layers of chocolate, strawberry, and vanilla. I love cutting into these to see the different colors. I love the challenge of getting all three flavors in my mouth at once, too.

1. In a medium mixing bowl, sift or whisk together the flour, baking powder, and salt.

2. In a large mixing bowl, using an electric mixer on medium speed or a wooden spoon, beat together the butter and sugar until light and creamy. This will take about 3 minutes if using an electric mixer or 5 to 6 minutes if creaming by hand. Add the egg and vanilla, and beat to combine. Add the dry ingredients and beat on low speed or by hand until the dough comes together, about 1 minute. Divide the dough into 3 equal balls.

3. Add the strawberry extract and food coloring to one dough ball, working them into the dough with a rubber spatula or your hands, until evenly distributed.

4. Add the cocoa powder to the second dough ball, working it into the dough until evenly distributed.

5. Place the plain dough ball between two sheets of wax paper or parchment paper. Using a rolling pin, roll out the dough into a 12-by-9-inch rectangle. Repeat with the other two dough balls.

6. Carefully place the vanilla dough rectangle on top of the strawberry dough rectangle. Place the chocolate rectangle on top so that all three are stacked.

7. Wrap the dough in the paper and refrigerate until firm, about 2 hours.

8. Preheat the oven to 350°F. Line a cookie sheet with parchment paper.

9. Slice the cookies about ½-inch thick and place them 2 inches apart on the prepared cookie sheet.

10. Bake for 18 to 19 minutes, until the edges are golden.

11. Let the cookies rest on the cookie sheets for 5 minutes before transferring them to wire racks to cool completely.

Get creative with the fruity extract! Replace the strawberry extract with raspberry, cherry, or even orange extract. If using orange, use orange gel paste food coloring instead of pink.

# Cinnamon Roll Slice 'n' Bake Cookies

**MAKES ABOUT 24 COOKIES**
Prep: 25 minutes
Chill: 2 hours 15 minutes
Bake: 17 to 18 minutes
Shelf Life: 4 to 5 days

**FOR THE COOKIES**

2 ¼ cups all-purpose flour

1 teaspoon baking powder

1 teaspoon cornstarch

½ teaspoon table salt

¾ cup (1 ½ sticks) unsalted butter, at room temperature

½ cup granulated sugar

½ cup confectioners' sugar

1 large egg

1 teaspoon pure vanilla extract

1 teaspoon cream cheese emulsion

**FOR THE FILLING**

5 tablespoons unsalted butter, melted

¾ cup packed light brown sugar

3 tablespoons all-purpose flour

1 tablespoon ground cinnamon

Easier and less time-consuming than cinnamon rolls made with yeast dough, these cookies include that familiar cinnamon swirl we all love. The cream cheese emulsion gives the dough a rich flavor. My husband and son could eat an entire batch of these in one sitting.

**TO MAKE THE COOKIES**

1. In a medium mixing bowl, sift or whisk together the flour, baking powder, cornstarch, and salt.

2. In a large mixing bowl, using an electric mixer on medium speed or a wooden spoon, beat together the butter and both sugars until light and creamy. This will take about 3 minutes if using an electric mixer or 5 to 6 minutes if creaming by hand. Add the egg, vanilla, and cream cheese emulsion, and beat to combine. Add the dry ingredients and beat on low speed or by hand until the dough comes together, about 1 minute.

3. Place the dough between two sheets of wax paper or parchment paper and roll it out to an even ¼-inch thickness. Wrap the dough in the paper and refrigerate until firm, about 15 minutes.

**TO MAKE THE FILLING**

1. In a small bowl, stir together the melted butter, brown sugar, flour, and cinnamon until combined.

2. Spread the cinnamon filling on top of the firm cookie dough and spread it all the way out to the edges. Starting from one long side of the dough, roll it up into a tight cylinder. Roll the dough back and forth to get rid of any air pockets. Wrap the dough in the paper again and refrigerate until firm, about 2 hours.

3. Preheat the oven to 350°F. Line a cookie sheet with parchment paper.

4. Slice the cookies ¼- to ½-inch thick and place them on the prepared cookie sheets, leaving about 2 inches between each cookie.

5. Bake for 17 to 18 minutes, until the edges are golden.

6. Let the cookies rest on the cookie sheets for 5 minutes before transferring them to wire racks to cool completely.

You can find bakery emulsions, like the cream cheese emulsion used in this recipe, in the cake baking and decorating section of many supermarkets, or at crafts stores like Michael's. You can also order them online.

# Thin Mints

**MAKES ABOUT 24 COOKIES**
Prep: 25 minutes
Bake: 14 to 15 minutes
Shelf Life: 4 to 5 days

**FOR THE COOKIES**

1 3/4 cups all-purpose flour

1/2 cup unsweetened cocoa powder

1 teaspoon baking powder

1 teaspoon cornstarch

1/2 teaspoon table salt

3/4 cup (1 1/2 sticks) unsalted butter, at room temperature

1 cup granulated sugar

1 large egg

1/2 teaspoon peppermint extract

**FOR THE CHOCOLATE COATING**

1 pound semisweet baking chocolate

3 teaspoons vegetable oil

These homemade "thin" mints are actually quite thick, which means that they hold their shape perfectly. They are soft chocolate-and-peppermint-flavored cookies enrobed in chocolate. The packaged version can't compare to these homemade ones. My favorite part is the smooth and shiny chocolate coating.

**TO MAKE THE COOKIES**

1. Preheat the oven to 350°F. Line a cookie sheet with parchment paper.

2. In a medium mixing bowl, sift or whisk together the flour, cocoa powder, baking powder, cornstarch, and salt.

3. In a large mixing bowl, using an electric mixer on medium speed or a wooden spoon, beat together the butter and sugar until light and creamy. This will take about 3 minutes if using an electric mixer or 5 to 6 minutes if creaming by hand. Add the egg and peppermint extract, and beat to combine. Add the dry ingredients and beat on low speed or by hand until the dough comes together, about 1 minute.

4. Place the dough between two sheets of wax paper or parchment paper. Using a rolling pin, roll out the dough to an even ½-inch thickness.

5. Using a 2-inch round cookie cutter, cut out the cookies and place them 2 inches apart on the prepared cookie sheet.

6. Bake for 14 to 15 minutes, until the center is set and the edges are firm to the touch.

7. Let the cookies rest on the cookie sheets for 5 minutes before transferring them to wire racks to cool completely.

### TO MAKE THE CHOCOLATE COATING

1. Combine the baking chocolate and vegetable oil in a small microwave-safe bowl and heat on 50 percent power in 30-second intervals, stirring in between, until melted and smooth.

2. Dip the cooled cookies into the melted chocolate and tap off the excess.

3. Place the coated cookies on a sheet of wax paper or parchment paper to set for 1 to 2 hours.

For some color contrast, add a little green. It can be green sprinkles or a green drizzle using candy melts. If you opt for a green drizzle, you can find green candy melts in the cake decorating section of most supermarkets. Put ¼ cup candy melts in a microwave-safe bowl and microwave on 50 percent power in 30-second intervals, stirring in between, until melted and smooth. Transfer the melted candy melts to a resealable plastic bag and snip off one corner of the bag. While the cookies are drying on the paper, drizzle the candy melt on top. Let dry for another 30 minutes.

# Classic Sugar Cookies

**MAKES ABOUT 45 COOKIES**
Prep: 20 minutes
Chill: 1 hour
Bake: 13 to 14 minutes
Shelf Life: 4 to 5 days

**FOR THE COOKIES**

4 cups all-purpose flour

1 ½ teaspoons baking powder

1 teaspoon cornstarch

½ teaspoon table salt

1 ½ cups (3 sticks) unsalted butter, at room temperature

1 ¾ cups granulated sugar

2 large eggs

1 tablespoon pure vanilla extract

**FOR THE FROSTING**

1 cup (2 sticks) unsalted butter, at room temperature

3 ½ cups confectioners' sugar

⅓ cup milk

2 teaspoons pure vanilla extract

Food coloring and sprinkles (optional)

These sugar cookies are soft, yet dense. They're perfect for decorating and hold their shape when baked. As a kid, I used to hate when I put in all the work to cut out my pretty cookie shapes only to see them get smooshed together and unidentifiable after baking.

**TO MAKE THE COOKIES**

1. In a medium mixing bowl, sift or whisk together the flour, baking powder, cornstarch, and salt.

2. In a large mixing bowl, using an electric mixer on medium speed or a wooden spoon, beat together the butter and sugar until light and creamy. This will take about 3 minutes if using an electric mixer or 5 to 6 minutes if creaming by hand. Add the eggs and vanilla, and beat to combine. Add the dry ingredients and beat on low speed or by hand until the dough comes together, about 1 minute.

3. Place the dough between two sheets of wax paper or parchment paper. Using a rolling pin, roll out the dough to an even ½-inch thickness. Wrap the dough in the paper and refrigerate until firm, about 1 hour.

4. Preheat the oven to 350°F. Line a cookie sheet with parchment paper.

5. Using a 2-inch round cookie cutter or your preferred shape, cut out the cookies and place them 2 inches apart on the prepared cookie sheet.

6. Bake for 13 to 14 minutes, until the edges are golden brown.

7. Let the cookies rest on the cookie sheets for 5 minutes before transferring them to wire racks to cool completely.

#### TO MAKE THE FROSTING

1. In a large mixing bowl, using an electric mixer on medium speed or a wooden spoon, beat together the butter, confectioners' sugar, milk, and vanilla until fluffy. This will take 1 to 2 minutes if using an electric mixer or 4 to 5 minutes if beating by hand.
2. When the cookies are completely cooled, spread the frosting evenly over their tops. Decorate them with your choice of colorings and sprinkles, if desired.

Does this recipe make too many cookies for your needs? Cut out the cookies and place them on a cookie sheet lined with parchment paper or wax paper as if you were going to bake them. Place the cookie sheet in the freezer. When they are frozen solid, quickly transfer them to a resealable plastic bag and store in the freezer until ready to use. They can be baked from frozen, but you may need to add a minute or two to the baking time.

# Peppermint Crunch Cut-Out Cookies

**MAKES ABOUT 24 COOKIES**
Prep: 15 minutes
Chill: 1 hour
Bake: 12 to 13 minutes
Shelf Life: 4 to 5 days

- 2 ¼ cups all-purpose flour
- 1 teaspoon baking powder
- 1 teaspoon cornstarch
- ½ teaspoon table salt
- ¾ cup (1 ½ sticks) unsalted butter, at room temperature
- 1 cup granulated sugar
- 1 large egg
- ¼ teaspoon peppermint extract
- ½ cup Andes peppermint crunch baking chips

For a fun finish, dip half of each cookie in white chocolate. Melt ¾ cup white chocolate candy melts (found in the baking aisle of the supermarket) in the microwave and dip half of each cookie in it. Tap off the excess chocolate and place the cookies on a sheet of wax paper or parchment paper to dry for 1 hour.

Perfect at Christmastime, these cookies have red bits of crunchy peppermint speckled throughout and a buttery peppermint flavor. The cookies are soft and slightly crumbly. This is a cookie that begs to be dipped in a cup of hot chocolate.

1. Preheat the oven to 350°F. Line a cookie sheet with parchment paper.
2. In a medium mixing bowl, sift or whisk together the flour, baking powder, cornstarch, and salt.
3. In a large mixing bowl, using an electric mixer on medium speed or a wooden spoon, beat together the butter and sugar until light and creamy. This will take about 3 minutes if using an electric mixer or 5 to 6 minutes if creaming by hand. Add the egg and peppermint extract, and beat to combine. Add the dry ingredients and beat on low speed or by hand until the dough comes together, about 1 minute. Using a rubber spatula, fold in the baking chips.
4. Place the dough between two sheets of wax paper or parchment paper. Using a rolling pin, roll out the dough to an even ½-inch thickness. Wrap the dough in the paper and refrigerate until firm, at least 1 hour.
5. Using a 2-inch round cookie cutter, cut out the cookies and place them 2 inches apart on the prepared cookie sheet.
6. Bake for 12 to 13 minutes, until the edges are golden.
7. Let the cookies rest on the cookie sheets for 5 minutes before transferring them to wire racks to cool completely.

# Chocolate-Vanilla Slice 'n' Bake Pinwheels

**MAKES ABOUT 28 COOKIES**
Prep: 25 minutes
Chill: 2 hours
Bake: 14 to 15 minutes
Shelf Life: 4 to 5 days

- 3½ cups all-purpose flour
- ½ teaspoon baking powder
- ½ teaspoon table salt
- 1½ cups (3 sticks) unsalted butter, at room temperature
- 1½ cups granulated sugar
- 1 large egg
- 1 tablespoon pure vanilla extract
- 4 ounces unsweetened baking chocolate, chopped

As my son says, these cookies look like zebras. But what I love about this recipe is that the cookies don't need to be baked immediately. Once the dough is rolled into a log, it can be refrigerated or frozen and then sliced and baked as needed.

1. In a medium mixing bowl, sift or whisk together the flour, baking powder, and salt.
2. In a large mixing bowl, using an electric mixer on medium speed or a wooden spoon, beat together the butter and sugar until light and creamy. This will take about 3 minutes if using an electric mixer or 5 to 6 minutes if creaming by hand. Add the egg and vanilla, and beat to combine. Add the dry ingredients and beat on low speed or by hand until the dough comes together, about 1 minute. Divide the dough in half, leaving one half in the bowl.
3. Put the baking chocolate in a small microwave-safe bowl and heat on 50 percent power in 30-second intervals, stirring in between, until melted and smooth.
4. Pour the melted chocolate into the dough in the bowl and beat it into the dough until it is evenly distributed.
5. Place the vanilla dough between two sheets of wax paper or parchment paper. Using a rolling pin, roll it out into a 14-by-9-inch rectangle. Do the same with the chocolate dough.

6. Keeping the bottom side of the chocolate rectangle stuck to the wax paper, flip it over onto the vanilla rectangle, lining up the edges. Starting from one of the long sides, tightly roll up the dough into a cylinder. Roll the dough back and forth a few times to help remove air pockets between the layers. Wrap the dough in the paper and refrigerate until firm, about 2 hours.

7. Preheat the oven to 350°F. Line a cookie sheet with parchment paper.

8. Slice the cookies about ½-inch thick and place them 2 inches apart on the prepared cookie sheet.

9. Bake for 14 to 15 minutes, until the edges are golden.

10. Let the cookies rest on the cookie sheets for 5 minutes before transferring them to wire racks to cool completely.

The unsweetened baking chocolate can be replaced with semisweet baking chocolate or milk chocolate baking chocolate. The sweeter the chocolate, the sweeter the cookie.

# Nutella Pinwheel Swirls

**MAKES ABOUT 20 COOKIES**
Prep: 25 minutes
Chill: 2 hours 15 minutes
Bake: 17 to 18 minutes
Shelf Life: 4 to 5 days

2 1/4 cups all-purpose flour
1 teaspoon baking powder
1 teaspoon cornstarch
1/2 teaspoon table salt
3/4 cup (1 1/2 sticks) unsalted butter, at room temperature
1 cup granulated sugar
1 large egg
1 teaspoon pure vanilla extract
1/2 cup Nutella

These pinwheel cookies are soft and tender. They're a slice-and-bake sugar cookie with a delicious, rich chocolate-hazelnut swirl. Once rolled out and formed into a log, these cookies can be stored in the refrigerator or freezer and sliced and baked as needed.

1. In a medium mixing bowl, sift or whisk together the flour, baking powder, cornstarch, and salt.

2. In a large mixing bowl, using an electric mixer on medium speed or a wooden spoon, beat together the butter and sugar until light and creamy. This will take about 3 minutes if using an electric mixer or 5 to 6 minutes if creaming by hand. Add the egg and vanilla, and beat to combine. Add the dry ingredients and beat on low speed or by hand until the dough comes together, about 1 minute.

3. Place the dough between two sheets of wax paper or parchment paper. Using a rolling pin, roll out the dough to an even 1/4-inch thickness. Wrap the dough in the paper and refrigerate until firm, about 15 minutes.

4. Spread the Nutella on top of the firm cookie dough, spreading it all the way to the edges. Starting from one of the long sides, tightly roll up the dough into a cylinder. Roll the dough back and forth to get rid of any air pockets in the swirl. Wrap the dough in the paper and refrigerate until firm, about 2 hours.

5. Preheat the oven to 350°F. Line a cookie sheet with parchment paper.

6. Slice the cookies ¼- to ½-inch thick and place them 2 inches apart on the prepared cookie sheet.

7. Bake for 17 to 18 minutes, until the edges are golden.

8. Let the cookies rest on the cookie sheets for 5 minutes before transferring them to wire racks to cool completely.

Don't care for chocolate and hazelnut? Use Hershey's chocolate spread or Reese's peanut butter–chocolate spread instead.

# Peanut Butter Cut-Out Cookies

**MAKES ABOUT 50 COOKIES**
Prep: 25 minutes
Chill: 2 hours
Bake: 13 to 14 minutes
Shelf Life: 4 to 5 days

4 ½ cups all-purpose flour

1 ½ teaspoons baking powder

1 teaspoon cornstarch

½ teaspoon table salt

1 ½ cups (3 sticks) unsalted butter, at room temperature

1 ½ cups creamy peanut butter

1 cup packed light brown sugar

1 cup granulated sugar

2 large eggs

2 teaspoons pure vanilla extract

**FOR THE FROSTING**

1 ½ cups (3 sticks) unsalted butter, at room temperature

4 cups confectioners' sugar

¾ cup unsweetened cocoa powder

⅓ cup milk

These cut-out cookies are dense and soft. I love to top them with chocolate frosting, but they taste equally delicious without it. This recipe makes a lot of cookies, so unless you're planning to serve them for a large event, be prepared to freeze some or share them with the whole town.

1. In a medium mixing bowl, sift or whisk together the flour, baking powder, cornstarch, and salt.
2. In a large mixing bowl, using an electric mixer on medium speed or a wooden spoon, beat together the butter, peanut butter, and both sugars until light and creamy. This will take about 3 minutes if using an electric mixer or 5 to 6 minutes if creaming by hand. Add the eggs and vanilla, and beat to combine. Add the dry ingredients and beat on low speed or by hand until the dough comes together, about 1 minute.
3. Place the dough between two sheets of wax paper or parchment paper. Using a rolling pin, roll out the dough to an even ½-inch thickness. Wrap the dough in the paper and refrigerate until firm, at least 2 hours.
4. Preheat the oven to 350°F. Line a cookie sheet with parchment paper.
5. Using a 2-inch round cookie cutter, cut out the cookies and place them 2 inches apart on the prepared cookie sheet.
6. Bake for 13 to 14 minutes, until the edges are golden.
7. Let the cookies rest on the cookie sheets for 5 minutes before transferring them to wire racks to cool completely.

**TO MAKE THE FROSTING**

1. While the cookies are cooling, in a large bowl, using an electric mixer on medium speed or a wire whisk, beat together the butter, confectioners' sugar, cocoa powder, and milk, until whipped and creamy, 1 to 2 minutes.

2. Once the cookies have cooled, spread the frosting over their tops.

If you or someone you're cooking for can't eat peanuts, you can replace the peanut butter with almond butter.

# Fruity Pebbles Cut-Out Cookies

**MAKES ABOUT 28 COOKIES**
Prep: 20 minutes
Chill: 1 hour
Bake: 12 to 13 minutes
Shelf Life: 4 to 5 days

2 1/4 cups all-purpose flour

1 teaspoon baking powder

1 teaspoon cornstarch

1/2 teaspoon table salt

3/4 cup (1 1/2 sticks) unsalted butter, at room temperature

1 cup granulated sugar

1 large egg

1 teaspoon pure vanilla extract

1/2 cup Fruity Pebbles cereal, crushed

These are a fun cut-out cookie. The Fruity Pebbles look like rainbow sprinkles in the dough and provide a sweet, fruity flavor. The cookies become chewy and get a slight crunch from the cereal. Kids adore this recipe!

1. In a medium mixing bowl, sift or whisk together the flour, baking powder, cornstarch, and salt.

2. In a large mixing bowl, using an electric mixer on medium speed or a wooden spoon, beat together the butter and sugar until light and creamy. This will take about 3 minutes if using an electric mixer or 5 to 6 minutes if creaming by hand. Add the egg and vanilla, and beat to combine. Add the dry ingredients and beat on low speed or by hand until the dough comes together, about 1 minute. Using a rubber spatula, fold in the Fruity Pebbles until evenly distributed.

3. Place the dough between two sheets of wax paper or parchment paper. Using a rolling pin, roll out the dough to an even ½-inch thickness. Wrap the dough in the paper and refrigerate until firm, at least 1 hour.

4. Preheat the oven to 350°F. Line a cookie sheet with parchment paper.

5. Using a 2-inch round cookie cutter, cut out the cookies and place them 2 inches apart on the prepared cookie sheet.

6. Bake for 12 to 13 minutes, until the edges are golden brown.

7. Let the cookies rest on the cookie sheets for 5 minutes before transferring them to wire racks to cool completely.

For a fun finish, drizzle the cookies with white chocolate. Melt ¾ cup white chocolate candy melts (found in the baking aisle of the supermarket) in the microwave. Transfer the melted chocolate to a resealable plastic bag and snip off one corner of the bag. Place the cooled cookies on a sheet of wax paper or parchment paper and drizzle the melted chocolate over the top. You can sprinkle additional crushed Fruity Pebbles on the wet white chocolate, too. Let dry for 30 minutes.

# Red Velvet Cut-Out Cookies

**MAKES ABOUT 30 COOKIES**
Prep: 25 minutes
Chill: 1 hour
Bake: 10 to 11 minutes
Shelf Life: 4 to 5 days

**FOR THE COOKIES**

2 cups all-purpose flour

¼ cup unsweetened cocoa powder

1 teaspoon baking powder

1 teaspoon cornstarch

½ teaspoon table salt

¾ cup (1 ½ sticks) unsalted butter, at room temperature

1 cup granulated sugar

1 large egg

2 teaspoons pure vanilla extract

1 tablespoon red velvet emulsion or red gel paste food coloring

**FOR THE GLAZE**

4 ounces cream cheese, at room temperature

1 cup confectioners' sugar

¼ cup milk

1 teaspoon pure vanilla extract

Like red velvet cake, these cookies have a deep red color and a light chocolate flavor. The cream cheese drizzle on top of the cookies tastes just like a cream cheese frosting.

**TO MAKE THE COOKIES**

1. In a medium mixing bowl, sift or whisk together the flour, cocoa powder, baking powder, cornstarch, and salt.

2. In a large mixing bowl, using an electric mixer on medium speed or a wooden spoon, beat together the butter, and sugar until light and creamy. This will take about 3 minutes if using an electric mixer or 5 to 6 minutes if creaming by hand. Add the egg, vanilla, and red velvet emulsion or food coloring, and beat to combine. Add the dry ingredients and beat on low speed or by hand until the dough comes together, about 1 minute.

3. Place the dough between two sheets of wax paper or parchment paper. Using a rolling pin, roll out the dough to an even ½-inch thickness. Wrap the dough in the paper and refrigerate until firm, at least 1 hour.

4. Preheat the oven to 350°F. Line a cookie sheet with parchment paper.

5. Using a 2-inch round cookie cutter, cut out the cookies and place them 2 inches apart on the prepared cookie sheet.

6. Bake for 10 to 11 minutes, until the edges are golden.

7. Let the cookies rest on the cookie sheets for 5 minutes before transferring them to wire racks to cool completely.

**TO MAKE THE GLAZE**

1. In a large mixing bowl, using an electric mixer on medium speed or a wooden spoon, cream together the cream cheese, confectioners' sugar, milk, and vanilla until smooth, 1 to 2 minutes.

2. Transfer the glaze to a resealable plastic bag and snip off the corner of the bag.

3. Drizzle the glaze onto the tops of the cookies.

If you like, you can use melted white chocolate in place of the glaze to decorate these cookies.

# Chocolate-Orange Cut-Out Cookies

**MAKES ABOUT 28 COOKIES**
Prep: 20 minutes
Chill: 30 minutes
Bake: 11 to 12 minutes
Shelf Life: 4 to 5 days

- 2 cups all-purpose flour
- ¼ cup unsweetened cocoa powder
- 1 teaspoon baking powder
- 1 teaspoon cornstarch
- ½ teaspoon table salt
- ¾ cup (1 ½ sticks) unsalted butter, at room temperature
- 1 cup granulated sugar
- 1 large egg
- 1 teaspoon orange extract
- 1 tablespoon grated orange zest (from about 2 oranges)

These remind me of chocolate candies filled with orange cream, which is one of my favorites! If you enjoy this flavor combination, too, you're sure to love these cookies. They're soft, but hold their shape well.

1. In a medium mixing bowl, sift or whisk together the flour, cocoa powder, baking powder, cornstarch, and salt.
2. In a large mixing bowl, using an electric mixer on medium speed or a wooden spoon, beat together the butter and sugar until light and creamy. This will take about 3 minutes if using an electric mixer or 5 to 6 minutes if creaming by hand. Add the egg, orange extract, and orange zest, and beat to combine. Add the dry ingredients and beat on low speed or by hand until the dough comes together, about 1 minute.
3. Place the dough between two sheets of wax paper or parchment paper. Using a rolling pin, roll out the dough to an even ½-inch thickness. Wrap the dough in the paper and refrigerate until firm, at least 30 minutes.
4. Preheat the oven to 350°F. Line a cookie sheet with parchment paper.
5. Using a 2-inch-round cookie cutter, cut out the cookies and place them 2 inches apart on the prepared cookie sheet.
6. Bake for 11 to 12 minutes, until the centers are set and the edges are firm to the touch.
7. Let the cookies rest on the cookie sheets for 5 minutes before transferring them to wire racks to cool completely.

Want a plain chocolate cut-out cookie? Substitute vanilla extract for the orange extract and omit the orange zest.

# S'mores Cut-Out Cookies

**MAKES ABOUT 30 COOKIES**
Prep: 20 minutes
Chill: 1½ hours
Bake: 11 to 12 minutes
Shelf Life: 4 to 5 days

- 1 ¾ cups all-purpose flour
- 1 teaspoon baking powder
- 1 teaspoon cornstarch
- ½ teaspoon table salt
- ½ teaspoon ground cinnamon
- ¾ cup (1 ½ sticks) unsalted butter, at room temperature
- ½ cup packed light brown sugar
- ½ cup granulated sugar
- 1 large egg
- 1 tablespoon honey
- 1 teaspoon pure vanilla extract
- ½ cup graham cracker crumbs
- ¾ cup milk chocolate chips
- ¾ cup Mallow Bits

These cut-outs are fun and unique. They have a graham cracker–infused flavor with milk chocolate chips and marshmallow bits throughout. They're the perfect treat for when classic s'mores aren't available!

1. In a medium mixing bowl, sift or whisk together the flour, baking powder, cornstarch, salt, and cinnamon.
2. In a large mixing bowl, using an electric mixer on medium speed or a wooden spoon, beat together the butter and both sugars until light and creamy. This will take about 3 minutes if using an electric mixer or 5 to 6 minutes if creaming by hand. Add the egg, honey, and vanilla, and beat to combine. Add the dry ingredients and the graham cracker crumbs and beat on low speed or by hand until incorporated, about 1 minute. Using a rubber spatula, fold in the chocolate chips and marshmallow bits until incorporated.
3. Place the dough between two sheets of wax paper or parchment paper. Using a rolling pin, roll out the dough to an even ½-inch thickness. Wrap the dough in the paper and refrigerate until firm, at least 1½ hours.
4. Preheat the oven to 350°F. Line a cookie sheet with parchment paper.
5. Using a 2-inch round cookie cutter, cut out the cookies and place them 2 inches apart on the prepared cookie sheet.
6. Bake for 11 to 12 minutes, until the edges are golden.
7. Let the cookies rest on the cookie sheets for 5 minutes before transferring them to wire racks to cool completely.

If you can't find marshmallow bits, use the marshmallow packs from a hot chocolate mix, or chopped mini marshmallows dusted in confectioners' sugar.

# Molasses Cut-Out Cookies

**MAKES ABOUT 36 COOKIES**
Prep: 20 minutes
Bake: 12 to 13 minutes
Shelf Life: 4 to 5 days

- 4 ½ cups all-purpose flour
- 1 teaspoon baking powder
- ½ teaspoon table salt
- 1 ½ teaspoons ground ginger
- 1 teaspoon ground cinnamon
- ¼ teaspoon ground cloves
- 1 cup (2 sticks) unsalted butter, at room temperature
- ¾ cup packed light brown sugar
- ½ cup granulated sugar
- 2 large eggs
- 1 cup molasses
- 2 teaspoons pure vanilla extract
- 4 ounces white baking chocolate, chopped

These cookies are soft, spicy, and loaded with the dark, sugary goodness of molasses. A drizzle of white chocolate on top gives these cookies a finished look. When making these, I like to stick to a full-flavor molasses rather than blackstrap. I find that the blackstrap molasses is just too concentrated and almost bitter.

1. Preheat the oven to 350°F. Line a cookie sheet with parchment paper.
2. In a medium mixing bowl, sift or whisk together the flour, baking powder, salt, ginger, cinnamon, and cloves.
3. In a large mixing bowl, using an electric mixer on medium speed or a wooden spoon, beat together the butter and both sugars until light and creamy. This will take about 3 minutes if using an electric mixer or 5 to 6 minutes if creaming by hand. Add the eggs, molasses, and vanilla, and beat to combine. Add the dry ingredients and beat on low speed or by hand until the dough comes together, about 1 minute.
4. Place the dough on a well-floured countertop. Sprinkle flour over the top of the dough and roll it out to an even ½-inch thickness. (You could roll the dough between sheets of wax paper or parchment paper as in other recipes, but this dough is especially sticky, so adding flour is necessary.)
5. Using a 2-inch round cookie cutter, cut out the cookies and place them 2 inches apart on the prepared cookie sheet.
6. Bake for 12 to 13 minutes, until the edges are golden brown.

7. Let the cookies rest on the cookie sheets for 5 minutes before transferring them to wire racks to cool completely.

8. While the cookies are cooling, put the white chocolate in a small microwave-safe bowl and microwave for 30-second intervals, stirring in between, until the chocolate is completely melted.

9. Put the melted white chocolate in a resealable plastic bag and cut off one of the corners. Drizzle the melted chocolate over the cookies.

Work with a quarter of the dough at a time. After you've cut out all the cookies from one quarter, add the bits and pieces of dough that are left to another quarter of the dough. This will help prevent the dough from getting too saturated with flour.

Buckeye Thumbprint Cookies, *page 164*

# Sandwich Cookies, Whoopie Pies, Thumbprints, and Macaroons

# Chocolate Sandwich Cookies

**MAKES 10 SANDWICH COOKIES**
Prep: 30 minutes
Bake: 11 to 12 minutes
Shelf Life: 4 to 5 days

**FOR THE COOKIES**

1 cup all-purpose flour

½ cup special dark cocoa powder

1 teaspoon baking soda

½ teaspoon table salt

½ cup (1 stick) unsalted butter, at room temperature

½ cup packed light brown sugar

½ cup granulated sugar

1 large egg

2 teaspoons pure vanilla extract

**FOR THE FILLING**

¼ cup (½ stick) unsalted butter, at room temperature

¼ cup vegetable shortening

2½ cups confectioners' sugar

1 tablespoon pure vanilla extract

1 tablespoon milk

These rich, chocolaty sandwich cookies are softer than the traditional Oreo cookie, but they're filled with a similar vanilla crème filling. I enjoy these with a cup of hot chocolate.

**TO MAKE THE COOKIES**

1. Preheat the oven to 350°F. Line a cookie sheet with parchment paper.
2. In a medium mixing bowl, sift or whisk together the flour, cocoa powder, baking soda, and salt.
3. In a large mixing bowl, using an electric mixer on medium speed or a wooden spoon, beat together the butter and both sugars until light and creamy. This will take about 3 minutes if using an electric mixer or 5 to 6 minutes if creaming by hand. Add the egg and vanilla, and beat to combine. Add the dry ingredients and beat on low speed or by hand until the dough comes together, about 1 minute.
4. Using a medium (1½-tablespoon) cookie scoop, scoop the dough into balls and drop them 2 inches apart on the prepared cookie sheet.
5. Bake for 11 to 12 minutes, until the centers are set and the edges are firm to the touch.
6. Let the cookies rest on the cookie sheets for 5 minutes before transferring them to wire racks to cool completely.

#### TO MAKE THE FILLING

1. In a large mixing bowl, using an electric mixer on medium or a wooden spoon, beat together the butter, shortening, confectioners' sugar, vanilla, and milk until light and fluffy, 2 to 4 minutes.

2. Transfer the frosting to a resealable plastic bag and snip off one corner of the bag. Once the cookies are completely cooled, pipe the frosting onto the bottom (flat) side of half of the cookies. Add a second cookie on top of the filling, flat-side down.

Go for a little pop of color by adding 2 to 3 tablespoons of rainbow sprinkles to the frosting before piping it into the cookies.

# PB&J Sandwich Cookies

**MAKES ABOUT 16 SANDWICH COOKIES**
Prep: 25 minutes
Bake: 12 to 13 minutes
Shelf Life: 2 to 3 days

**FOR THE COOKIES**

1 3/4 cups all-purpose flour
1/2 teaspoon baking powder
1/2 teaspoon baking soda
1/2 teaspoon table salt
1/2 cup (1 stick) unsalted butter, at room temperature
3/4 cup creamy peanut butter
1 cup packed light brown sugar
1/2 cup granulated sugar
2 large eggs
2 teaspoons pure vanilla extract

**FOR THE FILLINGS**

1 1/2 cups (3 sticks) unsalted butter, at room temperature
1/2 cup creamy peanut butter
1 1/2 cups confectioners' sugar
1 teaspoon pure vanilla extract
1/4 teaspoon table salt
3/4 cup grape jam
1 to 2 teaspoons warm water

Talk about nostalgia. These cookies take me back to brown-bag school lunches of peanut butter and jelly sandwiches. The peanut butter cookies are soft and pleasant to bite into. In the center of each cookie is a dollop of peanut butter frosting and a generous amount of jam.

**TO MAKE THE COOKIES**

1. In a medium mixing bowl, sift or whisk together the flour, baking powder, baking soda, and salt.
2. In a large mixing bowl, using an electric mixer on medium speed or a wooden spoon, beat together the butter, peanut butter, and both sugars until light and creamy. This will take about 3 minutes if using an electric mixer or 5 to 6 minutes if creaming by hand. Add the eggs and vanilla, and beat to combine. Add the dry ingredients and beat on low speed or by hand until the dough comes together, about 1 minute.
3. Preheat the oven to 350°F. Line a cookie sheet with parchment paper.
4. Using a medium (1½-tablespoon) cookie scoop, scoop the dough into balls and drop them 2 inches apart on the prepared cookie sheet.
5. Bake for 12 to 13 minutes, until the edges are golden brown.
6. Let the cookies rest on the cookie sheets for 5 minutes before transferring them to wire racks to cool completely.

**TO MAKE THE FILLINGS**

1. In a large mixing bowl, using an electric mixer on medium speed or with a wooden spoon, beat together the butter, peanut butter, confectioners' sugar, vanilla, and salt until light and fluffy, 2 to 5 minutes. Transfer the frosting to a resealable plastic bag.

2. In a small bowl, stir together the jam and warm water until well combined. Transfer the mixture to another resealable plastic bag.

3. Snip off one corner of each bag. Once the cookies are completely cooled, pipe a swirl of peanut butter frosting on the bottom (flat) side of half of the cookies, then pipe the jam mixture on top of the frosting. Top with the remaining cookies, flat-side down, and press down gently.

Not a peanut butter lover? Substitute the peanut butter in this recipe for almond butter or cashew butter.

# Caramel-Filled Sandwich Cookies

**MAKES ABOUT 6 SANDWICH COOKIES**
Prep: 20 minutes
Chill: 1 hour
Bake: 14 to 15 minutes
Shelf Life: 4 to 5 days

- ½ cup (1 stick) unsalted butter, at room temperature
- ⅓ cup confectioners' sugar
- 2 tablespoons granulated sugar
- 1 large egg yolk
- 2 teaspoons pure vanilla extract
- 1 ¼ cups all-purpose flour
- ½ teaspoon table salt
- ¾ cup dulce de leche

I love the simplicity of both the look and the flavor of these cookies. They are basic shortbread cookies that are super rich and buttery. Inside each cookie is a swirl of *dulce de leche*—caramelized sweetened condensed milk—that has a rich, caramel flavor and a thick consistency. The sandwich will squish down when you take a bite, so check for runaway caramel.

1. Preheat the oven to 350°F. Line a cookie sheet with parchment paper.
2. In a large mixing bowl, using an electric mixer on medium speed or a wooden spoon, beat together the butter and both sugars until light and creamy. This will take about 3 minutes if using an electric mixer or 5 to 6 minutes if creaming by hand. Add the egg yolk and vanilla, and beat to combine. Add the flour and salt and beat on low speed or by hand until the dough comes together, about 1 minute.
3. Place the dough between two sheets of wax paper or parchment paper. Using a rolling pin, roll out the dough to an even ½-inch thickness. Wrap the dough in the paper and refrigerate until firm, at least 1 hour.
4. Using a 2-inch round cookie cutter, cut out the cookies and place them 2 inches apart on the prepared cookie sheet.
5. Bake for 14 to 15 minutes, until the edges are golden brown.

6. Let the cookies rest on the cookie sheets for 5 minutes before transferring them to wire racks to cool completely.

7. Once the cookies are completely cooled, put the dulce de leche in a resealable plastic bag and snip off one corner of the bag. Pipe a swirl of dulce de leche on the bottom (flat) side of half of the cookies. Add a second cookie on top of the filling, flat-side down.

If you can't find dulce de leche in the international foods or baking section of your supermarket, you can easily make it yourself. Remove the label from a can of sweetened condensed milk. Place the unopened can in a saucepan and cover it with water. Bring the water to a boil over medium-low heat. Let it boil for 3 hours, making sure that the can is always completely submerged in the water. Let the can cool in the water before opening.

# Chocolate Chip Cookie Dough Sandwich Cookies

**MAKES ABOUT 16 SANDWICH COOKIES**
Prep: 35 minutes
Bake: 11 to 12 minutes
Shelf Life: 4 to 5 minutes

**FOR THE COOKIES**

2 1/4 cups all-purpose flour
1 teaspoon baking soda
1/2 teaspoon table salt
1/2 cup (1 stick) unsalted butter, at room temperature
1 cup packed light brown sugar
1/2 cup granulated sugar
2 large eggs
2 teaspoons pure vanilla extract
1 1/2 cups semisweet chocolate chips

**FOR THE FILLING**

1/2 cup (1 stick) unsalted butter, at room temperature
1/2 cup packed light brown sugar
1/2 cup confectioners' sugar
2 tablespoons milk
2 teaspoons pure vanilla extract
1 cup all-purpose flour
3/4 cup mini chocolate chips

If you love chocolate chip cookie dough as much as I do, you have to try these sandwich cookies! They're soft, tender chocolate chip cookies filled with a soft eggless chocolate chip cookie dough. They are highly addicting!

**TO MAKE THE COOKIES**

1. Preheat the oven to 350°F. Line a cookie sheet with parchment paper.
2. In a medium mixing bowl, sift or whisk together the flour, baking soda, and salt.
3. In a large mixing bowl, using an electric mixer on medium speed or a wooden spoon, beat together the butter and both sugars until light and creamy. This will take about 3 minutes if using an electric mixer or 5 to 6 minutes if creaming by hand. Add the eggs and vanilla, and beat to combine. Add the dry ingredients and beat on low speed or by hand until the dough comes together, about 1 minute. Using a rubber spatula, fold in the chocolate chips.
4. Using a medium (1½-tablespoon) cookie scoop, scoop the dough into balls and drop them 2 inches apart on the prepared cookie sheet.
5. Bake for 11 to 12 minutes, until the edges are golden brown.
6. Let the cookies rest on the cookie sheets for 5 minutes before transferring them to wire racks to cool completely.

**TO MAKE THE FILLING**

1. In a medium mixing bowl, using an electric mixer on medium speed or a wooden spoon, beat together the butter, both sugars, milk, vanilla, and flour until light and fluffy. This will take 1 to 2 minutes using an electric mixer, or 3 to 4 by hand. Using a rubber spatula, fold in the mini chocolate chips.

2. Transfer the filling to a resealable plastic bag and snip off one corner of the bag. Once the cookies are completely cooled, pipe a swirl of the filling on the bottom (flat) side of half of them. Top with the remaining cookies, flat-side down, and press down lightly.

For a prettier cookie, press 2 or 3 additional chocolate chips into each cookie while they are still warm from the oven.

# Carrot Cake Sandwich Cookies

**MAKES ABOUT 14 SANDWICH COOKIES**
Prep: 30 minutes
Bake: 15 to 16 minutes
Shelf Life: 4 to 5 days

**FOR THE COOKIES**

2 cups all-purpose flour

1 teaspoon ground cinnamon

½ teaspoon ground ginger

½ teaspoon baking powder

½ teaspoon table salt

½ cup (1 stick) unsalted butter, at room temperature

1 cup packed light brown sugar

½ cup granulated sugar

1 large egg

1 teaspoon pure vanilla extract

¾ cup grated carrots

**FOR THE FILLING**

½ cup (1 stick) unsalted butter, at room temperature

2 cups confectioners' sugar

3 tablespoons milk

1 teaspoon pure vanilla extract

These soft carrot cake cookies are spiced with a healthy dose of cinnamon and ginger. They're moist from the shredded carrots and have a rich color. Shred the carrots with the smallest grater possible for a more pleasant texture. The brown butter frosting adds a nice nutty flavor.

**TO MAKE THE COOKIES**

1. Preheat the oven to 350°F. Line a cookie sheet with parchment paper.
2. In a medium mixing bowl, sift or whisk together the flour, cinnamon, ginger, baking powder, and salt.
3. In a large mixing bowl, using an electric mixer on medium speed or a wooden spoon, beat together the butter and both sugars until light and creamy. This will take about 3 minutes if using an electric mixer or 5 to 6 minutes if creaming by hand. Add the egg and vanilla, and beat to combine. Add the dry ingredients and beat on low speed or by hand until the dough comes together, about 1 minute. With a rubber spatula, fold in the grated carrots.
4. Using a medium (1½-tablespoon) cookie scoop, scoop the dough into balls and drop them 2 inches apart on the prepared cookie sheet.
5. Bake for 15 to 16 minutes, until the edges are golden brown.
6. Let the cookies rest on the cookie sheets for 5 minutes before transferring them to wire racks to cool completely.

**TO MAKE THE FILLING**

1. In a small saucepan, melt the butter over medium heat. Cook the butter, swirling occasionally, until it begins to brown, 10 to 12 minutes.

2. In a medium mixing bowl, cream together the browned butter (leave the burnt bits in the bottom of the saucepan), confectioners' sugar, milk, and vanilla until light and fluffy, 1 to 2 minutes.

3. Transfer the filling mixture to a resealable plastic bag and snip off one corner of the bag. Once the cookies are completely cooled, pipe a swirl of the filling on the bottom (flat) side of half of the cookies. Add the remaining cookies on top, flat-side down, pressing down lightly.

TIP Brown butter frosting adds a delicious nutty flavor to the frosting, but can be intimidating to make. If you're not quite ready to try it, just skip the browning of the butter to make traditional frosting.

# Root Beer Float Sandwich Cookies

**MAKES ABOUT 15 SANDWICH COOKIES**

Prep: 1 hour

Chill: 30 minutes

Bake: 12 to 13 minutes

Shelf Life: 4 to 5 days

**FOR THE COOKIES**

2 ¼ cups all-purpose flour

1 teaspoon baking soda

½ teaspoon table salt

½ cup (1 stick) unsalted butter, at room temperature

1 cup granulated sugar

½ cup packed light brown sugar

2 large eggs

1 ½ teaspoons root beer extract

½ teaspoon pure vanilla extract

1 cup white chocolate chips

**FOR THE FILLING**

1 ½ cups white chocolate chips

5 tablespoons heavy cream

½ cup (1 stick) unsalted butter, at room temperature

1 teaspoon root beer extract

1 ½ cups confectioners' sugar

These cookies are soft, chewy, unique, and fun. I was intrigued the first time I saw root beer extract and knew I had to create a cookie that would highlight this irresistible flavor. I finally put it to good use and paired it with white chocolate to make a cookie with a flavor reminiscent of a root beer float.

**TO MAKE THE COOKIES**

1. Preheat the oven to 350°F. Line a cookie sheet with parchment paper.

2. In a medium mixing bowl, sift or whisk together the flour, baking soda, and salt.

3. In a large mixing bowl, using an electric mixer on medium speed or a wooden spoon, beat together the butter and both sugars until light and creamy. This will take about 3 minutes if using an electric mixer or 5 to 6 minutes if creaming by hand. Add the eggs, root beer extract, and vanilla, and beat to combine. Add the dry ingredients and beat on low speed or by hand until the dough comes together, about 1 minute. Using a rubber spatula, fold in the white chocolate chips.

4. Using a medium (1½-tablespoon) cookie scoop, scoop the dough into balls and drop them 2 inches apart on the prepared cookie sheet.

5. Bake for 12 to 13 minutes, until the edges are golden brown.

6. Let the cookies rest on the cookie sheets for 5 minutes before transferring them to wire racks to cool completely.

**TO MAKE THE FILLING**

1. Combine the white chocolate chips and cream in a medium microwave-safe bowl and heat on 50 percent power for 30-second intervals, stirring in between, until the chocolate is completely melted and the mixture is smooth. Refrigerate the mixture until firm, about 30 minutes.

2. Add the butter, root beer extract, and confectioners' sugar to the chilled chocolate and cream mixture and beat until fluffy, 1 to 2 minutes.

3. Transfer the frosting to a resealable plastic bag and snip off one corner of the bag. Once the cookies are completely cooled, pipe a swirl of the filling on the bottom (flat) side of half of the cookies. Add the remaining cookies on top, flat-side down, and press down lightly.

Turn these root beer float cookies into ice cream sandwiches by substituting vanilla ice cream for the filling. Let the ice cream soften on the countertop for about 10 minutes and then scoop some ice cream onto the bottom of a cookie. Press the top cookie onto the sandwich and eat immediately!

# Chocolate Whoopie Pies

**MAKES ABOUT 20 PIES**
Prep: 30 minutes
Bake: 13 to 14 minutes
Shelf Life: 4 to 5 days

**FOR THE COOKIES**

2 cups all-purpose flour

¾ cup unsweetened cocoa powder

1 teaspoon baking powder

½ teaspoon baking soda

½ teaspoon table salt

¾ cup (1 ½ sticks) unsalted butter

¾ cup light brown sugar

¾ cup granulated sugar

2 large eggs

2 teaspoons pure vanilla extract

¾ cup buttermilk

**FOR THE FILLING**

½ cup (1 stick) unsalted butter, at room temperature

2 cups confectioners' sugar

2 tablespoons milk

1 teaspoon pure vanilla extract

These whoopie pies are made of a rich, cake-like chocolate cookie and filled with a whipped vanilla frosting. These are very similar to the traditional chocolate whoopie pies that are sold in the supermarket, except that they're homemade—and we all know that homemade is better.

**TO MAKE THE COOKIES**

1. In a medium mixing bowl, sift or whisk together the flour, cocoa powder, baking powder, baking soda, and salt.

2. In a large mixing bowl, using an electric mixer on medium speed or a wooden spoon, beat together the butter and both sugars until light and creamy. This will take about 3 minutes if using an electric mixer or 5 to 6 minutes if creaming by hand. Add the eggs and vanilla, and beat to combine. Add
the buttermilk and dry ingredients in alternating batches, beating on low speed or by hand until incorporated.

3. Preheat the oven to 350°F. Line a cookie sheet with parchment paper.

4. Using a medium (1½-tablespoon) cookie scoop, scoop the dough into balls and drop them 2 inches apart on the prepared cookie sheet.

5. Bake for 13 to 14 minutes, until the tops are slightly cracked.

6. Let the cookies rest on the cookie sheets for 5 minutes before transferring them to wire racks to cool completely.

**TO MAKE THE FILLING**

1. In a large bowl, using an electric mixer on medium or a wooden spoon, beat together the butter, confectioners' sugar, milk, and vanilla until light and fluffy, 1 to 2 minutes.

2. Transfer the filling to a resealable plastic bag and snip off one corner of the bag. Once the cookies are completely cooled, pipe a swirl on the bottom (flat) side of half of the whoopie pies. Add the top cookies, flat-side down, and gently press together.

Make double chocolate whoopie pies by sprinkling semisweet chocolate chips on top of each cookie before baking. You'll need 1½ to 2 cups of semisweet chocolate chips.

# Jam Sandwich Cookies

**MAKES ABOUT 5 SANDWICH COOKIES**
Prep: 20 minutes
Chill: 1 hour
Bake: 14 to 15 minutes
Shelf Life: 4 to 5 days

½ cup (1 stick) unsalted butter, at room temperature

¼ cup granulated sugar

¼ cup confectioners' sugar

1 large egg yolk

1 teaspoon pure vanilla extract

¼ teaspoon almond extract

1 cup all-purpose flour

¼ teaspoon table salt

½ cup jam, any flavor

These cookies were inspired by a jam sandwich bar recipe that was handed down to me. These are made with rich, crumbly almond-flavored shortbread cookies. They're filled with a jam of your preference to make a classic sandwich cookie.

1. In a large mixing bowl, using an electric mixer on medium speed or a wooden spoon, beat together the butter and both sugars until light and creamy. This will take about 3 minutes if using an electric mixer or 5 to 6 minutes if creaming by hand. Add the egg yolk, vanilla, and almond extract, and beat to combine. Add the flour and salt and beat on low speed or by hand until the dough comes together, about 1 minute.
2. Place the dough between two sheets of wax paper or parchment paper. Using a rolling pin, roll out the dough to an even ⅛-inch thickness. Wrap the dough in the paper and refrigerate until firm, at least 1 hour.
3. Preheat the oven to 350°F. Line a cookie sheet with parchment paper.
4. Using a 2-inch round cookie cutter, cut out the cookies and place them 2 inches apart on the prepared cookie sheet.
5. Bake for 14 to 15 minutes, until the edges are golden brown.
6. Let the cookies rest on the cookie sheets for 5 minutes before transferring them to wire racks to cool completely.
7. Put the jam in a small bowl and stir to loosen it up. Once the cookies are completely cooled, spread the jam on the bottom (flat) side of half of the cookies, leaving a bit of space around the edges. Place the remaining cookies on top, flat-side down, and press down on each sandwich gently.

If you don't like almond extract, omit it or replace it with additional vanilla extract.

# Oatmeal Cream Pies

**MAKES ABOUT 17 SANDWICH COOKIES**
Prep: 35 minutes
Bake: 12 to 13 minutes
Shelf Life: 4 to 5 days

**FOR THE COOKIES**

2 cups all-purpose flour

½ teaspoon baking powder

½ teaspoon table salt

1 cup (2 sticks) unsalted butter, at room temperature

1 cup packed light brown sugar

½ cup granulated sugar

1 large egg

2 tablespoons molasses

½ teaspoon maple extract

1 ¾ cups old-fashioned rolled oats

**FOR THE FROSTING**

½ cup (1 stick) unsalted butter, at room temperature

7 ounces marshmallow crème (such as Marshmallow Fluff)

2 cups confectioners' sugar

2 teaspoons pure vanilla extract

These soft, chewy cream pies remind me of the ones my mom used to buy at the store, but these are so much better. The secret to a great oatmeal cream pie is a small amount of molasses and, of course, rich maple flavor. These pies are finished with a delicious frosting made with marshmallow crème.

**TO MAKE THE COOKIES**

1. Preheat the oven to 350°F. Line a cookie sheet with parchment paper.

2. In a medium mixing bowl, sift or whisk together the flour, baking powder, and salt.

3. In a large mixing bowl, using an electric mixer on medium speed or a wooden spoon, beat together the butter and both sugars until light and creamy. This will take about 3 minutes if using an electric mixer or 5 to 6 minutes if creaming by hand. Add the egg, molasses, and maple extract, and beat until combined. Add the dry ingredients and oats, and beat on low speed or by hand until the dough comes together.

4. Using a medium (1½-tablespoon) cookie scoop, scoop the dough into balls and drop them 2 inches apart on the prepared cookie sheet.

5. Bake for 12 to 13 minutes, until the edges are golden brown.

6. Let the cookies rest on the cookie sheets for 5 minutes before transferring them to wire racks to cool completely.

**TO MAKE THE FROSTING**

1. In a large mixing bowl, using an electric mixer on medium speed or a wooden spoon, beat together the butter, marshmallow crème, confectioners' sugar, and vanilla until combined.

2. Transfer the frosting to a resealable plastic bag and snip off one corner of the bag. Once the cookies are completely cooled, pipe a swirl of frosting onto the bottom (flat) side of half of the cookies. Add the remaining cookies on top, flat-side down, and gently press the cookies together.

Add ½ teaspoon ground cinnamon to the frosting along with the confectioners' sugar to make a cinnamon-marshmallow frosting.

# Red Velvet–Cream Cheese Whoopie Pies

**MAKES ABOUT 20 PIES**
Prep: 35 minutes
Bake: 13 to 14 minutes
Shelf Life: 4 to 5 days

Of course, there has to be a red velvet whoopie pie! These whoopie pies are soft to bite into and are filled with the classic rich cream cheese frosting, much like a traditional red velvet cake. They have a light chocolate flavor and a deep red color.

**FOR THE COOKIES**

2 1/4 cups all-purpose flour

1/2 cup unsweetened cocoa powder

1 teaspoon baking powder

1/2 teaspoon baking soda

1/2 teaspoon table salt

1/2 cup vegetable shortening

1/4 cup (1/2 stick) unsalted butter, at room temperature

3/4 cup packed light brown sugar

3/4 cup granulated sugar

2 large eggs

2 teaspoons pure vanilla extract

1 tablespoon red velvet emulsion or several drops of red gel paste food coloring

1 cup buttermilk

**FOR THE FROSTING**

8 ounces cream cheese, at room temperature

1/2 cup (1 stick) unsalted butter, at room temperature

2 1/2 cups confectioners' sugar

1 teaspoon vanilla

**TO MAKE THE COOKIES**

1. Preheat the oven to 350°F. Line a cookie sheet with parchment paper.

2. In a medium mixing bowl, sift or whisk together the flour, cocoa powder, baking powder, baking soda, and salt.

3. In a large mixing bowl, using an electric mixer on medium speed or a wooden spoon, cream together the shortening, butter, and both sugars until light and creamy. This will take about 3 minutes if using an electric mixer or 5 to 6 minutes if creaming by hand. Add the eggs, vanilla, and red velvet emulsion or food coloring, and beat to combine. Add the dry ingredients and buttermilk in several alternating batches, beating until incorporated.

4. Using a medium (1½-tablespoon) cookie scoop, scoop the dough into balls and drop them 2 inches apart on the prepared cookie sheet.

5. Bake for 13 to 14 minutes, until the tops are springy to the touch and no longer shiny.

6. Let the cookies rest on the cookie sheets for 5 minutes before transferring them to wire racks to cool completely.

**TO MAKE THE FROSTING**

1. In a large mixing bowl, using an electric mixer on medium speed or a wooden spoon, beat together the cream cheese, butter, confectioners' sugar, and vanilla until thick and fluffy, 2 to 5 minutes.

2. Transfer the frosting to a resealable plastic bag and snip off one corner of the bag. Once the cookies are completely cooled, pipe a swirl of frosting on the bottom (flat) side of half of the cookies. Add the remaining cookies on top, flat-side down, and press down gently.

Use a piping bag with an open star piping tip, such as Wilton 1M or Wilton #32, to add detail to your frosting.

# Pumpkin Whoopie Pies

**MAKES ABOUT 20 PIES**
Prep: 30 minutes
Bake: 12 to 13 minutes
Shelf Life: 4 to 5 days

**FOR THE COOKIES**

2 3/4 cups all-purpose flour

1 teaspoon baking powder

1/2 teaspoon baking soda

1/2 teaspoon table salt

1 teaspoon ground cinnamon

1/4 teaspoon ground ginger

1/4 teaspoon ground nutmeg

1/4 teaspoon ground cloves

1/2 cup (1 stick) unsalted butter, at room temperature

1 cup packed light brown sugar

1/4 cup granulated sugar

2 large eggs

2 teaspoons pure vanilla extract

1/2 cup canned pumpkin purée (not pumpkin pie filling)

**FOR THE FROSTING**

8 ounces cream cheese, at room temperature

1/2 cup (1 stick) unsalted butter, at room temperature

2 1/2 cups confectioners' sugar

1 teaspoon vanilla

These whoopie pies have a light pumpkin flavor, but the spices are what really stand out! (I learned that after trying to make a pumpkin cookie without any of the spices.) These cookies are soft and fluffy and filled with the same rich cream cheese frosting I use for the Red Velvet–Cream Cheese Whoopie Pies (page 140).

**TO MAKE THE COOKIES**

1. Preheat the oven to 350°F. Line a cookie sheet with parchment paper.

2. In a medium mixing bowl, sift or whisk together the flour, baking powder, baking soda, salt, cinnamon, ginger, nutmeg, and cloves.

3. In a large mixing bowl, using an electric mixer on medium speed or a wooden spoon, beat together the butter and both sugars until light and creamy. This will take about 3 minutes if using an electric mixer or 5 to 6 minutes if creaming by hand. Add the eggs, vanilla, and pumpkin purée, and beat to combine. Add the dry ingredients and beat on low speed or by hand until the dough comes together, about 1 minute.

4. Using a medium (1½-tablespoon) cookie scoop, scoop the dough into balls and drop them 2 inches apart on the prepared cookie sheet.

5. Bake for 12 to 13 minutes, until the edges are golden brown.

6. Let the cookies rest on the cookie sheets for 5 minutes before transferring them to wire racks to cool completely.

### TO MAKE THE FROSTING

1. In a large mixing bowl, using an electric mixer on medium speed or a wooden spoon, beat together the cream cheese, butter, confectioners' sugar, and vanilla until thick and fluffy, 2 to 5 minutes.

2. Transfer the cream cheese frosting to a resealable plastic bag and snip off one corner of the bag. Pipe a swirl of frosting on the bottom (flat) side of half of the cookies. Place the remaining cookies on top, flat-side down, and gently press down.

You can simplify by using 1½ teaspoons pumpkin pie spice in place of the cinnamon, ginger, nutmeg, and cloves.

# Funfetti Whoopie Pies

**MAKES ABOUT 17 PIES**

Prep: 35 minutes

Bake: 16 to 17 minutes

Shelf Life: 4 to 5 days

**FOR THE COOKIES**

2 3/4 cups all-purpose flour

1 teaspoon baking powder

1/2 teaspoon table salt

3/4 cup (1 1/2 sticks) unsalted butter, at room temperature

1 1/2 cups granulated sugar

2 large eggs

1 teaspoon butter vanilla emulsion

1/2 cup buttermilk

1/4 rainbow sprinkles

**FOR THE FILLING**

1/2 cup (1 stick) unsalted butter, at room temperature

1/2 cup yellow cake mix

1 1/2 cups confectioners' sugar

3 tablespoons milk

1/4 cup rainbow sprinkles

Everything is better with sprinkles! These vanilla cookies are light, fluffy, and loaded with colorful sprinkles. To finish off the whoopie pies, I whipped up a Funfetti cake batter frosting to stuff in between the two cookies using part of a box of cake mix.

**TO MAKE THE COOKIES**

1. Preheat the oven to 350°F. Line a cookie sheet with parchment paper.

2. In a medium mixing bowl, sift or whisk together the flour, baking powder, and salt.

3. In a large mixing bowl, using an electric mixer on medium speed or a wooden spoon, beat together the butter and sugar until light and creamy. This will take about 3 minutes if using an electric mixer or 5 to 6 minutes if creaming by hand. Add the eggs and butter vanilla emulsion, and beat to combine. Add the buttermilk and dry ingredients in alternating batches and beat on low speed or by hand until the dough comes together, about 1 minute. Using a rubber spatula, fold in the sprinkles.

4. Using a medium (1½-tablespoon) cookie scoop, scoop the dough into balls and drop them 2 inches apart on the prepared cookie sheet.

5. Bake for 16 to 17 minutes, until the edges are golden brown.

6. Let the cookies rest on the cookie sheets for 5 minutes before transferring them to wire racks to cool completely.

**TO MAKE THE FILLING**

1. In a large mixing bowl, using an electric mixer on medium or a wooden spoon, cream together the butter, cake mix, confectioners' sugar and milk until light and fluffy, 1 to 2 minutes. Fold in the sprinkles.

2. Transfer the filling to a resealable plastic bag and snip off one corner of the bag. Once the cookies are completely cooled, pipe a swirl of the filling onto the bottom (flat) side of half of the cookies. Add the remaining cookies on top, flat-side down, and press together lightly.

What can you do with the leftover cake mix? Use ¼ cup to ½ cup in your favorite vanilla milkshake recipe and top with sprinkles for a cake batter milkshake.

# S'mores Whoopie Pies

**MAKES ABOUT 19 PIES**
Prep: 35 minutes
Bake: 15 to 16 minutes
Shelf Life: 4 to 5 days

**FOR THE COOKIES**

1 3/4 cups all-purpose flour

3/4 cup unsweetened cocoa powder

1 teaspoon baking powder

1/2 teaspoon table salt

1/2 teaspoon ground cinnamon

1/2 cup graham cracker crumbs

3/4 cup (1 1/2 sticks) unsalted butter, at room temperature

3/4 cup packed light brown sugar

3/4 cup granulated sugar

2 large eggs

1 tablespoon honey

2 teaspoons pure vanilla extract

3/4 cup buttermilk

**FOR THE FILLING**

1/2 cup (1 stick) unsalted butter, at room temperature

7 ounces marshmallow crème or Marshmallow Fluff

2 cups confectioners' sugar

2 teaspoons pure vanilla extract

If you like s'mores or whoopie pies, you're going to love this mashup of the two. The chocolate cookies have graham cracker crumbs incorporated into them, providing the perfect amount of graham cracker flavor. The marshmallow crème frosting in the center brings everything together for the full s'mores experience.

**TO MAKE THE COOKIES**

1. Preheat the oven to 350°F. Line a cookie sheet with parchment paper.
2. In a medium mixing bowl, sift or whisk together the flour, cocoa powder, baking powder, salt, and cinnamon. Stir in the graham cracker crumbs.
3. In a large mixing bowl, using an electric mixer on medium speed or a wooden spoon, beat together the butter and both sugars until light and creamy. This will take about 3 minutes if using an electric mixer or 5 to 6 minutes if creaming by hand. Add the eggs, honey, and vanilla, and beat to combine. Add the dry ingredients and buttermilk in alternating batches, beating to combine.
4. Using a medium (1½-tablespoon) cookie scoop, scoop the dough into balls and drop them 2 inches apart on the prepared cookie sheet.
5. Bake for 15 to 16 minutes, until the edges are golden brown.
6. Let the cookies rest on the cookie sheets for 5 minutes before transferring them to wire racks to cool completely.

**TO MAKE THE FILLING**

1. In a large mixing bowl, using an electric mixer on medium or a wooden spoon, beat together the butter, marshmallow crème, confectioners' sugar, and vanilla until light and fluffy, 1 to 2 minutes.

2. Transfer the filling to a resealable plastic bag and snip off one corner of the bag. Once the cookies have completely cooled, pipe a swirl of the filling on the bottom (flat) side of half of the cookies. Add the remaining cookies on top, flat-side down, and gently press together.

For a fun surprise, add two squares of a Hershey's milk chocolate bar in the center of the frosting before adding the top cookie. You'll need 4 (1.55-ounce) chocolate bars for one batch of whoopie pies.

# Butterfinger Whoopie Pies

**MAKES ABOUT 20 PIES**
Prep: 30 minutes
Bake: 13 to 14 minutes
Shelf Life: 4 to 5 days

**FOR THE COOKIES**

2 cups all-purpose flour

¾ cup unsweetened cocoa powder

1 teaspoon baking powder

½ teaspoon baking soda

½ teaspoon table salt

¾ cup vegetable shortening

1 cup packed light brown sugar

½ cup granulated sugar

3 large eggs

2 teaspoons pure vanilla extract

1 cup buttermilk

**FOR THE FILLING**

1 ½ cups (1 stick) unsalted butter, at room temperature

½ cup creamy peanut butter

1 ½ cups confectioners' sugar

1 teaspoon pure vanilla extract

¼ teaspoon table salt

1 cup Butterfinger baking bits

These chocolate whoopie pies are fluffy and cake-like. I initially tried adding bits of Butterfinger candy to the cookies, but quickly realized that they melt into unpleasantly hard pellets. Instead, the Butterfingers are mixed into the peanut butter frosting—and people go crazy for the unique flavor!

**TO MAKE THE COOKIES**

1. Preheat the oven to 350°F. Line a cookie sheet with parchment paper.
2. In a medium mixing bowl, sift or whisk together the flour, cocoa powder, baking powder, baking soda, and salt.
3. In a large mixing bowl, using an electric mixer on medium speed or a wooden spoon, beat together the shortening and both sugars until light and creamy. This will take about 3 minutes if using an electric mixer or 5 to 6 minutes if creaming by hand. Add the eggs and vanilla, and beat to combine. Add the dry ingredients and the buttermilk in alternating batches, beating to combine.
4. Using a medium (1½-tablespoon) cookie scoop, scoop the dough into balls and drop them 2 inches apart on the prepared cookie sheet.
5. Bake for 13 to 14 minutes, until the tops are slightly cracked.
6. Let the cookies rest on the cookie sheets for 5 minutes before transferring them to wire racks to cool completely.

**TO MAKE THE FILLING**

1. In a large mixing bowl, using an electric mixer or wooden spoon, beat together the butter, peanut butter, confectioners' sugar, vanilla extract, and salt until light and fluffy, 1 to 2 minutes. Fold in the Butterfinger baking bits.

2. Transfer the filling to a resealable plastic bag and snip off one corner of the bag. Once the cookies are completely cooled, pipe a swirl of the filling on the bottom (flat) side of half of the cookies. Add the remaining cookies on top, flat-side down, and gently press them together.

If you don't have buttermilk on hand, you can make your own by adding 1 tablespoon of lemon juice or white vinegar to 1 scant cup of milk and letting it sit for 5 to 10 minutes, until it thickens and curdles.

# Tiramisu Whoopie Pies

**MAKES ABOUT 22 PIES**
Prep: 30 minutes
Bake: 14 to 15 minutes
Shelf Life: 4 to 5 days

**FOR THE COOKIES**

2 3/4 cups all-purpose flour

1 teaspoon baking powder

1/2 teaspoon table salt

3/4 cup vegetable shortening

1 cup packed light brown sugar

1/2 cup granulated sugar

3 large eggs

2 teaspoons pure vanilla extract

1 teaspoon instant coffee granules

3/4 cup buttermilk

**FOR THE FILLING**

1 tablespoon milk

1/2 teaspoon instant coffee granules

1/2 cup (1 stick) unsalted butter, at room temperature

8 ounces mascarpone cheese

2 cups confectioners' sugar

1 teaspoon pure vanilla extract

These whoopie pies are fluffy and full of coffee flavor. And they wouldn't be tiramisu without a little mascarpone cheese, right? Here you'll find it in the creamy, coffee-flavored frosting. This frosting is what makes these whoopie pies stand out—and also what requires them to be refrigerated.

**TO MAKE THE COOKIES**

1. Preheat the oven to 350°F. Line a cookie sheet with parchment paper.
2. In a medium mixing bowl, sift or whisk together the flour, baking powder, and salt.
3. In a large mixing bowl, using an electric mixer on medium speed or a wooden spoon, cream together the vegetable shortening and both sugars until light and creamy. This will take about 3 minutes if using an electric mixer or 5 to 6 minutes if creaming by hand. Add the eggs and vanilla, and beat to combine.
4. Stir the coffee into the buttermilk. Add the buttermilk mixture and the dry ingredients in alternating batches, beating to combine.
5. Using a medium (1½-tablespoon) cookie scoop, scoop the dough into balls and drop them 2 inches apart on the prepared cookie sheet.
6. Bake for 14 to 15 minutes, until the edges are golden brown.
7. Let the cookies rest on the cookie sheets for 5 minutes before transferring them to wire racks to cool completely.

**TO MAKE THE FILLING**

1. In a small bowl, stir together the milk and instant coffee.

2. In a large mixing bowl, using an electric mixer on medium or a wooden spoon, beat together the butter, mascarpone cheese, confectioners' sugar, vanilla, and the coffee-milk until light and fluffy, 1 to 2 minutes.

3. Transfer the filling to a resealable plastic bag and snip off one corner of the bag. Once the cookies are completely cooled, pipe a swirl of the filling on the bottom (flat) side of half of the cookies. Place the remaining cookies on top, flat-side down, and gently press them together.

Finish off the cookies with a dusting of either unsweetened cocoa powder or a sweetened chocolate mix like Nesquik or hot chocolate mix.

# Gingerbread Whoopie Pies

**MAKES ABOUT 18 PIES**
Prep: 30 minutes
Bake: 14 to 15 minutes
Shelf Life: 4 to 5 days

**FOR THE COOKIES**

3 cups all-purpose flour

1 teaspoon baking powder

½ teaspoon table salt

1 teaspoon ground cinnamon

½ teaspoon ground ginger

¼ teaspoon ground nutmeg

¼ teaspoon ground cloves

¾ cup (1½ sticks) unsalted butter, at room temperature

¾ cup packed light brown sugar

¾ cup granulated sugar

2 large eggs

½ cup molasses

1 teaspoon pure vanilla extract

¾ cup buttermilk

**FOR THE FILLING**

½ cup (1 stick) unsalted butter, at room temperature

8 ounces cream cheese, at room temperature

2½ cups confectioners' sugar

1 teaspoon pure vanilla extract

¼ teaspoon ground cinnamon

Get your freshly brewed coffee and enjoy a perfect fall day with these whoopie pies. They have a spicy pop of ginger and a rich molasses flavor. Sandwiched in the middle of these pies is a smooth cream cheese frosting that brings everything together nicely and balances out the ginger flavor.

**TO MAKE THE COOKIES**

1. Preheat the oven to 350°F. Line a cookie sheet with parchment paper.

2. In a medium mixing bowl, sift or whisk together the flour, baking powder, salt, cinnamon, ginger, nutmeg, and cloves.

3. In a large mixing bowl, using an electric mixer on medium speed or a wooden spoon, beat together the butter and both sugars until light and creamy. This will take about 3 minutes if using an electric mixer or 5 to 6 minutes if creaming by hand. Add the eggs, molasses, and vanilla, and beat to combine. Add half of the dry ingredients and beat on low speed or by hand until the dough comes together, about 1 minute. Add the buttermilk and mix on low until combined. Add the remaining half of the dry ingredients and mix until combined.

4. Using a medium (1½-tablespoon) cookie scoop, scoop the dough into balls and drop them 2 inches apart on the prepared cookie sheet.

5. Bake for 14 to 15 minutes, until the top is springy to the touch and no longer shiny.

6. Let the cookies rest on the cookie sheets for 5 minutes before transferring them to wire racks to cool completely.

### TO MAKE THE FILLING

1. In a large bowl, using an electric mixer on medium or a wooden spoon, beat together the butter, cream cheese, confectioners' sugar, vanilla, and cinnamon until light and fluffy, 1 to 2 minutes.

2. Transfer the filling to a resealable plastic bag and snip off one corner of the bag. Once the cookies are completely cooled, pipe a swirl of the filling on the bottom (flat) side of half of the cookies. Add the remaining cookies on top, flat-side down, and gently press them together.

Use full-flavored molasses rather than blackstrap molasses in these cookies, to avoid overpowering all the other flavors in the cookie.

# Chocolate-Dipped Macaroons

**MAKES ABOUT 24 COOKIES**
Prep: 10 minutes
Bake: 16 to 17 minutes
Shelf Life: 4 to 5 days

- 4 large egg whites
- 2 tablespoons granulated sugar
- ¾ cup sweetened condensed milk
- ½ teaspoon table salt
- 1 teaspoon pure vanilla extract
- 5 cups sweetened coconut flakes
- ½ cup all-purpose flour
- 8 ounces semisweet baking chocolate, chopped

These coconut macaroons are perfect for the coconut lover in your life. These mounds of coconut are sweet, chewy, and just look like piles of shredded coconut. Don't let their appearance fool you, as they hold together quite well thanks to the egg whites and flour. They are incredibly simple to make, too!

1. Preheat the oven to 325°F. Line a cookie sheet with parchment paper.
2. In a large mixing bowl, using an electric mixer or a wooden spoon, beat the egg whites, sugar, and sweetened condensed milk until frothy. This will take about 2 minutes with an electric mixer or about 4 minutes by hand. Add the salt and vanilla, and beat until combined. Using a rubber spatula, fold in the coconut and stir to coat completely with the egg mixture. Add the flour and stir until thoroughly incorporated.
3. Using a medium (1½-tablespoon) cookie scoop, scoop out balls of the dough and drop them 2 inches apart on the prepared cookie sheet.
4. Bake for 16 to 17 minutes, until you see golden-brown bits of coconut on the edges and on top.

## Chocolate-Dipped Macaroons *continued*

5. Let the cookies rest on the cookie sheets for 5 minutes before transferring them to wire racks to cool completely.

6. Put the chocolate in a small microwave-safe bowl and heat on 50 percent power in 30-second intervals, stirring in between, until the chocolate is melted and smooth.

7. Once the cookies are completely cooled, dip the bottom of each cookies in the melted chocolate and then place them on a sheet of wax paper to dry. If you like, you can also drizzle some chocolate on the tops of the cookies.

Love Almond Joy candy bars? I've got you! Finely chop 1½ cups of almonds. Once the macaroons are dipped in chocolate, dip them in the chopped nuts and then place on the wax paper to dry.

# Lime Macaroons

**MAKES ABOUT 26 COOKIES**
Prep: 15 minutes
Bake: 17 to 18 minutes
Shelf Life: 4 to 5 days

4 large egg whites

2 tablespoons granulated sugar

¾ cup sweetened condensed milk

Grated zest and juice of 2 limes

½ teaspoon table salt

5 cups sweetened coconut flakes

½ cup all-purpose flour

2 ounces white baking chocolate, chopped (optional)

Add a sweet, nutty flavor to your macaroons by toasting the coconut before adding it to the cookie dough. Set your oven to 325°F and toast the coconut for 5 minutes. Stir and toast for another 5 minutes.

Are you ready for a summer party? The lime and the coconut are. These tangy coconut macaroons stand out for their bright, citrusy flavor! The cookies look like they could crumble any second, but rest assured, they hold together well.

1. Preheat the oven to 325°F. Line a cookie sheet with parchment paper.

2. In a large mixing bowl, using an electric mixer or a wooden spoon, beat the egg whites, sugar, and sweetened condensed milk until frothy. This will take about 2 minutes with an electric mixer or about 4 minutes by hand. Add the lime zest, lime juice, and salt and beat until combined. Using a rubber spatula, fold in the coconut and stir to coat completely with the egg mixture. Add the flour and stir until thoroughly incorporated.

3. Using a medium (1½-tablespoon) cookie scoop, scoop the dough into balls and drop them 2 inches apart on the prepared cookie sheet.

4. Bake for 17 to 18 minutes, until you see golden brown bits of coconut on the edges and on top.

5. Let the cookies rest on the cookie sheets for 5 minutes before transferring them to wire racks to cool completely.

6. Put the white chocolate, if using, in a small microwave-safe bowl and heat on 50 percent power in 30-second intervals, stirring in between, until the chocolate is melted and smooth. Transfer the chocolate to a resealable plastic bag and snip off one corner of the bag. Drizzle the chocolate on top of the cookies.

# Samoa Macaroons

**MAKES ABOUT 30 COOKIES**

Prep: 15 minutes

Bake: 15 to 16 minutes

Shelf Life: 4 to 5 days

- 4 large egg whites
- ¾ cup dulce de leche
- ½ teaspoon table salt
- 1 teaspoon pure vanilla extract
- 5 cups sweetened coconut flakes
- ¼ cup all-purpose flour
- 1 cup caramel bits or caramel squares, quartered
- 8 ounces semisweet baking chocolate, chopped

This fun twist on classic macaroons reminds me of the Girl Scout cookies, minus the shortbread! Dulce de leche, also known as caramelized sweetened condensed milk, is incorporated into these macaroons, along with bits of caramel. After they're baked and cooled, they're dipped in and drizzled with semisweet chocolate.

1. Preheat the oven to 325°F. Line a cookie sheet with parchment paper.
2. In a large mixing bowl, using an electric mixer or a wooden spoon, beat the egg whites and dulce de leche until frothy. This will take about 2 minutes with an electric mixer or about 4 minutes by hand. Add the salt and vanilla, and beat until combined. Using a rubber spatula, fold in the coconut and mix until it is completely coated with the egg mixture. Add the flour and caramel bits, and stir until thoroughly incorporated.
3. Using a medium (1½-tablespoon) cookie scoop, scoop the dough into balls and drop them 2 inches apart on the prepared cookie sheet.
4. Bake for 15 to 16 minutes, until bits of coconut around the edges and on top have turned golden brown.

5. Let the cookies rest on the cookie sheets for 5 minutes before transferring them to wire racks to cool completely.

6. Put the chocolate in a small microwave-safe bowl and heat on 50 percent power in 30-second intervals, stirring in between, until the chocolate is melted and smooth.

7. Once the macaroons are completely cooled, dip the bottoms of the cookies in the melted chocolate and then place them on wax paper to dry. Drizzle any leftover chocolate on top of the cookies.

If you can't find dulce de leche in the international foods or baking section of your supermarket, you can easily make it yourself. Remove the label from a can of sweetened condensed milk can. Place the unopened can in a saucepan and cover it with water. Bring the water to a bowl over medium-low. Let it boil for 3 hours, making sure that the can is always completely submerged in the water. Let the can cool in the water before opening.

# Shaping Dough

Shaping dough for cookies like Classic Thumbprint Cookies (page 162) can sometimes be difficult. It's nice to have them all uniform in size to ensure even baking, and it's also more pleasing to the eye. A cookie scoop is especially helpful here.

Depending on what you're filling the cookies with, you can add the filling before or after you bake them. If it's after, you may need to gently press the center of the cookie back down so there's room to fill your cookies. We'll be doing both in our recipes.

To get perfect thumbprint cookies, first you'll want to get out your cookie scoop or measuring spoons. I use a medium (1½-tablespoon) cookie scoop and scoop out all of my dough balls first. Doing this ensures that the cookies are all the same size.

Next, roll the dough between your palms until each ball is perfectly round and smooth. If the dough begins to crumble, work it between your hands a few times and try rolling it into a ball again. (If you're dipping the thumbprints into sugar or sprinkles, do this now.)

Press the balls down to flatten out the top. Using the back of a ½-teaspoon measuring spoon, make an indentation in the center of each cookie, forming a well to hold the filling. If you're using jam for the filling, fill the cookies before baking. If you're using something like a kiss or marshmallow crème, wait to fill the cookies until after baking them.

# Strawberry Jam Thumbprint Cookies

**MAKES ABOUT 40 COOKIES**
Prep: 20 minutes
Chill: 30 minutes
Bake: 14 to 15 minutes
Shelf Life: 4 to 5 days

2 3/4 cups all-purpose flour
1/2 teaspoon baking powder
1/2 teaspoon table salt
1/2 cup (1 stick) unsalted butter, at room temperature
1/4 cup vegetable shortening
8 ounces cream cheese, room temperature
1 1/2 cups granulated sugar, plus more for dipping
1 large egg
2 teaspoons pure vanilla extract
3/4 cup strawberry jam

Here are a couple of my favorite flavors together in a cookie: cream cheese and strawberry jam. The cookies take on a creamy, but dense texture, and the strawberry jam center swoops in to add a nice pop of fruity flavor.

1. In a medium mixing bowl, sift or whisk together the flour, baking powder, and salt.

2. In a large mixing bowl, using an electric mixer on medium speed or a wooden spoon, beat together the butter, shortening, cream cheese, and sugar until light and creamy. This will take about 3 minutes if using an electric mixer or 5 to 6 minutes if creaming by hand. Add the egg and vanilla, and beat to combine. Add the dry ingredients and beat on low speed or by hand until the dough comes together, about 1 minute. Wrap the dough with plastic wrap and refrigerate until firm, at least 30 minutes.

3. Preheat the oven to 350°F. Line a cookie sheet with parchment paper.

4. Using a medium (1½-tablespoon) cookie scoop, scoop the dough into balls and roll them between your palms until they are round and smooth. Place the dough balls 2 inches apart on the prepared cookie sheet and flatten the tops slightly. Dip a ½-teaspoon measuring spoon in a bit of water and then in sugar and press into the center of each cookie ball. Spoon the jam into the indentations in the cookies.

5. Bake for 14 to 16 minutes, until the edges are golden brown.

6. Let the cookies rest on the cookie sheets for 5 minutes before transferring them to wire racks to cool completely.

You can put the jam in a resealable plastic bag, snip off one corner of the bag, and pipe the jam into the cookies.

# Classic Thumbprint Cookies

**MAKES ABOUT 28 COOKIES**
Prep: 20 minutes
Bake: 14 to 16 minutes
Shelf Life: 4 to 5 days

- 1 cup (2 sticks) unsalted butter, at room temperature
- 1 cup granulated sugar
- 1 large egg yolk
- 1 teaspoon pure vanilla extract
- 2½ cups all-purpose flour
- ½ teaspoon table salt
- Your choice of filling: Hershey's Kisses, caramel, marshmallow crème, jelly or jam, chocolate spread, etc.

These classic thumbprint cookies are so soft and tender. The cookie base itself is flavored with vanilla, and it basically goes with everything. It can be filled with chocolates, candies, caramel, chocolate spread, and more. My all-time favorite filling for these cookies is strawberry jam.

1. Preheat the oven to 350°F. Line a cookie sheet with parchment paper.
2. In a large mixing bowl, using an electric mixer on medium speed or a wooden spoon, beat together the butter and sugar until light and creamy. This will take about 3 minutes if using an electric mixer or 5 to 6 minutes if creaming by hand. Add the egg yolk and vanilla, and beat to combine. Add the flour and salt and beat on low speed or by hand until the dough comes together, about 1 minute.
3. Using a medium (1½-tablespoon) cookie scoop, scoop the dough into balls and roll them between your palms until the balls are smooth and round. Flatten each ball slightly as you place it on the prepared cookie sheet, 2 inches apart. Press a ½-teaspoon measuring spoon into the center of each flattened ball for the "thumbprint."

4. If you're filling the thumbprint with jam, do that now. If you're using a candy, caramel, or something else that won't hold up to the oven, leave it out for now.

5. Bake for 14 to 16 minutes, until the edges are golden brown.

6. Remove the cookies from the oven. If any of the thumbprint indentations have puffed up, use the measuring spoon to gently press it back down while the cookie is still hot. If you didn't fill the cookies before baking them, immediately fill them now with your choice of filling.

7. Let the cookies rest on the cookie sheets for 5 minutes before transferring them to wire racks to cool completely.

If you want a bigger "thumbprint," use a 1-teaspoon measuring spoon. You can also use your finger to form the thumbprint.

# Buckeye Thumbprint Cookies

**MAKES ABOUT 28 COOKIES**
Prep: 25 minutes
Bake: 15 to 16 minutes
Shelf Life: 4 to 5 days

**FOR THE PEANUT BUTTER FILLING**

½ cup creamy peanut butter

½ cup confectioners' sugar

1 teaspoon pure vanilla extract

**FOR THE COOKIES**

2 cups all-purpose flour

½ cup unsweetened cocoa powder

½ teaspoon table salt

1 cup (2 sticks) unsalted butter, at room temperature

1 cup granulated sugar

1 large egg yolk

1 teaspoon pure vanilla extract

4 ounces semisweet baking chocolate, chopped

These tender chocolate thumbprint cookies are inspired by the famous buckeye peanut butter balls. They have a ball of peanut butter baked inside! As the cookies bake, they spread, leaving a gap, which is then filled with a chocolate drizzle.

**TO MAKE THE FILLING**

In a small bowl, beat together the peanut butter, confectioners' sugar, and vanilla until smooth. Set aside.

**TO MAKE THE COOKIES**

1. Preheat the oven to 350°F. Line a cookie sheet with parchment paper.

2. In a medium mixing bowl, sift or whisk together the flour, cocoa powder, and salt.

3. In a large mixing bowl, using an electric mixer on medium speed or a wooden spoon, beat together the butter and sugar until light and creamy. This will take about 3 minutes if using an electric mixer or 5 to 6 minutes if creaming by hand. Add the egg yolk and vanilla, and beat to combine. Add the dry ingredients and beat on low speed or by hand until the dough comes together, about 1 minute.

4. Using a medium (1½-tablespoon) cookie scoop, scoop the dough into balls and drop them 2 inches apart on the prepared cookie sheet. Flatten the top of the dough balls. Using the back of a ½-teaspoon measuring spoon, make an indentation in the center of each dough ball.

5. Scoop out 1 teaspoon of the peanut butter mixture and roll it into a ball. Press this into the indentation in the center of a dough ball. Repeat with the remaining cookies.

6. Bake for 15 to 16 minutes, until the edges are firm to the touch.

7. Let the cookies rest on the cookie sheets for 5 minutes before transferring them to wire racks to cool completely.

8. Put the chocolate in a small microwave-safe bowl and heat on 50 percent power in 30-second intervals, stirring in between, until the chocolate is melted and smooth.

9. Transfer the chocolate to a resealable plastic bag and snip off one corner out of the bag. Once the cookies have cooled completely, drizzle them with the melted chocolate.

Substitute chunky peanut butter for the creamy peanut butter to add a crunch to the center of the cookies.

# Mocha Thumbprint Cookies

**MAKES ABOUT 28 COOKIES**
Prep: 25 minutes
Bake: 15 to 16 minutes
Shelf Life: 4 to 5 days

**FOR THE COOKIES**

2 cups all-purpose flour

½ cup unsweetened cocoa powder

1 teaspoon instant coffee granules

½ teaspoon table salt

1 cup (2 sticks) unsalted butter, at room temperature

1 cup granulated sugar

1 large egg yolk

1 teaspoon pure vanilla extract

**FOR THE FILLING**

1 cup milk chocolate chips

¼ cup heavy cream

¼ teaspoon instant coffee granules

Mocha is always a hit with my blog readers, so I wanted to create a new cookie recipe incorporating it. These mocha cookies have a rich, chocolate flavor with a subtle hint of coffee. But they don't stop there. The mocha ganache filling will satisfy both the chocolate lover and the coffee lover.

**TO MAKE THE COOKIES**

1. Preheat the oven to 350°F. Line a cookie sheet with parchment paper.

2. In a medium mixing bowl, sift or whisk together the flour, cocoa powder, instant coffee, and salt.

3. In a large mixing bowl, using an electric mixer on medium speed or a wooden spoon, beat together the butter and sugar until light and creamy. This will take about 3 minutes if using an electric mixer or 5 to 6 minutes if creaming by hand. Add the egg yolk and vanilla, and beat to combine. Add the dry ingredients and beat on low speed or by hand until the dough comes together, about 1 minute.

4. Using a medium (1½-tablespoon) cookie scoop, scoop the dough into balls and drop them 2 inches apart on the prepared cookie sheet. Flatten the top of the dough balls. Using the back of a ½-teaspoon measuring spoon, make an indentation in the center of each dough ball.

5. Bake for 15 to 16 minutes, until the edges are firm to the touch.

6. Use the measuring spoon to gently press down any indentations that may have puffed up while baking.

7. Let the cookies rest on the cookie sheets for 5 minutes before transferring them to wire racks to cool completely.

**TO MAKE THE FILLING**

1. In a small microwave-safe bowl, combine the chocolate chips, heavy cream, and instant coffee. Heat on 50 percent power in 30-second intervals, stirring in between, until the chocolate is completely melted and the mixture is smooth.

2. Transfer the filling mixture to a resealable plastic bag and snip off one corner of the bag. Once the cookies are completely cooled, pipe the ganache filling into the indentations in the cookies.

Not a coffee lover? Make a simple double chocolate thumbprint cookie by omitting the instant coffee in the cookie and in the filling.

# Fluffernutter Thumbprint Cookies

**MAKES ABOUT 30 COOKIES**
Prep: 20 minutes
Bake: 13 to 14 minutes
Shelf Life: 4 to 5 days

2 cups all-purpose flour
½ teaspoon baking powder
½ teaspoon table salt
½ cup (1 stick) unsalted butter, at room temperature
¼ cup vegetable shortening
¾ cup creamy peanut butter
1 cup granulated sugar
¼ cup packed light brown sugar
1 large egg yolk
2 teaspoons pure vanilla extract
¾ cup marshmallow crème (such as Marshmallow Fluff)

Peanut butter and marshmallow crème make the perfect team, which is obviously why the Fluffernutter sandwich was invented. These peanut butter cookies are soft and tender, and the thumbprint centers are filled with marshmallow crème! I love using Marshmallow Fluff, even though I do have a recipe for making your own marshmallow crème on my blog.

1. Preheat the oven to 350°F. Line a cookie sheet with parchment paper.

2. In a medium mixing bowl, sift or whisk together the flour, baking powder, and salt.

3. In a large mixing bowl, using an electric mixer on medium speed or a wooden spoon, beat together the butter, shortening, peanut butter, and both sugars until light and creamy. This will take about 3 minutes if using an electric mixer or 5 to 6 minutes if creaming by hand. Add the egg yolk and vanilla, and beat to combine. Add the dry ingredients and beat on low speed or by hand until the dough comes together, about 1 minute.

4. Using a medium (1½-tablespoon) cookie scoop, scoop the dough into balls and then roll the balls between your palms to make them round and smooth. Place them 2 inches apart on the prepared cookie sheet and flatten their tops.

5. Using the back of a ½-teaspoon measuring spoon, make an indentation in the center of each dough ball.

6. Bake for 13 to 14 minutes, until the edges are golden brown.

7. If the indentations have puffed up, gently press them down with the measuring spoon.

8. Let the cookies rest on the cookie sheets for 5 minutes before transferring them to wire racks to cool completely.

9. Put the marshmallow crème in a resealable plastic bag and snip off one corner of the bag. Once the cookies have completely cooled, pipe some marshmallow crème into each indentation.

Look for marshmallow crème near the peanut butter and jams or near the marshmallows in your supermarket.

# German Chocolate Thumbprint Cookies

**MAKES ABOUT 26 COOKIES**
Prep: 35 minutes
Bake: 13 to 14 minutes
Shelf Life: 4 to 5 days

**FOR THE FILLING**

¾ cup packed light brown sugar

2 large egg yolks

1 (14-ounce) can sweetened condensed milk

½ cup (1 stick) unsalted butter, at room temperature

1 teaspoon pure vanilla extract

1½ cups sweetened coconut flakes

**FOR THE COOKIES**

2 cups all-purpose flour

½ cup unsweetened cocoa powder

½ teaspoon table salt

1 cup (2 sticks) unsalted butter, at room temperature

1 cup granulated sugar

1 large egg yolk

1 teaspoon pure vanilla extract

Oh hey, I just transformed German chocolate cake into thumbprint cookies! They're rich, chocolate cookies filled with a thick, gooey caramel-coconut filling—and they taste amazing. The cookie starts out soft, but the filling makes it even more tender.

**TO MAKE THE FILLING**

1. In a medium saucepan, stir together the brown sugar and egg yolks until combined.
2. Add the sweetened condensed milk, and butter, and bring to a boil over medium heat, stirring frequently. Let boil, stirring constantly, for 5 minutes. Remove from the heat and stir in the vanilla and coconut flakes. Set aside to cool.

**TO MAKE THE COOKIES**

1. Preheat the oven to 350°F. Line a cookie sheet with parchment paper.
2. In a medium mixing bowl, sift or whisk together the flour, cocoa powder, and salt.
3. In a large mixing bowl, using an electric mixer on medium speed or a wooden spoon, beat together the butter and sugar until light and creamy. This will take about 3 minutes if using an electric mixer or 5 to 6 minutes if creaming by hand. Add the egg yolk and vanilla, and beat to combine. Add the dry ingredients and beat on low speed or by hand until the dough comes together, about 1 minute.

4. Using a medium (1½-tablespoon) cookie scoop, scoop the dough into balls and roll them between your palms to make them round and smooth. Arrange them 2 inches apart on the prepared cookie sheet. Flatten the top of each dough ball. Using the back of a ½-teaspoon measuring spoon, make an indentation in the center of each cookie ball.

5. Bake for 13 to 14 minutes, until the edges are golden brown.

6. Use the measuring spoon to gently press down any indentations that have puffed up.

7. Let the cookies rest on the cookie sheets for 5 minutes before transferring them to wire racks to cool completely.

8. Transfer the cooled coconut filling to a resealable plastic bag and snip off one corner of the bag. Once the cookies are completely cooled, pipe the filling into the indentation in each cookie.

For a finished look, add a drizzle of chocolate to the top of each thumbprint cookie. Melt 4 ounces of semisweet baking chocolate in the microwave on 50 percent power in 30-second intervals, stirring in between, until melted and smooth. Transfer the melted chocolate to a resealable plastic bag and snip off one corner of the bag. Place the cookies on a sheet of wax paper or parchment paper and drizzle the chocolate over the tops of the cookies.

Gingerbread Men, *page 222*

# Christmas and Other Holiday Cookies

# Sugary Mint Shamrocks

**MAKES ABOUT 12 COOKIES**

Prep: 15 minutes

Chill: 1½ hours

Bake: 17 to 18 minutes

Shelf Life: 4 to 5 days

- 3 ¾ cups all-purpose flour
- 1 teaspoon cornstarch
- ½ teaspoon table salt
- 1 ½ cups (1 stick) unsalted butter, at room temperature
- 1 ¾ cups granulated sugar
- 1 large egg
- 2 teaspoons pure vanilla extract
- ½ teaspoon peppermint extract
- 1 or 2 drops green gel paste food coloring
- ¼ cup green sanding sugar

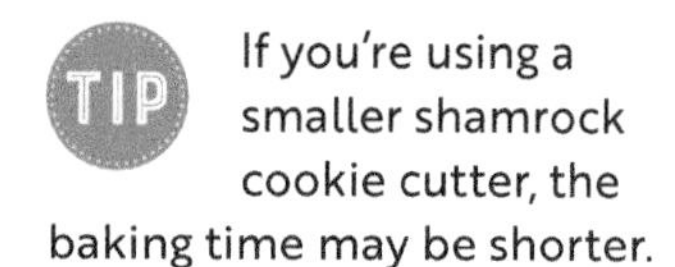

If you're using a smaller shamrock cookie cutter, the baking time may be shorter.

Step aside, Shamrock Shakes. I've got these minty shamrock cookies that are perfect for celebrating St. Patrick's Day! They sparkle from the green sanding sugar, making it impossible not to grab one. The sugar also provides a bit of crunch, which I welcome in any cookie.

1. In a medium mixing bowl, sift or whisk together the flour, cornstarch, and salt.

2. In a large mixing bowl, using an electric mixer on medium speed or a wooden spoon, beat together the butter and sugar until light and creamy. This will take about 3 minutes if using an electric mixer or 5 to 6 minutes if creaming by hand. Add the egg, vanilla, peppermint extract, and food coloring, and beat to combine. Add the dry ingredients and beat on low speed or by hand until the dough comes together, about 1 minute.

3. Place the dough between two sheets of wax paper or parchment paper. Using a rolling pin, roll out the dough to an even ½-inch thickness. Wrap the dough in the paper and refrigerate until firm, about 1½ hours.

4. Preheat the oven to 350°F. Line a cookie sheet with parchment paper.

5. Using a 3½-by-4-inch shamrock-shaped cookie cutter, cut out the cookies and place them 2 inches apart on the prepared cookie sheet. Coat the tops of the cookies with the green sanding sugar.

6. Bake for 17 to 18 minutes, until the edges are golden brown.

7. Let the cookies rest on the cookie sheets for 5 minutes before transferring them to wire racks to cool completely.

# Tie-Dye Easter Egg Cookies

**MAKES ABOUT 11 LARGE COOKIES**
Prep: 25 minutes
Chill: 1 hour
Bake: 14 to 15 minutes
Shelf Life: 4 to 5 days

- 2 ¼ cups all-purpose flour
- 1 teaspoon baking powder
- 1 teaspoon cornstarch
- ½ teaspoon table salt
- ¾ cup (1 ½ sticks) unsalted butter, at room temperature
- 1 cup granulated sugar
- 1 large egg
- 1 teaspoon pure vanilla extract
- 1 or 2 drops each of teal, green, pink, and yellow gel paste food coloring

If you're a lover of pastel colors and tie-dye, you're going to go crazy for these Easter egg cookies! They are buttery and soft sugar cookies loaded with swirls of color. What I love the most about the marbled effect is that no two cookies are identical.

1. In a medium mixing bowl, sift or whisk together the flour, baking powder, cornstarch, and salt.

2. In a large mixing bowl, using an electric mixer on medium speed or a wooden spoon, beat together the butter and sugar until light and creamy. This will take about 3 minutes if using an electric mixer or 5 to 6 minutes if creaming by hand. Add the egg and vanilla, and beat to combine. Add the dry ingredients and beat on low speed or by hand until the dough comes together, about 1 minute.

3. Divide the dough into 4 equal parts. Add a different food coloring to each of the dough balls and work it in until there are streaks of color. You'll want to still be able to see some of the cookie dough, too.

4. Lay out a sheet of wax paper or parchment paper and tear off pieces of the different colored doughs, smooshing them together on the wax paper. Keep adding the dough until it's all used. Place a second piece of wax paper or parchment paper on top. Using a rolling pin, roll out the dough. Fold the dough twice, then roll it out again to an even ¼-inch thickness. Wrap the dough in the paper and refrigerate until firm, at least 1 hour.

5. Preheat the oven to 350°F. Line a cookie sheet with parchment paper.

## Tie-Dye Easter Egg Cookies *continued*

6. Using a large egg-shaped cookie cutter, cut out the cookies and place them 2 inches apart on the prepared cookie sheet.

7. Bake for 14 to 15 minutes, until the edges are golden brown.

8. Let the cookies rest on the cookie sheets for 5 minutes before transferring them to wire racks to cool completely.

Can't find one of the gel paste food coloring colors recommended? Omit it or replace it with either purple or blue.

# Marbled Patriotic Stars

**MAKES ABOUT 22 COOKIES**
Prep: 25 minutes
Chill: 1½ hours
Bake: 11 to 12 minutes
Shelf Life: 4 to 5 days

2 ¼ cups all-purpose flour
1 teaspoon cornstarch
½ teaspoon table salt
¾ cup (1 ½ sticks) unsalted butter, at room temperature
1 cup granulated sugar
1 large egg
1 teaspoon lemon extract
½ teaspoon raspberry extract
Red gel paste food coloring
Blue gel paste food coloring
White gel paste food coloring (optional)

Cookie platters should be mandatory at every cookout. These red, white, and blue stars are the perfect cookie for the 4th of July and a great grab-and-go sweet. They're jazzed up with a raspberry lemonade flavor that brightens up the cookie and will surely be a pleasant surprise.

1. In a medium mixing bowl, sift or whisk together the flour, cornstarch, and salt.

2. In a large mixing bowl, using an electric mixer on medium speed or a wooden spoon, beat together the butter and sugar until light and creamy. This will take about 3 minutes if using an electric mixer or 5 to 6 minutes if creaming by hand. Add the egg, lemon extract, and raspberry extract, and beat to combine. Add the dry ingredients and beat on low speed or by hand until the dough comes together, about 1 minute. Divide the dough into 3 equal parts.

3. Add red food coloring to one of the dough balls, blue food coloring to the next, and white food coloring, if using, to the third. Work in each color so that the dough has dark and light color streaks in it as well as some natural color peeking through.

## Marbled Patriotic Stars *continued*

4. Lay out a sheet of wax paper or parchment paper. Tear off pieces of the colored balls of dough and smoosh them together on the paper. Add a second piece of paper on top. Using a rolling pin, roll out the dough to an even ¼-inch thickness. Wrap the dough in the paper and refrigerate until firm, about 1½ hours.

5. Preheat the oven to 350°F. Line a cookie sheet with parchment paper.

6. Using a star-shaped cookie cutter, cut out the cookies and place them 2 inches apart on the prepared cookie sheet.

7. Bake for 11 to 12 minutes, until the edges are golden brown.

8. Let the cookies rest on the cookie sheets for 5 minutes before transferring them to wire racks to cool completely.

The raspberry and lemon extracts add a bright, fruity flavor to the cookies, but either one or both can be replaced with vanilla extract.

# Slice 'n' Bake American Flags

**MAKES ABOUT 20 COOKIES**
Prep: 1 hour
Chill: 2½ hours
Bake: 14 to 15 minutes
Shelf Life: 4 to 5 days

- 3¾ cups all-purpose flour
- 1 tablespoon cornstarch
- ½ teaspoon table salt
- 1½ cups (1 stick) unsalted butter, at room temperature
- 1¾ cups granulated sugar
- 1 large egg
- 2 teaspoons pure vanilla extract
- Red gel paste food coloring
- Blue gel paste food coloring
- 2 tablespoons star-shaped sprinkles

Let's take our American flag cookies seriously, why don't we? I broke out my ruler for this cookie. It's crucial, otherwise you'll be ready to rip your hair out after spending an hour of prep time with nothing more than a heap of cookie dough to show for it.

1. In a medium mixing bowl, sift or whisk together the flour, cornstarch, and salt.
2. In a large mixing bowl, using an electric mixer on medium speed or a wooden spoon, beat together the butter and sugar until light and creamy. This will take about 3 minutes if using an electric mixer or 5 to 6 minutes if creaming by hand. Add the egg and vanilla, and beat to combine. Add the dry ingredients and beat on low speed or by hand until the dough comes together, about 1 minute. Divide the dough into 4 equal pieces.
3. Color one quarter of the dough a deep blue color using the blue food coloring.
4. Cut another quarter of the dough in half and add one half to each of the two remaining quarters of dough. Color one of the dough balls a vibrant red using the red food coloring. Leave the other dough ball as is.
5. Place the red dough between two sheets of wax paper or parchment paper. Using a rolling pin, roll out the dough to a 13½-by-10-inch rectangle. Trim off any extra dough and use it elsewhere to help make a perfect rectangle. Wrap the rectangle in the paper and refrigerate until firm, about 30 minutes.

6. Place the plain dough between two sheets of wax paper or parchment paper. Using a rolling pin, roll out the dough to a 12-by-10-inch rectangle. Trim off any extra dough and use it elsewhere to help make a perfect rectangle. Wrap the rectangle in the paper and refrigerate until firm, about 30 minutes.

7. Form the blue dough into a 1-inch square. Wrap it in wax paper or parchment paper and refrigerate until firm, about 30 minutes.

8. Using a pizza cutter and ruler, cut 3 strips of the red dough that are 2½ by 10 inches. Next, cut 4 strips of the red dough that are 1½ by 10 inches. Return the red dough to the refrigerator.

9. Again using the pizza cutter and ruler, cut 3 strips of the plain dough that are 2½ by 10 inches. Next, cut 3 strips of the plain dough that are 1½ by 10 inches.

10. Line a cookie sheet with wax paper. Lay down a 2½-inch-wide strip of red cookie dough. Lay a 2½-inch-wide strip of plain cookie dough on top of it. Add the rest of the 2½-inch-wide strips of red and plain cookie dough, stacking them up and alternating the colors. The last strip should be plain.

11. Place the blue square of cookie dough on the top left corner of the dough.

12. Add a strip of red 1½-inch-wide dough on top of the plain dough on the right-hand side, next to the blue square. Continue adding all of the 1½-inch-wide red and plain strips, stacking them up and alternating the colors. The last strip you add should be red. If the dough gets too soft, place it in the refrigerator until it has firmed back up.

13. Gently press everything together. Gently tap the sides on a flat surface to remove any air pockets. Wrap up the little flag in the wax paper and refrigerate until firm, about 2 hours.

14. Preheat the oven to 350°F. Line a cookie sheet with parchment paper.

15. Slice the cookie dough into ¼-inch-thick slabs and place them 2 inches apart on the prepared cookie sheet. Scatter the star-shaped sprinkles on the blue part of the flag.

16. Bake for 14 to 15 minutes, until the edges are golden brown.

17. Let the cookies rest on the cookie sheets for 5 minutes before transferring them to wire racks to cool completely.

These cookies are quite time consuming, but they freeze really well! Make the cookie dough and assemble the flag ahead of time. Wrap the dough tightly in plastic wrap and place it in a resealable plastic bag. Freeze for up to 3 months. Thaw in the refrigerator for an hour or two before slicing.

# Ghost Meringues

**MAKES ABOUT 21 COOKIES**
Prep: 15 minutes
Bake: 1¾ to 2 hours
Shelf Life: 2 to 3 days

2 egg whites, at room temperature

¼ teaspoon cream of tartar

½ cup granulated sugar

**TIP** If you don't have an edible food writer, use 1 tablespoon of dark candy melts melted in a microwave on 50 percent power in 30-second intervals, stirring in between, until smooth. Put the melted chocolate in a resealable plastic bag and snip off one corner of the bag. Pipe the eyes and mouths onto the meringues.

Do you have a little extra time on your hands and a day without a lot of humidity? Try out these cookies. They're piped into ghost shapes with a wide bottom and a pointy top. The cookies are crunchy on the outside with a melt-in-your-mouth interior. You'll need a piping bag fitted with a 1A round piping tip and a black edible food writer.

1. Preheat the oven to 200°F. Line a cookie sheet with parchment paper.
2. In a mixing bowl, using an electric mixer on high speed or a wire whisk, whip the egg whites until soft peaks form. While continuing to whip, add the cream of tartar and then gradually add the granulated sugar. Continue to whip until stiff peaks form. This will take about 4 minutes total using an electric mixer or 10 to 12 minutes by hand.
3. Transfer the egg white mixture to a piping bag fit with a 1A round piping tip.
4. Pipe 1½- to 2-inch-tall stacks of meringue onto the prepared cookie sheet, spacing them about ½ inch apart. Make sure the tops come up to a point for the ghostly effect.
5. Bake for 1¾ to 2 hours. When the meringues are done, they will be easy to lift off of the parchment paper. Transfer to a wire rack to cool completely.
6. Add little eyes and a round mouth with a black edible writer.
7. Store these meringues in an airtight container with low humidity. Otherwise, they will become a sticky mess quickly.

# Peppermint Candy Swirl Cookies

**MAKES ABOUT 45 COOKIES**

Prep: 25 minutes

Chill: 2 hours

Bake: 11 to 12 minutes

Shelf Life: 4 to 5 days

2 ½ cups all-purpose flour

1 teaspoon cornstarch

½ teaspoon table salt

¾ cup (1 ½ sticks) unsalted butter, at room temperature

1 cup granulated sugar

1 large egg

1 teaspoon pure vanilla extract

1 teaspoon peppermint extract

Red gel paste food coloring

These cookies remind me of peppermint candies in both appearance and taste. They are adorable wrapped up in small pieces of parchment paper like the true candy would be. Don't plan on storing them wrapped, but please do take them to a party like that. They'll be a hit!

1. In a medium mixing bowl, sift or whisk together the flour, cornstarch, and salt.

2. In a large mixing bowl, using an electric mixer on medium speed or a wooden spoon, beat together the butter and sugar until light and creamy. This will take about 3 minutes if using an electric mixer or 5 to 6 minutes if creaming by hand. Add the egg, vanilla, and peppermint extract, and beat to combine. Add the dry ingredients and beat on low speed or by hand until the dough comes together, about 1 minute.

3. Divide the dough in half and add red food coloring to one half, working it in with your hands. Roll each dough ball into a 9-inch-long log. Cut both logs in half lengthwise and then swap a red half with a white half. Now you have two logs that are partially red and partially white. Cut each half into thirds crosswise. Swap the center sections with its opposite color. Gently press the three pieces of each half back together and then press the halves back together. Pinch it in places if you need to. Roll it back and forth to help it come back together. Wrap the log in wax paper or plastic wrap and refrigerate until firm, at least 2 hours.

4. Preheat the oven to 350°F. Line a cookie sheet with parchment paper.

5. Slice the cookies into ¼-inch-thick slices and place them 1 inch apart on the prepared cookie sheet.

6. Bake for 11 to 12 minutes, until the edges are golden.

7. Let the cookies rest on the cookie sheets for 5 minutes before transferring them to wire racks to cool completely.

Using the icing in the Christmas Tree Cookies recipe (see page 209), pipe white lines in the middle of the red, and red lines in the middle of the white. Let the icing dry. This will make the cookies really stand out.

# Slice 'n' Bake Christmas Ornament Cookies

**MAKES ABOUT 28 COOKIES**
Prep: 45 minutes
Chill: 3 hours
Bake: 14 to 15 minutes
Shelf Life: 4 to 5 days

¾ cup (1½ sticks) unsalted butter, at room temperature

1¾ cups granulated sugar

1 large egg

2 teaspoons pure vanilla extract

3¾ cups all-purpose flour

½ teaspoon table salt

Red or green gel paste food coloring

¾ cup nonpareil sprinkles

These are great to make ahead of time. You can store them in the refrigerator or freezer, and then just slice and bake them when you need them. They are a delicious sugar cookie with a cute ornament design in the center. For a finishing touch, the log is rolled in nonpareils before chilling.

1. In a large mixing bowl, using an electric mixer on medium speed or a wooden spoon, beat together the butter and sugar until light and creamy. This will take about 3 minutes if using an electric mixer or 5 to 6 minutes if creaming by hand. Add the egg and vanilla, and beat to combine. Add the flour and salt and beat on low speed or by hand until the dough comes together, about 1 minute.

2. Divide the dough into thirds. Leave 2 of the 3 balls plain. Add a few drops of food coloring to the third dough ball, working it in well.

3. Place the colored dough between two sheets of wax paper or parchment paper. Using a rolling pin, roll out the dough to an even ½-inch thickness. Wrap the dough in the paper and refrigerate until firm, about 30 minutes.

4. Using a round cookie cutter, cut out the cookies and stack them 4 or 5 high on the prepared cookie sheet, neatly aligning them so that they are in an even tower. You should have 9 or 10 ornaments. Return them to the refrigerator and chill for another 30 minutes.

5. Create long, narrow ropes of uncolored cookie dough by rolling the dough between your hands and the countertop. Place the ropes lengthwise on the ornaments, taking care to push the narrow ropes into any corners that the ornaments may have, to avoid holes in the finished cookie. Add ropes around the entire surface of the ornament cookie and additional ones to help form a round cookie out of the plain cookie dough. Gently roll the dough back and forth to help smooth out the ropes while the ornament cookies are still firm. Press the sprinkles into the sides of the cookie dough log, coating it evenly.

6. Wrap the cookie dough in wax paper or plastic wrap and refrigerate until firm, at least 2 hours.

7. Preheat the oven to 350°F. Line a cookie sheet with parchment paper.

8. Slice the cookies about ¼-inch thick and place them 2 inches apart on the prepared cookie sheet.

9. Bake for 14 to 15 minutes, until the edges are golden.

10. Let the cookies rest on the cookie sheets for 5 minutes before transferring them to wire racks to cool completely.

You can use other small cookie cutters in place of the ornament cutter. Try to avoid cutters with a lot of details. Ideal cutters would be a Christmas tree, candy cane, bell, etc.

# Peppermint Twisted Candy Canes

**MAKES ABOUT 24 COOKIES**

Prep: 35 minutes

Chill: 20 minutes

Bake: 13 to 14 minutes

Shelf Life: 4 to 5 days

- 1 cup (2 sticks) unsalted butter, at room temperature
- 1 ¾ cups confectioners' sugar
- 1 large egg
- 1 teaspoon peppermint extract
- 1 tablespoon milk
- 2 ½ cups all-purpose flour
- ½ teaspoon table salt
- 3 to 7 drops red gel paste food coloring

These are among my favorite cookies! They're so buttery and crumbly in my mouth, I just can't resist them. Red and white peppermint-flavored lengths of cookie dough are twisted together and shaped into a candy cane. Don't be alarmed if the first couple of cookies are hideous. Mine were, but I got the hang of it, and you will, too.

1. In a large mixing bowl, using an electric mixer on medium speed or a wooden spoon, beat together the butter and sugar until light and creamy. This will take about 3 minutes if using an electric mixer or 5 to 6 minutes if creaming by hand. Add the egg, peppermint extract, and milk and beat to combine. Add the flour and salt, and beat on low speed or by hand until the dough comes together, about 1 minute.

2. Divide dough in half. Set one half of the dough aside. Work 3 to 5 drops of red gel paste food coloring into the other ball of dough until thoroughly incorporated. If the color needs to be intensified, add 1 to 2 additional drops of the food coloring.

3. Place the dough between two sheets of wax paper or parchment paper and flatten it out with your hand until it is an even ½-inch thick. Wrap the dough in the paper and refrigerate until firm, about 20 minutes.

4. Preheat the oven to 350°F. Line a cookie sheet with parchment paper.

5. Using a small (1-tablespoon) cookie scoop, scoop out one ball of each color dough. Roll each color into a 6- to 6½-inch rope. Place the two colors side by side and roll them to twist the colors together. If the dough breaks, pinch it back together. Place the dough on the prepared cookie sheet and shape it like a candy cane. Space the cookies 2 inches apart.

6. Bake for 13 to 14 minutes, until the edges are golden brown.

7. Let the cookies cool on the cookie sheet for 10 minutes before transferring to a wire rack to cool completely.

If you find that making the candy cane shape is a hassle, make peppermint sticks instead.

# Sweetheart Linzer Cookies

**MAKES ABOUT 9 SANDWICH COOKIES**

Prep: 25 minutes

Chill: 1 hour

Bake: 14 to 15 minutes

Shelf Life: 3 to 4 days

1 cup (2 sticks) unsalted butter, at room temperature

1 cup confectioners' sugar

1 ½ teaspoons lemon extract

1 teaspoon grated lemon zest

2 cups all-purpose flour

½ teaspoon table salt

¾ cup strawberry jam

Sweetheart cookies for your sweetheart on Valentine's Day! These buttery cookies have a cute heart in the center with strawberry jam peeking out. You'll need a large heart-shaped cookie cutter and a small heart-shaped cookie cutter for these cookies.

1. In a large mixing bowl, using an electric mixer on medium speed or a wooden spoon, beat together the butter and sugar until light and creamy. This will take about 3 minutes if using an electric mixer or 5 to 6 minutes if creaming by hand. Add the lemon extract and lemon zest, and beat to combine. Add the flour and salt, and beat on low speed or by hand until the dough comes together, a bout 1 minute.

2. Place the dough between two sheets of wax paper or parchment paper. Using a rolling pin, roll out the dough to an even ½-inch thickness. Wrap the dough in the paper and refrigerate until firm, at least 1 hour.

3. Preheat the oven to 350°F. Line a cookie sheet with parchment paper.

4. Using a large heart-shaped cookie cutter, cut out the cookies and place them 2 inches apart on the prepared cookie sheet. Using a small heart-shaped cookie cutter, cut out hearts from the centers of half of the cookies.

5. Bake for 14 to 15 minutes, until the edges are golden brown.

6. Let the cookies rest on the cookie sheets for 5 minutes before transferring them to wire racks to cool completely.

7. In a small bowl, stir the jam to loosen it up.

8. Spread the jam on the cookies without the center cut-outs, going almost, but not quite, to the outer edges. Place the cutout cookies on top of the jam and press down lightly.

You can substitute any flavor of jam you like for the strawberry jam. In fact, Linzer cookies are traditionally filled with raspberry jam.

# Bunny Tail Cookies

**MAKES ABOUT 12 COOKIES**
Prep: 20 minutes
Chill: 1 hour
Bake: 14 to 15 minutes
Shelf Life: 4 to 5 days

½ cup (1 stick) unsalted butter, at room temperature
½ cup confectioners' sugar
¼ teaspoon lemon extract
1 cup plus 2 tablespoons all-purpose flour
¼ teaspoon table salt
¼ cup white sanding sugar

These buttery shortbread cookies are coated with a sparkly white sanding sugar. The cookies are slightly rounded and look like cute little bunny tails. The sugar coating provides a crunchy outside and the shortbread gives them a rich, crumbly interior.
I created a similar recipe for my blog and every Easter it is revisited.

1. In a large mixing bowl, using an electric mixer on medium speed or a wooden spoon, beat together the butter and sugar until light and creamy. This will take about 3 minutes if using an electric mixer or 5 to 6 minutes if creaming by hand. Add the lemon extract and beat to combine. Add the flour and salt and beat on low speed or by hand until the dough comes together, about 1 minute. Wrap the dough in plastic wrap and refrigerate until firm, about 1 hour.

2. Preheat the oven to 350°F. Line a cookie sheet with parchment paper.

3. Using a medium (1½-tablespoon) cookie scoop, scoop the dough into balls and roll them in the sanding sugar to coat. Place them 2 inches apart on the prepared cookie sheet.

4. Bake for 14 to 15 minutes, until the edges are golden brown.

5. Let the cookies rest on the cookie sheets for 5 minutes before transferring them to wire racks to cool completely.

Can't find sanding sugar? Use white nonpareils instead.

# Pumpkin Pie Cookie Slices

**MAKES ABOUT 44 COOKIES**
Prep: 15 minutes
Chill: 1 hour
Bake: 10 to 11 minutes
Shelf Life: 4 to 5 days

- 2½ cups all-purpose flour
- 1 teaspoon cornstarch
- ½ teaspoon table salt
- ½ teaspoon pumpkin pie spice
- ¾ cup (1½ sticks) unsalted butter, at room temperature
- 1 cup granulated sugar
- 1 large egg
- 1 teaspoon pure vanilla extract
- 1½ cups butterscotch chips
- 2 teaspoons vegetable shortening
- ¼ cup white candy melts

These tiny slices of pumpkin pie shortbread cookies have pumpkin pie spice sprinkled in them for a slight flavor boost. Most of the flavor comes from the layer of butterscotch on top, which also provides the color for the pie.

1. In a medium mixing bowl, sift or whisk together the flour, cornstarch, salt, and pumpkin pie spice.

2. In a large mixing bowl, using an electric mixer on medium speed or a wooden spoon, beat together the butter and sugar until light and creamy. This will take about 3 minutes if using an electric mixer or 5 to 6 minutes if creaming by hand. Add the egg and vanilla, and beat to combine. Add the dry ingredients and beat on low speed or by hand until the dough comes together, about 1 minute.

3. Place the dough between two sheets of wax paper or parchment paper. Using a rolling pin, roll out the dough to an even ½-inch thickness. Wrap the dough in the paper and refrigerate until firm, at least 1 hour.

4. Preheat the oven to 350°F. Line a cookie sheet with parchment paper.

5. Using a 4-inch round cookie cutter, cut out the cookies. Using a knife, cut each circle into 4 wedges and place them 2 inches apart on the prepared cookie sheet.

6. Bake for 10 to 11 minutes, until the edges are golden brown.

7. Let the cookies rest on the cookie sheets for 5 minutes before transferring them to wire racks to cool completely.

8. In a small microwave safe bowl, combine the butterscotch chips and shortening and heat on 50 percent power in 30-second intervals, stirring in between, until melted and smooth. Transfer the butterscotch mixture to a resealable plastic bag and snip off one corner of the bag. Pipe the butterscotch on top of each pie slice, leaving a small gap around the edges. Use a toothpick to spread the butterscotch out to fill any gaps.

9. Put the white candy melts in a small microwave-safe bowl and heat on 50 percent power in 30-second intervals, stirring in between, until melted and smooth. Transfer the melted white chocolate to a resealable plastic bag and snip off one corner of the bag. Pipe the white on the top of the cookie where the whipped cream would go.

10. Let dry completely.

You can flick your wrist back and forth or make small circles while piping the white chocolate to make different designs.

# Robin's Nest Cookies

**MAKES ABOUT 14 NESTS**
Prep: 20 minutes
Shelf Life: 4 to 5 days

1 cup butterscotch chips
½ cup milk chocolate chips
½ cup creamy peanut butter
4 cups chow mein noodles
42 speckled candy eggs (M&Ms or mini malted milk eggs)

These cookies are similar to Butterscotch Haystacks (page 40), but with chocolate incorporated as well. After coating the chow mein noodles with a mixture of butterscotch and chocolate for color and flavor, shape the noodles into little nests. Finish off this spring/Easter cookie with speckled candy eggs in the center of each nest.

1. Lay out a sheet of wax paper or parchment paper.
2. In a medium microwave-safe bowl, combine the butterscotch chips and milk chocolate chips. Heat on 50 percent power for 30-second intervals, stirring in between, until completely melted and smooth. Add the peanut butter and stir to combine well. Stir in the chow mein noodles.
3. Lay out a piece of wax paper or parchment paper. Using a medium (1½-tablespoon) cookie scoop, scoop the mixture into balls and drop them 2 inches apart on the paper. Use a toothpick to shape the balls into nests. Place 2 or 3 candies in the center of each nest.
4. Let the cookies dry completely on the paper, about 2 hours.

In a hurry? You can speed up the drying of the cookies by placing them in the refrigerator for 30 minutes to an hour.

## Decorating Cookies

We have cookies and we have frosting—now let's learn how to decorate.

### FLOODING

Using a piping bag fitted with a small round tip, outline the parts of the cookie that you'll want covered with icing. For the Christmas Tree Cookies (page 209), I outlined everything except for the tree trunk.

With heavier pressure than what you were using to outline the cookies, fill in the area you just outlined. If you have a few bare spots, don't worry.

Use a toothpick and move the icing around to fill in any blank spots. Make small circles with the toothpick. *Tip: If there are ripples in the frosting, give the cookies a few gentle taps to smooth them out.*

## WET-ON-WET ICING

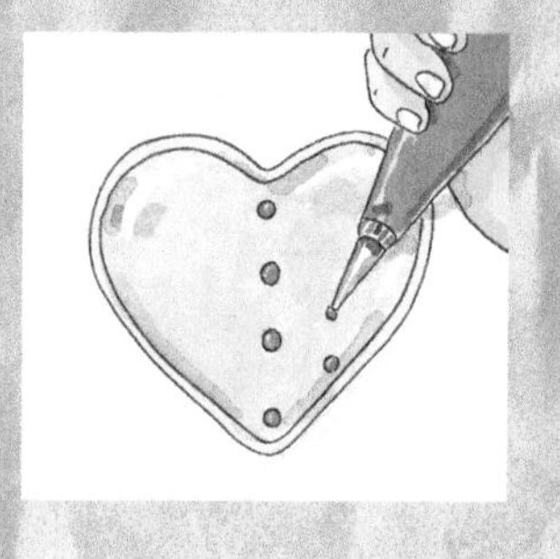

With two colors of icing ready, flood the cookie as in the previous technique and working quickly, add a different color on top of the first color of icing. It will sink in.

Using a toothpick, move the color around. Be careful to not over-flood your cookie or the icing will run off..

## RAISED ICING

Flood the cookies as above and let dry for 10 to 15 minutes, giving the icing plenty of time to crust. Add another layer of icing on top of the dried icing. *Tip: As a finishing touch, cover the second layer of icing with sprinkles or sanding sugar.*

## QUILTING

Mark the cookies with a toothpick or edible writer in a quilted or checkerboard design.

Fill in some parts of the design that aren't going to be touching each other. Let those dry for 10 to 15 minutes, until crusted.

Fill in more parts of the quilt. This time it can be touching the crusted icing, but not other freshly piped parts. Repeat until your design is finished.

# Be Mine Glazed Red Heart Cookies

**MAKES ABOUT 26 COOKIES**
Prep: 35 minutes
Chill: 1 hour
Bake: 15 to 16 minutes
Shelf Life: 4 to 5 days

**FOR THE COOKIES**

1½ cups unsalted butter, at room temperature

1¾ cups granulated sugar

2 large eggs

1 tablespoon pure vanilla extract

4 cups all-purpose flour

½ teaspoon table salt

**FOR THE GLAZE**

½ cup boiling water

1 (3-ounce) package gelatin dessert mix, any red or pink flavor

2 cups confectioners' sugar

Sprinkles (optional)

**FOR THE ICING**

2 cups confectioners' sugar

2 teaspoons corn syrup

2 tablespoons milk

1 teaspoon pure vanilla extract

Here is a basic sugar cookie that's amped up with a delicious sweet glaze. They are easy to glaze and fun to decorate! There are so many Jell-O flavors that come in red and pink colors for Valentine's Day, too. You'll need a piping bag fitted with a #3 round piping tip for this recipe.

**TO MAKE THE COOKIES**

1. In a large mixing bowl, using an electric mixer on medium speed or a wooden spoon, beat together the butter and sugar until light and creamy. This will take about 3 minutes if using an electric mixer or 5 to 6 minutes if creaming by hand. Add the eggs and vanilla, and beat to combine. Add the flour and salt and beat on low speed or by hand until the dough comes together, about 1 minute.

2. Place the dough between two sheets of wax paper or parchment paper. Using a rolling pin, roll out the dough to an even ¼-inch thickness. Wrap the dough in the paper and refrigerate until firm, at least 1 hour.

3. Preheat the oven to 350°F. Line a cookie sheet with parchment paper.

4. Using a heart-shaped cookie cutter, cut out the cookies and place them on the prepared cookie sheet.

5. Bake for 15 to 16 minutes, until the edges are golden brown.

6. Let the cookies rest on the cookie sheets for 5 minutes before transferring them to wire racks to cool completely.

#### TO MAKE THE GLAZE

1. In a large bowl, combine the boiling water and gelatin mix. Stir until the gelatin mix is completely dissolved. Add the confectioners' sugar and whisk until all the lumps are gone and the glaze is smooth. Let cool for 5 to 10 minutes.

2. Once the cookies are completely cooled, dip their tops into the glaze. Tap to let the excess drip off. If you are using sprinkles, add them now. Place on a sheet of wax paper to dry.

#### TO MAKE THE ICING

1. In a large mixing bowl, stir together the confectioners' sugar, corn syrup, milk, and vanilla until smooth. You may need to stir for a bit to get rid of any lumps.

2. Once the glaze has crusted, transfer the icing to a piping bag with a #3 round piping tip. Pipe cute little sayings on the cookies.

You can also use melted candy melts to pipe onto the cookies. The vanilla would go great with this glaze.

# Monster Cookie Sandwiches

**MAKES ABOUT 15 COOKIES**
Prep: 45 minutes
Bake: 9 to 10 minutes
Shelf Life: 4 to 5 days

**FOR THE COOKIES**

2 ¼ cups all-purpose flour
1 teaspoon baking soda
½ teaspoon table salt
½ cup (1 stick) unsalted butter, at room temperature
1 cup packed light brown sugar
½ cup granulated sugar
2 large eggs
1 teaspoon pure vanilla extract
1 or 2 drops electric green gel paste food coloring
30 jumbo candy eyes
¼ cup light green candy melts

**FOR THE FROSTING**

½ cup (1 stick) unsalted butter, at room temperature
2 cups confectioners' sugar
2 tablespoons milk
1 teaspoon pure vanilla extract
3 to 5 drops red gel paste food coloring
¾ cup sliced almonds

These monster cookie sandwiches are a hit with the kids! They're a soft flat cookie, decorated with large candy eyes, sliced almond teeth, and a red frosting tongue. These are a must-bring to any Halloween party, especially if there are kids there to appreciate them. You'll need a piping bag and a 1A round piping tip for these.

**TO MAKE THE COOKIES**

1. Preheat the oven to 350°F. Line a cookie sheet with parchment paper.
2. In a medium mixing bowl, sift or whisk together the flour, baking soda, and salt.
3. In a large mixing bowl, using an electric mixer on medium speed or a wooden spoon, beat together the butter and both sugars until light and creamy. This will take about 3 minutes if using an electric mixer or 5 to 6 minutes if creaming by hand. Add the eggs, vanilla, and green food coloring, and beat to combine. Add the dry ingredients and beat on low speed or by hand until the dough comes together, about 1 minute.
4. Using a medium (1½-tablespoon) cookie scoop, scoop the dough into balls and drop them 2 inches apart on the prepared cookie sheet.
5. Bake for 9 to 10 minutes, until the edges are golden brown.
6. Let the cookies rest on the cookie sheets for 5 minutes before transferring them to wire racks to cool completely.
7. When the cookies are completely cooled, stand 2 eyes up on top of half of the cookies, gently pressing them down into the cookie.

8. Put the green candy melts in a small microwave-safe bowl and heat on 50 percent power in 30-second intervals, stirring in between, until melted and smooth. Transfer to a resealable plastic bag and snip off one corner of the bag. Pipe a line of green candy melts behind each eye. Hold them if they won't stand on their own until the candy melts firm up.

### TO MAKE THE FROSTING

1. In a large mixing bowl, using an electric mixer on medium or wooden spoon, beat together the butter, confectioners' sugar, milk, and vanilla until light and fluffy, 1 to 2 minutes. Add the red food coloring and mix until thoroughly incorporated. Add more red food coloring if the frosting isn't vibrant.

2. Transfer the frosting to a piping bag fitted with a 1A round piping tip. Pipe the frosting on the bottom (flat) side of the cookies that don't have eyes. This is going to be the inside of the mouth.

3. Cut sliced almonds in half to make teeth and add a row of 4 sliced almonds to each mouth. Press the almonds in gently. If they aren't standing, add a line of melted green candy melt to the backside of the almonds.

4. Add 5 sliced almond halves to the bottom (flat) side of the cookies that have eyes. Press the almonds in gently. Add a line of melted green candy melts to the backside of the teeth if they aren't standing on their own.

5. Press the top of the cookie on the filling. Apply more pressure to the backside of the cookie to help push the frosting towards the mouth opening. The cookies should be at a 45-degree angle to each other.

You can color some piping gel found in the cake decorating aisle red and squeeze the gel between the teeth for a bloody mouth.

# Piñata (Surprise Inside) Tombstone Cookies

**MAKES ABOUT 6 LARGE COOKIES**

Prep: 45 minutes

Chill: 1½ hours

Bake: 17 to 18 minutes

Shelf Life: 4 to 5 days

- 2 ¼ cups all-purpose flour
- ¼ cup unsweetened cocoa powder
- 1 teaspoon cornstarch
- ½ teaspoon table salt
- ¾ cup (1 ½ sticks) unsalted butter, at room temperature
- 1 cup granulated sugar
- 1 large egg
- 1 teaspoon banana extract (or vanilla extract)
- 1 or 2 drops black gel paste food coloring
- ¼ teaspoon chocolate candy melts
- ⅓ cup sprinkles or small candies

These cookies are made by stacking three cookies on top of each other, held together with melted chocolate. The secret is that the middle cookie is hollowed out to make room for a stash of sprinkles or small candies. After they're all put together, be sure to give them the signature tombstone "RIP" with chocolate.

1. In a medium mixing bowl, sift or whisk together the flour, cocoa powder, cornstarch, and salt.

2. In a large mixing bowl, using an electric mixer on medium speed or a wooden spoon, beat together the butter and sugar until light and creamy. This will take about 3 minutes if using an electric mixer or 5 to 6 minutes if creaming by hand. Add the eggs, banana extract, and black food coloring, and beat to combine. Add the dry ingredients and beat on low speed or by hand until the dough comes together, about 1 minute.

3. Place the dough between two sheets of wax paper or parchment paper. Using a rolling pin, roll out the dough to an even ¼-inch thickness. Wrap the dough in the paper and refrigerate until firm, about 1½ hours.

4. Preheat the oven to 350°F. Line a cookie sheet with parchment paper.

5. Using a 3½-inch tombstone-shaped cookie cutter, cut out the cookies and place them 2 inches apart on the prepared cookie sheet. Use a knife to cut the center out of one-third of the cookies, leaving about ½-inch of cookie around the edges.

6. Bake for 17 to 18 minutes, until the edges are golden brown.

7. Let the cookies rest on the cookie sheets for 5 minutes before transferring them to wire racks to cool completely.

8. Put the candy melts in a microwave-safe bowl and heat on 50 percent power in 30-second intervals, stirring in between, until melted and smooth. Transfer the melted chocolate to a resealable plastic bag and snip off one corner of the bag. Pipe a small line of chocolate around the edge of one-third of the cookies. Top those with the cookies with the centers cut out. The chocolate will serve as the glue to hold them together. Fill cookies with the sprinkles or small candies. Pipe chocolate around the edge of the cutout cookies. Top the filled cookies with the remaining whole cookies.

9. Let the chocolate set up, and then write "RIP" on the tops of the tombstones using the melted chocolate, and add a little crack at the top.

Can't find a tombstone cookie cutter? Use a round cookie cutter and cut straight sides and a straight bottom to make your own tombstones. Try to keep the size the same since they will be stacked.

# Witches' Broomsticks

MAKES ABOUT 28 COOKIES
Prep: 30 minutes
Chill: 1½ hours
Bake: 8 to 9 minutes
Shelf Life: 4 to 5 days

½ cup (1 stick) unsalted butter, at room temperature
¼ cup confectioners' sugar
1 cup all-purpose flour
¼ teaspoon table salt
½ cup butterscotch chips
1 ½ cups chow mein noodles

These delicate shortbread cookies are so much fun, but be careful with them because they break easily. The chow mein noodles provide the bristles of the broom and add a ton a character with the bristles going every which way. To hold everything together, melted butterscotch chips come to the rescue.

1. In a large mixing bowl, using an electric mixer on medium speed or a wooden spoon, beat together the butter and sugar until light and creamy. This will take about 3 minutes if using an electric mixer or 5 to 6 minutes if creaming by hand. Add the flour and salt, and beat on low speed or by hand until the dough comes together, about 1 minute. Wrap the dough in plastic wrap and chill for at least 1½ hours.

2. Preheat the oven to 350°F. Line a cookie sheet with parchment paper.

3. Using a 1-teaspoon measuring spoon, scoop out the dough and roll it into a 4-inch-long rope. Place it on the prepared cookie sheet. Pinch off a small piece of dough and roll it into a ball. Place the ball at the end of the rope and press it down flat. Repeat to make the remaining broomsticks.

4. Bake for 8 to 9 minutes, until golden brown.

5. Let the cookies rest on the cookie sheets for 5 minutes before transferring them to wire racks to cool completely.

6. Put the butterscotch chips in a small microwave-safe bowl and heat on 50 percent power in 30-second intervals, stirring in between, until melted and smooth. Transfer the melted butterscotch chips to a resealable plastic bag and snip off one corner of the bag. Pipe the butterscotch onto the flattened ball at the end of the cookie rope, coating it completely. Add a layer of chow mein noodles. Try to arrange the noodles into a triangle. Add a line of butterscotch on top of the noodles and cover with one last layer of chow mein noodles.

7. Let dry completely.

You can also use small pretzel sticks for the chow mein noodles to make the bristles of the broom.

# Creepy Eyeballs

**MAKES ABOUT 16 COOKIES**
Prep: 30 minutes
Bake: 10 to 11 minutes
Shelf Life: 4 to 5 days

½ cup (1 stick) unsalted butter, at room temperature

½ cup confectioners' sugar, divided

2 ¼ cups all-purpose flour

¼ cup light green or yellow candy melts

16 Junior Mints

Red gel paste food coloring

Creepy is right. These eyeball cookies are not overly sweet, but they come together after all the decorations are added. They are rolled in confectioners' sugar prior to baking to appear white, then topped with a Junior Mint and green candy melts.

1. Preheat the oven to 350°F. Line a cookie sheet with parchment paper.

2. In a large mixing bowl, using an electric mixer on medium speed or a wooden spoon, beat together the butter and ¼ cup of the confectioners' sugar until light and creamy. This will take about 3 minutes if using an electric mixer or 5 to 6 minutes if creaming by hand. Add the flour and beat on low speed or by hand until the dough comes together, about 1 minute.

3. Using a medium (1½-tablespoon) cookie scoop, scoop the dough into balls and roll them between your palms to form smooth, round balls.

4. Put the remaining ¼ cup of confectioner's sugar in a shallow dish and roll each of the balls in it to coat thoroughly. Place the coated balls 2 inches apart on the prepared cookie sheet.

5. Bake for 10 to 11 minutes, until firm to the touch.

6. Let the cookies rest on the cookie sheets for 5 minutes before transferring them to wire racks to cool completely.

7. Put the candy melts in a small microwave-safe bowl and heat on 50 percent power in 30-second intervals, stirring in between, until melted and smooth. Transfer the melted candy melts to a resealable plastic bag and snip off one corner of the bag. When the cookies are completely cooled, pipe a small circle on top of each cookie. Let it sit to dry slightly and then place a Junior Mint on top. The green should peek out the sides of the Junior Mint.

8. Using a toothpick and the red food coloring, add a few lines to the sides of each eye to make them look bloodshot.

You can use red decorating gel found in the baking aisle to substitute for the red gel paste food coloring for the bloodshot effect.

# Christmas Tree Cookies

**MAKES ABOUT 18 COOKIES**
Prep: 20 minutes
Chill: 1 hour
Bake: 13 to 14 minutes
Shelf Life: 4 to 5 days

**FOR THE COOKIES**

2 1/4 cups all-purpose flour

1 teaspoon cornstarch

1/4 teaspoon baking powder

1/2 teaspoon table salt

3/4 cup (1 1/2 sticks) unsalted butter, at room temperature

1 cup granulated sugar

1 large egg

2 teaspoons pure vanilla extract

1/2 cup rainbow sprinkles

**FOR THE ICING**

2 cups confectioners' sugar

2 teaspoons corn syrup

2 tablespoons milk

1 teaspoon pure vanilla extract

1 or 2 drops green gel paste food coloring

Easy to cut out and fun to decorate with a quick-drying icing, these are my favorite holiday cookies to make with my son. When you're working with kids, things need to be quick-drying to remain fun. Otherwise, you'll just be left with a mess and undecorated cookies. You'll need a piping bag and a round piping tip for these.

**TO MAKE THE COOKIES**

1. In a medium mixing bowl, sift or whisk together the flour, cornstarch, baking powder, and salt.

2. In a large mixing bowl, using an electric mixer on medium speed or a wooden spoon, beat together the butter and sugar until light and creamy. This will take about 3 minutes if using an electric mixer or 5 to 6 minutes if creaming by hand. Add the egg and vanilla, and beat to combine. Add the dry ingredients and beat on low speed or by hand until the dough comes together, about 1 minute.

3. Place the dough between two sheets of wax paper or parchment paper. Using a rolling pin, roll out the dough to an even ½-inch thickness. Wrap the dough in the paper and refrigerate until firm, at least 1 hour.

4. Preheat the oven to 350°F. Line a cookie sheet with parchment paper.

5. Using a Christmas tree–shaped cookie cutter, cut out the cookies and place them 2 inches apart on the prepared cookie sheet.

6. Bake for 13 to 14 minutes, until the edges are golden brown.

7. Let the cookies rest on the cookie sheets for 5 minutes before transferring them to wire racks to cool completely.

## Christmas Tree Cookies *continued*

**TO MAKE THE ICING**

1. In a large mixing bowl, stir together the confectioners' sugar, corn syrup, milk, and vanilla until smooth. You may need to stir for a bit to get rid of any lumps. Add the green food coloring and stir until well incorporated. Transfer the icing to a piping bag fitted with a round piping tip.

2. Use the icing to outline the cookies and then fill in the center. Use a toothpick to help blend in any bare spots and gently tap the cookie to even out the icing. I recommend doing one at a time since they crust so quickly. Add sprinkles to the cookie before the icing dries.

Before coloring all the icing green, set aside 3 tablespoons of icing and cover with plastic wrap so it doesn't crust over before you're ready to use it. Add white garlands on the trees with the icing or color it with 1 to 2 drops of gel paste food coloring to make a colored garland.

# Spritz Cookie Wreaths

**MAKES 9 LARGE WREATHS**
Prep: 15 minutes
Bake: 13 to 14 minutes
Shelf Life: 4 to 5 days

- 1 cup (2 sticks) unsalted butter, at room temperature
- ½ cup granulated sugar
- ¼ cup confectioners' sugar
- 2 egg yolks
- 1 teaspoon pure vanilla extract
- 2 cups all-purpose flour
- ½ teaspoon table salt
- 1 to 3 drops green gel paste food coloring
- 1 tablespoon red nonpareil sprinkles

These are delicate, buttery shortbread cookies that are tinted green and piped into festive wreaths. You'll need a piping bag fitted with a 1M piping tip—and a little muscle—to pipe these cookies. Adding red nonpareils gives the appearance of holly berries, which really brings these cookies to life.

1. Preheat the oven to 350°F. Line a cookie sheet with parchment paper.
2. In a large mixing bowl, using an electric mixer on medium speed or a wooden spoon, beat together the butter and both sugars until light and creamy. This will take about 3 minutes if using an electric mixer or 5 to 6 minutes if creaming by hand. Add the egg yolks and vanilla, and beat to combine. Add the flour and salt and beat on low speed or by hand until the dough comes together, about 1 minute. Add the green food coloring and work it in.
3. Transfer the cookie dough to a piping bag fitted with a 1M piping tip. The bag needs to be strong or double bagged because the dough can blow out otherwise.
4. Pipe a 2- to 2½-inch circle onto the prepared cookie sheet, leaving 2 inches of space in between cookies. Using the same piping tip, pipe small stars on top of each circle by using even pressure and pulling up. Sprinkle the nonpareils on top of the wreaths.
5. Bake for 13 to 14 minutes, until the edges are golden brown.
6. Let the cookies cool on the cookie sheet for 10 to 15 minutes before transferring them to a wire rack to cool completely.

You can make smaller wreaths by using a smaller open star piping tip and piping smaller circles.

# Easy Turkey Cookies

**MAKES ABOUT 26 COOKIES**
Prep: 45 minutes
Chill: 30 minutes
Bake: 16 to 17 minutes
Shelf Life: 4 to 5 days

**FOR THE COOKIES**

3 ¾ cups all-purpose flour

2 teaspoons cornstarch

½ teaspoon table salt

1 ½ cups unsalted butter, at room temperature

1 ¾ cups granulated sugar

1 large egg

2 teaspoons vanilla

**FOR THE FROSTING**

2 cups confectioners' sugar

¼ cup unsweetened cocoa powder

½ cup (1 stick) unsalted butter, at room temperature

2 tablespoons milk

1 teaspoon pure vanilla extract

1 (15-ounce) bag Reese's Pieces

39 Tootsie Roll Midgees, unwrapped

2 tablespoons white candy melts

2 tablespoons orange candy melts

2 tablespoons red candy melts

This is a great recipe to make with the kids! They're creative and fun and don't require any special techniques or cutters. The hardest part of making these with your children is that you constantly have to peel the Tootsie Rolls out of their little fists. Be smart and buy extra!

**TO MAKE THE COOKIES**

1. In a medium mixing bowl, sift or whisk together the flour, cornstarch, and salt.

2. In a large mixing bowl, using an electric mixer on medium speed or a wooden spoon, beat together the butter and sugar until light and creamy. This will take about 3 minutes if using an electric mixer or 5 to 6 minutes if creaming by hand. Add the egg and vanilla, and beat to combine. Add the dry ingredients and beat on low speed or by hand until the dough comes together, about 1 minute.

3. Place the dough between two sheets of wax paper or parchment paper. Using a rolling pin, roll out the dough to an even ½-inch thickness. Wrap the dough in the paper and refrigerate until firm, about 30 minutes.

4. Preheat the oven to 350°F. Line a cookie sheet with parchment paper.

5. Using a 3-inch round cookie cutter, cut out the cookies and place them 2 inches apart on the prepared cookie sheet.

6. Bake for 16 to 17 minutes, until the edges are golden brown.

7. Let the cookies rest on the cookie sheets for 5 minutes before transferring them to wire racks to cool completely.

**TO MAKE THE FROSTING**

1. In a medium mixing bowl, sift or whisk together the confectioners' sugar and cocoa powder. Add the butter, milk, and vanilla, and cream together using an electric mixer on medium or a wooden spoon, until light and fluffy, about 1 to 2 minutes.

2. Once the cookies are completely cooled, spread the frosting on top of them.

3. Add two rows of 8 Reese's Pieces along the top of each cookie.

4. Roll a Tootsie Roll until it's 2 inches long. Cut it in half. Roll another Tootsie Roll into a ball. Attach the ball to half of the previous Tootsie Roll. This will be the head and neck. Attach it to the bottom center of the cookie.

5. Put the white candy melts in a small microwave-safe bowl and heat on 50 percent power in 30-second intervals, stirring in between, until melted and smooth. Repeat with the orange and red candy melts. Transfer each batch of melted candy melts into its own resealable plastic bag and snip off one corner of the bag.

6. Using the orange candy melts, pipe a triangle into the center of each Tootsie Roll ball. Using the red, add a little red line along the side and top of the orange. Add two white eyes using the white candy melts.

You can use the premade eyes that are in the cake section, though they may be slightly large and cartoonish.

# Turkey Leg Cookies

**MAKES ABOUT 14 COOKIES**
Prep: 35 minutes
Chill: 1 hour
Bake: 17 to 18 minutes
Shelf Life: 4 to 5 days

- 2½ cups all-purpose flour
- 1 teaspoon cornstarch
- ½ teaspoon table salt
- ¾ cup (1½ sticks) unsalted butter, at room temperature
- 1 cup granulated sugar
- 1 large egg
- 2 teaspoons pure vanilla extract
- 6 (2-ounce) squares vanilla almond bark
- 1 cup graham cracker crumbs

These cookies look just like drumsticks and will be a hit at Thanksgiving. They are coated with white chocolate and graham cracker crumbs. You can find the almond bark in the baking aisle of your supermarket, or substitute white candy melts.

1. In a medium mixing bowl, sift or whisk together the flour, cornstarch, and salt.

2. In a large mixing bowl, using an electric mixer on medium speed or a wooden spoon, beat together the butter and sugar until light and creamy. This will take about 3 minutes if using an electric mixer or 5 to 6 minutes if creaming by hand. Add the egg and vanilla, and beat to combine. Add the dry ingredients and beat on low speed or by hand until the dough comes together, about 1 minute. Wrap the dough in plastic wrap and refrigerate until firm, about 1 hour.

3. Preheat the oven to 350°F. Line a cookie sheet with parchment paper.

4. Using a large (3-tablespoon) cookie scoop, scoop the dough into balls and roll them between your palms to make them round and smooth.

5. Shape each ball into the shape of a turkey leg 4 to 5 inches long, leaving one side thick and the other thin. It should almost look like a cone. Using a butter knife, press a little indentation in the thinner end. Place the cookies 3 inches apart on the prepared cookie sheet.

6. Bake for 17 to 18 minutes, until the edges are golden brown. The cookie will flatten out some.

7. Let the cookies rest on the cookie sheets for 5 minutes before transferring them to wire racks to cool completely.

8. Put the vanilla almond bark in a microwave-safe bowl and heat on 50 percent power in 30-second intervals, stirring in between, until thoroughly melted. Dip the tops of the cooled cookies into the melted vanilla almond bark, letting any excess drip back into the bowl. Coat the thick half of the drumstick in graham cracker crumbs. Set the cookies on a piece of wax paper to dry.

You can use corn flakes or butter cookies instead of graham cracker crumbs.

# 3-D Chocolate Pilgrim Hats

**MAKES 8 COOKIES**
Prep: 45 minutes
Chill: 45 minutes
Bake: 34 to 35 minutes
Shelf Life: 4 to 5 days

- Nonstick cooking spray
- 2 cups all-purpose flour
- ¼ cup Hershey's Special Dark cocoa powder
- 1 teaspoon cornstarch
- ½ teaspoon table salt
- ¾ cup (1 ½ sticks) unsalted butter, at room temperature
- 1 cup granulated sugar
- 1 large egg
- 2 teaspoons pure vanilla extract
- ¼ cup chocolate candy melts
- ¼ cup orange candy melts
- 1 tablespoon yellow candy melts

These cute chocolate hats make the perfect pilgrim hats for Thanksgiving. They're stuck together with a little chocolate and decorated with candy melts. To make these, you will need an 8-well nonstick mini cheesecake pan, which can be found on Amazon or at a cake decorating store.

1. Preheat the oven to 350°F. Spray an 8-well nonstick mini cheesecake pan with cooking spray.

2. In a medium mixing bowl, sift or whisk together the flour, cocoa powder, cornstarch, and salt.

3. In a large mixing bowl, using an electric mixer on medium speed or a wooden spoon, beat together the butter and sugar until light and creamy. This will take about 3 minutes if using an electric mixer or 5 to 6 minutes if creaming by hand. Add the egg and vanilla, and beat to combine. Add the dry ingredients and beat on low speed or by hand until the dough comes together, about 1 minute.

4. Press dough into each of the 8 wells of the cheesecake pan to make a shell (you will use about half of the dough). Cut off any overhang so that the crust doesn't rise up over the top of the well. Bake for 20 minutes. The cookies will have puffed up inside the cavities.

5. Let the cookies cool in the pan for 10 to 15 minutes before transferring them to a wire rack to cool completely. Remove the pan bottoms after they've cooled completely.

6. Place the remaining dough between two sheets of wax paper or parchment paper. Using a rolling pin, roll out the dough to an even ½-inch thickness. Wrap the dough in the paper and refrigerate until firm, about 45 minutes.

7. Line a cookie sheet with parchment paper.

8. Using a 3-inch round cutter, cut out 8 cookies and place them about 2 inches apart on the prepared cookie sheet.

9. Bake for 14 to 15 minutes, until the center is set and the edges are firm to the touch.

10. Let the cookies rest on the cookie sheets for 5 minutes before transferring them to wire racks to cool completely.

11. Put the chocolate candy melts in a small microwave-safe bowl heat on 50 percent power in 30-second intervals, stirring in between, until melted and smooth. Transfer the melted chocolate to a resealable plastic bag and snip off one corner of the bag. Once the cookies are completely cooled, pipe the chocolate around the edge of the bottom of the cookie part that came out of the cheesecake pan. Place a round cookie on top of the chocolate to make the brim of the hat. Turn the cookie right side up and let it sit until the chocolate sets.

12. Put the orange and yellow candy melts in separate microwave-safe bowls and heat each on 50 percent power on 30-second intervals, stirring in between, until melted and smooth. Transfer each to a separate a resealable plastic bag and snip off one corner of each bag. Pipe a band of orange candy melts around the bottom brim of the hat.

13. Use the yellow candy melts to pipe a tiny yellow square onto the center of the orange strip to make a buckle. Use a toothpick to sharpen up the corners of the square. Let the cookies sit until the candy melts harden.

You can use colored frosting to decorate the hats if you don't have candy melts available.

# Basket Weave Fall Leaves

**MAKES ABOUT 30 COOKIES**
Prep: 1 hour 20 minutes
Chill: 2½ hours
Bake: 14 to 15 minutes
Shelf Life: 4 to 5 days

- 3¾ cups all-purpose flour
- ½ teaspoon table salt
- ½ teaspoon ground cinnamon
- 1½ cups unsalted butter, at room temperature
- 1¾ cups granulated sugar
- 1 large egg
- 1 teaspoon pure vanilla extract
- 1 teaspoon maple extract
- Red, brown, green, and orange gel paste food coloring

These cookies are a little time consuming, but beautiful! They taste like maple and cinnamon and have a nice crunch. They sort of remind me of Cinnamon Toast Crunch cereal if I had to put my finger on it. The basket weave pattern is everything on these cookies.

1. In a medium mixing bowl, sift or whisk together the flour, salt, and cinnamon.

2. In a large mixing bowl, using an electric mixer on medium speed or a wooden spoon, beat together the butter and sugar until light and creamy. This will take about 3 minutes if using an electric mixer or 5 to 6 minutes if creaming by hand. Add the egg, vanilla, and maple extract, and beat to combine. Add the dry ingredients and beat on low speed or by hand until the dough comes together, about 1 minute. Divide the dough into 4 equal parts.

3. Working with one dough ball at a time, add 1 or 2 drops of coloring and work it in thoroughly. Do that with each color so that you have one dough ball in each color. You'll need to add more coloring to the red to get a nice red color, rather than pink.

4. Place each dough ball between two sheets of wax paper or parchment paper. Using a rolling pin, roll out the dough to a 12-by-8-inch rectangle that is an even ¼-inch thick. Wrap the dough in the paper and refrigerate until firm, about 30 minutes.

5. Line 2 cookie sheets with parchment paper.

6. Cut each color of dough into 1-inch-wide strips using a pizza cutter or knife.

7. For the first layer, lay the red and green strips side by side, alternating colors. For the second layer, lay the brown and orange strips, again alternating colors, but perpendicular to the strips in the first layer. Using the red and green ends as a guide, use a pizza cutter to cut across the brown and orange strips to create squares on the surface. Next, create a checkerboard pattern by exposing the red and green layer underneath. To accomplish this, use a toothpick to carefully remove every other square in the orange row, and then remove every other brown square alternating with the orange.

8. Return the dough to the refrigerator and chill for 2 more hours.

9. Preheat the oven to 350°F.

10. Using a leaf-shaped cookie cutter, cut out as many leaves as possible. Place the leaves 2 inches apart on the prepared cookie sheet.

11. Take any remaining dough, ball it up, roll it out and cut out as many more leaves as you can. This time you will get a more marbled effect.

12. Bake for 14 to 15 minutes, until the edges are golden brown.

13. Let the cookies rest on the cookie sheets for 5 minutes before transferring them to wire racks to cool completely.

You'll be working with the dough a lot for this cookie. If the dough starts to become too soft to work with at any point, place it in the freezer for 10 minutes to firm up. If you work on a piece of parchment paper, it's easier to transfer it to a cookie sheet and into the freezer.

# Ugly Sweater Cookies

**MAKES ABOUT 12 COOKIES**
Prep: 20 minutes
Chill: 1 hour
Bake: 14 to 15 minutes
Shelf Life: 4 to 5 days

2 1/4 cups all-purpose flour

1/4 cup unsweetened cocoa powder

1 teaspoon cornstarch

1/2 teaspoon table salt

3/4 cup (1 1/2 sticks) unsalted butter, at room temperature

1 cup granulated sugar

1 large egg

2 teaspoons pure vanilla extract

1/2 cup white candy melts

Green and red sanding sugar

Round candies

Even the least artistic person will be able to decorate these successfully, because we're aiming for ugly anyway. Let's not forget that they're delicious chocolate cookies, too. Since ugly sweaters are all the rage, it's easy to find sweater-shaped cutters during the holiday season at any store that carries cookie cutters.

1. In a medium mixing bowl, sift or whisk together the flour, cocoa powder, cornstarch, and salt.

2. In a large mixing bowl, using an electric mixer on medium speed or a wooden spoon, beat together the butter and sugar until light and creamy. This will take about 3 minutes if using an electric mixer or 5 to 6 minutes if creaming by hand. Add the egg and vanilla, and beat to combine. Add the dry ingredients and beat on low speed or by hand until the dough comes together, about 1 minute.

3. Place the dough between two sheets of wax paper or parchment paper. Using a rolling pin, roll out the dough to an even ½-inch thickness. Wrap the dough in the paper and refrigerate until firm, at least 1 hour.

4. Preheat the oven to 350°F. Line a cookie sheet with parchment paper.

5. Using a sweater-shaped cookie cutter, cut out the cookies and place them 2 inches apart on the prepared cookie sheet. Generously cover the cookies with Christmas sprinkles.

6. Bake for 14 to 15 minutes, until the center is set and the edges are firm to the touch.

7. Let the cookies rest on the cookie sheets for 5 minutes before transferring them to wire racks to cool completely.

8. Put the candy melts in a small microwave-safe bowl and heat on 50 percent power in 30-second intervals, stirring in between, until melted and smooth. Transfer the melted candy to a resealable plastic bag and snip off one corner of the bag.

9. Once the cookies are completely cooled, pipe Christmas tree shapes on some of the cookies and coat the wet candy melts with green sanding sugar. Add round candies as Christmas tree ornaments. Pipe candy cane stripes on other sweaters using red sanding sugar to make the red lines and the melted candy melts for the white lines. Let dry.

For a reindeer sweater, break twisted pretzels apart for horns and use the candy melts to stick them to a cookie. Add a red M&M for the nose, and pop on some candy eyes.

# Gingerbread Men

**MAKES ABOUT 26 COOKIES**
Prep: 25 minutes
Chill: 2 hours
Bake: 14 to 15 minutes
Shelf Life: 4 to 5 days

**FOR THE COOKIES**

4 ¼ cups all-purpose flour

1 teaspoon baking powder

½ teaspoon table salt

2 teaspoons ground cinnamon

2 teaspoons ground ginger

¼ teaspoon ground cloves

1 cup (2 sticks) unsalted butter, at room temperature

¾ cup packed light brown sugar

½ cup granulated sugar

2 large eggs

¾ cup molasses

1 teaspoon pure vanilla extract

½ cup sprinkles

**FOR THE ICING**

2 cups confectioners' sugar

2 teaspoons corn syrup

2 tablespoons milk

1 teaspoon pure vanilla extract

Who doesn't love making gingerbread men? These are soft, spicy, and fun to decorate for the holidays. The cookies hold their shape well. Kids love to decorate these guys with icing and sprinkles. (Though I think my son Lucian's goal is to get as much icing on it as possible and then gobble it down.) Use a piping bag fitted with a #3 round piping tip for these.

**TO MAKE THE COOKIES**

1. In a medium mixing bowl, sift or whisk together the flour, baking powder, salt, cinnamon, ginger, and cloves.

2. In a large mixing bowl, using an electric mixer on medium speed or a wooden spoon, beat together the butter and both sugars until light and creamy. This will take about 3 minutes if using an electric mixer or 5 to 6 minutes if creaming by hand. Add the eggs, molasses, and vanilla, and beat to combine. Add the dry ingredients and beat on low speed or by hand until the dough comes together, about 1 minute.

3. Place the dough between two sheets of wax paper or parchment paper. Using a rolling pin, roll out the dough to an even ½-inch thickness. Wrap the dough in the paper and refrigerate until firm, at least 2 hours.

4. Preheat the oven to 350°F. Line a cookie sheet with parchment paper.

5. Using a 3-inch gingerbread man cookie cutter, cut out the cookies and place them 2 inches apart on the prepared cookie sheet.

6. Bake for 14 to 15 minutes, until the edges are golden.

7. Let the cookies rest on the cookie sheets for 5 minutes before transferring them to wire racks to cool completely.

### TO MAKE THE ICING

1. In a large mixing bowl, stir together the confectioners' sugar, corn syrup, milk, and vanilla until smooth. You may need to stir for a bit to get rid of any lumps.

2. Put the icing in a piping bag fitted with a #3 round tip. Once the cookies have cooled completely, pipe the icing onto them to make them outfits or do the traditional white outline. Add some festive sprinkles, too.

Turn these into creepy skeleton gingerbread men by using the frosting to pipe bones, including rib cages, on them!

Pecan Pie Bars, *page 240*

# Brownies and Bars

# White Chocolate Brownies

**MAKES 9 BROWNIES**
Prep: 20 minutes
Bake: 40 to 45 minutes
Shelf Life: 4 to 5 days

Nonstick cooking spray

½ cup (1 stick) unsalted butter, melted

8 ounces white chocolate baking bars, chopped

1 cup granulated sugar

2 large eggs

2 teaspoons pure vanilla extract

1 ½ cups all-purpose flour

½ teaspoon table salt

These dense brownies are for the white chocolate lovers out there. They are rich and fluffy and have a nice white chocolate flavor. These brownies have the signature meringue crinkle top, but it's a nice golden brown color. They taste amazing topped with some fresh berries.

1. Preheat the oven to 350°F. Line an 8-inch square baking pan with aluminum foil and coat it with cooking spray.
2. Combine the butter and white chocolate in a large microwave-safe bowl and heat on 50 percent power in 30-second intervals, stirring in between, until melted and smooth. Add the sugar, eggs, and vanilla, and beat until thick and creamy, 2 to 3 minutes. Add the flour and salt and beat on low speed or by hand just until the flour is incorporated, about 1 minute. Spread the batter evenly in the prepared pan.
3. Bake for 40 to 45 minutes, until the top is golden brown and a skewer or toothpick inserted into the center comes out with moist crumbs but no batter.
4. Let cool to room temperature and then cut into 9 brownies.

The tops of these brownies brown up. If you prefer a lighter brown top, lay a piece of aluminum foil over the top of the pan as it bakes.

# Chocolate Chip Blondies

**MAKES 9 BLONDIES**
Prep: 10 minutes
Bake: About 25 minutes
Shelf Life: 4 to 5 days

Nonstick cooking spray

½ cup (1 stick) unsalted butter, melted

1 ¼ cups packed light brown sugar

2 large eggs

1 teaspoon pure vanilla extract

1 cup all-purpose flour

½ teaspoon table salt

½ cup semisweet chocolate chips

Blondies are good without the chocolate chips, but that little hit of chocolate does something wonderful for these bars. They're transformed into kind of a giant chocolate chip cookie, but thicker and denser. You better believe my son loves these. The best part is the beautiful, shiny meringue top.

1. Preheat the oven to 350°F. Line an 8-inch square baking pan with aluminum foil and spray with cooking spray.
2. In a large mixing bowl, using an electric mixer on medium speed or a wooden spoon, beat together the melted butter, sugar, eggs, and vanilla until the mixture thickens and lightens in color. This will take about 1 minute if using an electric mixer or 2 minutes if beating by hand. Add the flour and salt, and beat on low speed or by hand until the dough comes together, about 1 minute.
3. Transfer the batter to the prepared baking pan and sprinkle the chocolate chips over the top.
4. Bake for about 25 minutes, until the top is set.
5. Let the blondies cool to room temperature in the pan before cutting into 9 squares.

If you love nuts, stir ½ cup chopped walnuts into the batter before transferring to the baking pan.

# Classic Brownies

**MAKES 9 BROWNIES**
Prep: 20 minutes
Bake: About 30 minutes
Shelf Life: 4 to 5 days

Nonstick cooking spray

½ cup flour

½ cup unsweetened cocoa powder

½ teaspoon table salt

½ cup (1 stick) unsalted butter, melted

1 ¼ cups granulated sugar

2 large eggs

1 teaspoon pure vanilla extract

Everyone needs a go-to brownie recipe to work from. This is mine. It can easily be tweaked with several variations to create your perfect brownie, whether it's soft and cakey, or dense and chewy. As-is, it has the perfect meringue-like crinkle topping and rich chocolate flavor.

1. Preheat the oven to 350°F. Line an 8-inch square baking pan with aluminum foil and spray with cooking spray.
2. In a medium mixing bowl, sift together the flour, cocoa powder, and salt.
3. In a large bowl, using an electric mixer on medium speed or a wooden spoon, beat together the melted butter, granulated sugar, eggs, and vanilla until the mixture thickens and lightens in color, 1 to 2 minutes. Add the dry ingredients and beat on low speed or by hand just until the flour is incorporated, about 1 minute.
4. Spread the batter evenly in the prepared pan.
5. Bake for about 30 minutes, until a toothpick comes out clean or with moist crumbs.
6. Let the brownies cool to room temperature in the pan and then cut into 9 squares.

You can add about ½ cup chopped walnuts, pecans, or candy to the brownies.

## The Perfect Brownie

Everyone has their own idea of the perfect brownie. Whether you like yours dense and chewy or soft and cakey, the chart below can help you make your perfect brownie.

Classic Brownies (page 228).

Transform the Classic Brownie it into a cakey brownie by adding an additional egg.

Love a chewy brownie? Substitute brown sugar for the granulated sugar.

Oh, we can't forget about the perfect rich brownie! Just add ½ cup of melted chocolate chips into the batter!

# Cheesecake Swirled Brownies

**MAKES 9 BROWNIES**
Prep: 25 minutes
Bake: About 30 minutes
Shelf Life: 4 to 5 days

**FOR THE BROWNIE BATTER**

Nonstick cooking spray

½ cup flour

½ cup unsweetened cocoa powder

½ teaspoon table salt

½ cup (1 stick) unsalted butter, melted

4 ounces semisweet baking chocolate, chopped

1 ¼ cups granulated sugar

2 large eggs

1 teaspoon pure vanilla extract

**FOR THE CHEESECAKE BATTER**

8 ounces cream cheese, at room temperature

⅓ cup granulated sugar

1 large egg

You can never go wrong with these brownies. The brownie is rich, dense, and chocolaty. Swirled into the brownie batter is a simple vanilla cheesecake that's distributed throughout, so that you get a little bit of cheesecake and chocolate in every bite. Wash these rich brownies down with a glass of milk.

**TO MAKE THE BROWNIE BATTER**

1. Preheat the oven to 350°F. Line an 8-inch square baking pan with aluminum foil and spray with cooking spray.

2. In a medium mixing bowl, sift or whisk together the flour, cocoa powder, and salt.

3. In a large microwave-safe mixing bowl, combine the butter and chocolate and heat on 50 percent power in 30-second intervals, stirring in between, until melted and smooth. Add the granulated sugar, eggs, vanilla, and dry mixture from step 2, and beat until the mixture thickens and lightens in color, 1 to 2 minutes.

4. Reserve about ¼ cup of the brownie batter for the top. Transfer the remaining brownie batter to the prepared pan.

**TO MAKE THE CHEESECAKE BATTER**

1. In a large mixing bowl, using an electric mixer on medium speed or a wooden spoon, beat together the cream cheese and sugar until smooth, about 1 minute. Add the egg and beat until smooth.

2. Add the cheesecake batter in dollops on top of the brownie batter. Add a spoonful of the remaining ¼ cup of the brownie batter in the center of each cheesecake dollop. Using a skewer or butter knife, swirl the batters together.

3. Bake for about 30 minutes, until the top is set.

4. Let the brownies cool to room temperature in the pan and then refrigerate for 1 to 2 hours to set. Cut into 9 squares. Serve chilled or let the brownies come to room temperature before serving.

The semisweet baking chocolate helps create a rich, dense brownie, but you can omit it if you prefer a lighter brownie.

# Gooey Caramel Brownies

**MAKES 9 BROWNIES**
Prep: 25 minutes
Bake: About 30 minutes
Shelf Life: 4 to 5 days

These brownies have the gooey going on! A thick layer of caramel is sandwiched between the brownie layers, making for a sweet surprise. I love that when you bite into the brownies, a string of caramel trails from them. These didn't even make it to the testers due to how fast they disappeared.

### FOR THE BROWNIE BATTER

- Nonstick cooking spray
- ½ cup all-purpose flour
- ½ cup unsweetened cocoa powder
- ½ teaspoon table salt
- ½ cup (1 stick) unsalted butter, melted
- 1 ¼ cups granulated sugar
- 2 large eggs
- 1 teaspoon pure vanilla extract

### FOR THE CARAMEL FILLING

- 1 (11-ounce) package caramel squares
- ¼ cup heavy cream

### TO MAKE THE BROWNIE BATTER

1. Preheat the oven to 350°F. Line an 8-inch square baking pan with aluminum foil and spray with cooking spray.
2. In a medium bowl, sift or whisk together the flour, cocoa powder, and salt.
3. In a large mixing bowl, using an electric mixer on medium speed or a wooden spoon, beat together the melted butter, sugar, eggs, and vanilla until the mixture thickens and lightens in color, 1 to 2 minutes. Add the dry ingredients and beat on low speed or by hand just until the flour is incorporated, about 1 minute.
4. Transfer half of the brownie batter to the prepared pan.
5. Bake for 10 minutes.

## Gooey Caramel Brownies *continued*

**TO MAKE THE CARAMEL FILLING**

1. In a large microwave-safe bowl, combine the caramels and cream. Heat in the microwave on 50 percent power in 30-second intervals, stirring in between, until melted and smooth.

2. Remove the brownies from the oven and add the caramel mixture on top, spreading it into an even layer. Top with the remaining brownie batter.

3. Bake for about 20 minutes, until the top is set.

4. Let the brownies cool to room temperature in the pan and then refrigerate for 1 to 2 hours to set. Cut into 9 squares. Serve chilled, or let the brownies come to room temperature before serving.

Can't find caramel squares? Use the caramel bits located in the baking aisle instead.

# Mint Chocolate Chip Brownies

**MAKES 9 BROWNIES**
Prep: 25 minutes
Bake: About 30 minutes
Shelf Life: 4 to 5 days

**FOR THE BROWNIE BATTER**

Cooking spray

½ cup all-purpose flour

½ cup unsweetened cocoa powder

½ teaspoon table salt

½ cup (1 stick) unsalted butter, melted

1 ¼ cups granulated sugar

2 large eggs

1 teaspoon pure vanilla extract

**FOR THE CHEESECAKE BATTER**

8 ounces cream cheese, at room temperature

⅓ cup granulated sugar

1 large egg

¼ teaspoon peppermint extract

1 or 2 drops green gel paste food coloring

½ cup mini semisweet chocolate chips

Pretty brownies are allowed, right? These brownies have a pop of green color signifying the mint that's in them. The green, minty cheesecake swirl is creamy and has mini chocolate chips throughout it for a mint-chip appearance. The brownie itself is rich, dense, and chocolaty.

**TO MAKE THE BROWNIE BATTER**

1. Preheat the oven to 350°F. Line an 8-inch square baking pan with aluminum foil and spray with cooking spray.

2. In a medium mixing bowl, sift or whisk together the flour, cocoa powder, and salt.

3. In a large mixing bowl, using an electric mixer on medium speed or a wooden spoon, beat together the melted butter, granulated sugar, eggs, and vanilla until the mixture thickens and lightens in color, 1 to 2 minutes. Add the dry ingredients and beat on low speed or by hand, just until the flour is incorporated, 30 seconds to 1 minute.

4. Transfer the brownie batter to the prepared pan, reserving ¼ cup of the batter for the top.

## Mint Chocolate Chip Brownies *continued*

**TO MAKE THE CHEESECAKE BATTER**

1. In a large mixing bowl, using an electric mixer on medium or a wooden spoon, beat together the cream cheese and sugar until incorporated, 30 seconds to 1 minute. Add the egg, peppermint extract, and green food coloring and beat until smooth. Stir in the chocolate chips.

2. Add the cheesecake batter in dollops on top of the brownie batter. Add a spoonful of the remaining ¼ cup of the brownie batter in the center of each cheesecake dollop. Using a skewer or butter knife, swirl the batters together.

3. Bake for about 30 minutes, until the top is set.

4. Let the brownies cool to room temperature in the pan and then refrigerate for 1 to 2 hours to set. Cut into 9 squares. Serve chilled or let the brownies come to room temperature before serving.

Add more chocolate to create a rich, dense brownie. Melt 4 ounces of semisweet baking chocolate in with the butter.

# Chocolate–Peanut Butter Brownies

**MAKES 9 BROWNIES**
Prep: 20 minutes
Bake: 28 to 32 minutes
Shelf Life: 4 to 5 days

Nonstick cooking spray

½ cup flour

½ cup unsweetened cocoa powder

½ teaspoon table salt

½ cup (1 stick) unsalted butter, melted

4 ounces semisweet baking chocolate, chopped

1 ¼ cups granulated sugar

2 large eggs

1 teaspoon pure vanilla extract

¼ cup creamy peanut butter

These are rich, chocolaty brownies with a gorgeous peanut butter swirl on top. The swirls provide just the right amount of peanut butter flavoring without requiring a lot of extra work. While testing this recipe, I tried adding a variety of peanut butter ingredients, but in the end settled on a simple swirl.

1. Preheat the oven to 350°F. Line an 8-inch square baking pan with aluminum foil and spray it with cooking spray.

2. In a medium mixing bowl, sift together the flour, cocoa powder, and salt.

3. Combine the butter and chocolate in a large microwave-safe bowl and heat on 50 percent power in 30-second intervals, stirring in between, until melted and smooth. Add the granulated sugar, eggs, and vanilla, and beat until the mixture thickens and lightens in color, 1 to 2 minutes. Add the dry ingredients and beat until just incorporated.

4. Spread the brownie batter in the prepared pan.

5. Put the peanut butter in a small microwave-safe bowl and heat for 20 seconds to thin it. Drizzle the peanut butter on top of the brownie batter. Using a skewer or butter knife, swirl the peanut butter into the batter.

6. Bake for 28 to 32 minutes, until the top is set.

7. Let the brownies cool in the pan to room temperature. To serve, cut into 9 brownies.

Substitute chunky peanut butter for the creamy peanut butter to add some crunch.

# Coffee Cheesecake Swirled Brownies

**MAKES 9 BROWNIES**
Prep: 25 minutes
Bake: About 35 minutes
Shelf Life: 4 to 5 days

**FOR THE BROWNIES**

Nonstick cooking spray

½ cup all-purpose flour

½ cup unsweetened cocoa powder

½ teaspoon table salt

½ cup (1 stick) unsalted butter, melted

1 ¼ cups granulated sugar

2 large eggs

1 teaspoon pure vanilla extract

¼ teaspoon instant coffee granules

**FOR THE CHEESECAKE**

8 ounces cream cheese, at room temperature

⅓ cup granulated sugar

1 large egg

½ teaspoon instant coffee granules

Chocolaty brownies swirled with a rich coffee cheesecake—can it get any better? The coffee enhances the chocolate flavor of the brownies while providing its own wonderful flavor. What I love most is that my coffee is in a cheesecake batter. Who doesn't love a little cheesecake with their brownies?

**TO MAKE THE BROWNIES**

1. Preheat the oven to 350°F. Line an 8-inch square baking pan with aluminum foil and spray it with cooking spray.

2. In a medium mixing bowl, sift or whisk together the flour, cocoa powder, and salt.

3. In a large mixing bowl, using an electric mixer on medium speed or a wooden spoon, beat together the melted butter, sugar, eggs, vanilla, and coffee granules until thick and creamy. This will take about 2 minutes if using an electric mixer or 4 to 5 minutes if creaming by hand. Add the dry ingredients and beat on low speed or by hand until incorporated, about 30 seconds.

4. Reserve about ¼ cup of the brownie batter for the top. Transfer the remaining brownie batter to the prepared pan and smooth it out into an even layer.

**TO MAKE THE CHEESECAKE**

1. In a large mixing bowl, using an electric mixer on medium speed or a wooden spoon, beat together the cream cheese and sugar until light and creamy. This will take about 1 minute if using an electric mixer or 2 to 3 minutes if creaming by hand. Add the egg and instant coffee, and beat to incorporate.

2. Using a spoon, dollop the cheesecake batter on top of the brownie mix. Add a dollop of the reserved ¼ cup of the brownie batter in the center of each cheesecake dollop. Using a skewer or butter knife, swirl the batters together.

3. Bake for about 35 minutes, until the top is set.

4. Let the brownies cool to room temperature and then refrigerate for 1 to 2 hours to set. To serve, cut into 9 bars. Serve the bars chilled or let them come to room temperature before serving.

Add more chocolate to create a rich, dense brownie. Do so by melting 4 ounces of semisweet baking chocolate with the butter.

# Pecan Pie Bars

**MAKES 12 BARS**
Prep: 20 minutes
Bake: About 1 hour 10 minutes
Shelf Life: 4 to 5 days

**FOR THE CRUST**

Nonstick cooking spray

½ cup (1 stick) unsalted butter, at room temperature

4 ounces cream cheese, at room temperature

½ cup packed light brown sugar

¼ cup granulated sugar

2 cups all-purpose flour

½ teaspoon table salt

**FOR THE FILLING**

1 cup packed light brown sugar

¾ cup dark corn syrup

4 large eggs

3 tablespoons unsalted butter, melted

2 cups chopped pecans

These bars have the same irresistible pecan pie filling that's in a traditional pecan pie, but it's layered on top of a creamy cream cheese shortbread cookie crust rather than a pie crust. Did I mention how much easier they are to make than a pie? Hello, new Thanksgiving dessert!

**TO MAKE THE CRUST**

1. Preheat the oven to 350°F. Line an 11-by-7-inch baking pan with aluminum foil and spray with cooking spray.

2. In a large mixing bowl, using an electric mixer on medium or a wooden spoon, beat together the butter, cream cheese, and both sugars until well combined, 1 to 2 minutes. Add the flour and salt, and beat on low speed or by hand just until the flour is incorporated, about 1 minute. Press the crust dough evenly into the prepared pan, covering the bottom of the pan completely.

3. Bake for 20 minutes.

**TO MAKE THE FILLING**

1. In a large bowl, whisk together the brown sugar, corn syrup, eggs, and melted butter until well combined, about 1 minute. Stir in the pecans.

2. When the crust comes out of the oven, pour the filling on top, spreading it out into an even layer.

3. Bake for about 50 minutes, until the top is set.

4. Let cool to room temperature in the pan and then refrigerate for 2 to 3 hours until set. To serve, cut into 12 bars. Serve chilled or let the bars come to room temperature before serving.

Whisk 1 teaspoon of maple extract into the filling for a light maple-flavored pecan pie bar.

# Butterscotch Pudding Cookie Bars

**MAKES 12 BARS**
Prep: 20 minutes
Bake: 45 to 50 minutes
Shelf Life: 4 to 5 days

Nonstick cooking spray
2 ¼ cups all-purpose flour
1 (3.4-ounce) package butterscotch pudding mix
½ teaspoon baking soda
½ teaspoon baking powder
¼ teaspoon table salt
1 cup (2 sticks) unsalted butter, at room temperature
1 cup packed light brown sugar
1 teaspoon pure vanilla extract
2 large eggs
1 cup butterscotch chips

Since I've discovered using pudding mixes in cookies and cakes, I want to add them to everything, which brings me to these bars. They're full of butterscotch flavor, from the pudding to the chips. They're moist and fluffy and have a rich brown color from the butterscotch pudding.

1. Preheat the oven to 350°F. Line an 11-by-7-inch baking pan with aluminum foil and spray it with cooking spray.
2. In a medium mixing bowl, sift or whisk together the flour, dry pudding mix, baking soda, baking powder, and salt.
3. In a large mixing bowl, using an electric mixer on medium speed or a wooden spoon, beat together the butter and sugar until light and creamy. This will take about 3 minutes if using an electric mixer or 5 to 6 minutes if creaming by hand. Add the eggs and vanilla, and beat to combine. Add the dry ingredients, and beat on low speed or by hand until the dough comes together, about 1 minute. Using a rubber spatula, fold in the butterscotch chips.
4. Spread the cookie dough out in an even layer in the prepared pan.
5. Bake for 45 to 50 minutes, until the top is golden and a skewer or toothpick inserted into the center comes out clean or with crumbs, but not wet batter.
6. Let cool to room temperature, 1 to 2 hours. To serve, cut into 12 bars.

For a finished look, melt 1 cup of butterscotch chips in the microwave at 50 percent power in 30 second-intervals, stirring in between, until melted and smooth. Transfer the melted butterscotch to a resealable plastic bag and snip off one corner of the bag. Pipe a butterscotch drizzle on top of the bars.

# Turtle Bars

**MAKES 12 BARS**
Prep: 25 minutes
Chill: 1 hour
Bake: 35 minutes
Shelf Life: 4 to 5 days

**FOR THE CRUST**

Cooking spray

1 cup (2 sticks) unsalted butter, at room temperature

1 cup granulated sugar

2 cups all-purpose flour

¼ teaspoon table salt

**FOR THE CARAMEL**

1 (11-ounce) package caramel squares

¼ cup heavy cream

½ cup chopped pecans

**FOR THE GANACHE**

2 cups semisweet chocolate chips

¾ cup heavy cream

It has finally happened! I turned the brilliant idea of turtle candies into beautiful layered bars. They have a thin buttery shortbread base with a layer of gooey caramel-pecan filling on top. They're topped off with a healthy dose of chocolate ganache and refrigerated until they've set.

**TO MAKE THE CRUST**

1. Preheat the oven to 350°F. Line an 11-by-7-inch rectangular baking pan with aluminum foil and spray it with cooking spray.

2. In a large mixing bowl, using an electric mixer on medium speed or a wooden spoon, beat together the butter and sugar until light and creamy. This will take about 3 minutes if using an electric mixer or 5 to 6 minutes if creaming by hand. Add the flour and salt, and beat on low speed or by hand until the dough comes together, about 1 minute.

3. Press the crust dough evenly into the prepared pan, covering the bottom of the pan completely.

4. Bake for 35 minutes. Set aside to cool.

### TO MAKE THE CARAMEL

1. Combine the caramels and cream in a medium microwave-safe bowl and heat on 50 percent power in 30-second intervals, stirring in between, until the caramel is melted and the mixture is smooth. Stir in the pecans.
2. Pour the caramel on top of the crust.

### TO MAKE THE GANACHE

1. Combine the chocolate chips and cream in a medium microwave-safe bowl and heat on 50 percent power in 30-second intervals, stirring in between, until the chocolate is melted and the mixture is smooth. Pour the ganache on top of the caramel.
2. Refrigerate for about 2 hours to set up. To serve, cut into 12 bars. Serve chilled or at room temperature.

Can't find caramel squares? Use the caramel bits located in the baking aisle instead.

# Caramel Apple Bars

**MAKES 15 BARS**
Prep: 40 minutes
Bake: 45 minutes
Shelf Life: 4 to 5 days

**FOR THE CRUST**

Nonstick cooking spray

1 cup (2 sticks) unsalted butter, at room temperature

½ cup packed light brown sugar

1 teaspoon pure vanilla extract

2 cups all-purpose flour

½ teaspoon table salt

**FOR THE FILLING**

10 Granny Smith apples, peeled, cored, and sliced

1 (11-ounce) package caramel squares

¼ cup all-purpose flour

**FOR THE TOPPING**

½ cup (1 stick) unsalted butter, at room temperature

½ cup packed light brown sugar

1 cup all-purpose flour

1 cup individually wrapped caramels, unwrapped

These bars start with a brown sugar shortbread base. Sandwiched in the middle are the caramel apple slices, and on top is a brown sugar crumble. The apples add a nice texture to the bars and the caramel drizzle on top really makes the caramel stand out.

**TO MAKE THE CRUST**

1. Preheat the oven to 350°F. Line a 9-by-13-inch baking pan with aluminum foil and spray it with cooking spray.

2. In a large mixing bowl, using an electric mixer on medium speed or a wooden spoon, beat together the butter, brown sugar, and vanilla until light and creamy. This will take about 3 minutes if using an electric mixer or 5 to 6 minutes if creaming by hand. Add the flour and salt, and beat on low speed or by hand until the dough comes together, about 1 minute.

3. Press the crust dough evenly into the prepared pan, covering the bottom of the pan completely.

4. Bake for 15 minutes.

**TO MAKE THE FILLING**

1. Combine the apples, caramels, and flour in a saucepan and cook over medium heat, stirring, until the caramels melt and thicken slightly, about 16 minutes.

2. Pour the mixture over the hot crust.

#### TO MAKE THE TOPPING

1. In a large mixing bowl, using an electric mixer on medium speed or a wooden spoon, beat together the butter and brown sugar until light and creamy. This will take about 3 minutes if using an electric mixer or 5 to 6 minutes if creaming by hand. Add the flour and beat for about 45 seconds, until the mixture is in coarse crumbles. Sprinkle the topping over the apples.
2. Bake for about 30 minutes, until the crumble is browned.
3. Remove from the oven and let cool to room temperature.
4. Put the caramels in a microwave-safe bowl and heat on 50 percent power in 30-second intervals, stirring in between, until melted and smooth. Drizzle the caramel on top of the cooled bars.
5. To serve, cut into 15 bars.

Tart apples such as Granny Smiths make the best apple for these bars, but just about any sweet apples can be substituted.

# S'mores Bars

**MAKES 15 BARS**
Prep: 25 minutes
Bake: 30 to 35 minutes
Shelf Life: 4 to 5 days

Nonstick cooking spray

4 cups all-purpose flour

2 teaspoons baking soda

1 teaspoon table salt

1 teaspoon ground cinnamon

1 cup (2 sticks) unsalted butter, at room temperature

2 cups packed light brown sugar

1 cup granulated sugar

3 large eggs

2 tablespoons honey

2 teaspoons pure vanilla extract

½ cup graham cracker crumbs

1 (15-ounce) jar marshmallow crème (such as Marshmallow Fluff)

7 (1.55-ounce) milk chocolate bars (such as Hershey's)

How can a bar that tastes this good be tricky? Let me tell you. The ooey-gooey chocolate marshmallow inside can make or break these bars! The graham cracker cookie needs to seal in the marshmallow well, otherwise it'll find its way out and blow a nice-size hole in your bar.

1. Preheat the oven to 350°F. Line a 9-by-13-inch baking pan with aluminum foil and spray it with cooking spray.

2. In a medium mixing bowl, sift or whisk together the flour, baking soda, salt, and cinnamon.

3. In a large mixing bowl, using an electric mixer on medium speed or a wooden spoon, beat together the butter and both sugars until light and creamy. This will take about 3 minutes if using an electric mixer or 5 to 6 minutes if creaming by hand. Add the eggs, honey, and vanilla, and beat to combine. Add the dry ingredients and the graham cracker crumbs and beat on low speed or by hand until the dough comes together, about 1 minute.

4. Spread half of the cookie dough in the bottom of the prepared pan. If it's hard to spread, use wax paper or parchment paper to press it down and even it out.

5. Spread the marshmallow crème on top of the cookie.

6. Lay the candy bars on top of the marshmallow.

7. Add the remaining cookie dough on top of the chocolate. Be sure to fill all the holes and edges. Use a piece of wax paper to get it evenly spread out and pinch any holes together.

8. Bake for 30 to 35 minutes, until the top is golden.

9. Remove from the oven and let cool in the pan for 1 to 2 hours until room temperature. To serve, cut into 15 bars.

Forgot to get chocolate bars? Use a generous layer of chocolate chips instead. I like milk chocolate chips, but semisweet chocolate would work, too.

# Honey Bun Bars

**MAKES 12 BARS**
Prep: 30 minutes
Bake: About 50 minutes
Shelf Life: 4 to 5 days

Nonstick cooking spray
2 ½ cups all-purpose flour
½ teaspoon baking powder
½ teaspoon table salt
½ cup (1 stick) unsalted butter, at room temperature
4 ounces cream cheese, at room temperature
1 ¼ cups granulated sugar
1 large egg
2 teaspoons pure vanilla extract
½ cup packed light brown sugar
2 teaspoons ground cinnamon

**FOR THE GLAZE**

1 cup confectioners' sugar
1 tablespoon milk
1 teaspoon pure vanilla extract

Bars that can be eaten as a breakfast or dessert are officially the best kind of bars. I enjoyed the cinnamon-sugar layer in the center of these dense cookie bars so much that I added a generous sprinkle on top, too. The finishing touch was a vanilla glaze drizzled on top.

1. Preheat the oven to 350°F. Line a 9-by-13-inch baking pan with aluminum foil and spray it with cooking spray.
2. In a medium mixing bowl, sift or whisk together the flour, baking powder, and salt.
3. In a large mixing bowl, using an electric mixer on medium speed or a wooden spoon, beat together the butter, cream cheese, and granulated sugar until light and creamy. This will take about 3 minutes if using an electric mixer or 5 to 6 minutes if creaming by hand. Add the egg and vanilla, and beat to combine. Add the dry ingredients and beat on low speed or by hand just until incorporated, about 1 minute.
4. Press half of the cookie dough into the bottom of the prepared pan, spreading it evenly.

5. In a small bowl, stir together the brown sugar and cinnamon. Sprinkle three-quarters of it on the top of the cookie dough.

6. Spoon the remaining cookie dough on the top of the cinnamon sugar and carefully spread it out.

7. Sprinkle the remaining cinnamon-sugar on the top of the cookie dough.

8. Bake for about 50 minutes, until the edges are golden brown and a toothpick inserted in the center comes out clean.

**TO MAKE THE GLAZE**

In a small bowl, stir together the confectioners' sugar, milk, and vanilla. Drizzle the glaze over the warm bars. To serve, cut into 12 bars.

These taste especially good served warm. Heat individual bars in the microwave for 15 to 20 seconds.

# Lemony Lemon Bars

**MAKES 12 BARS**
Prep: 25 minutes
Bake: About 55 minutes
Shelf Life: 4 to 5 days

**FOR THE CRUST**

- Nonstick cooking spray
- 1 cup (2 sticks) unsalted butter, at room temperature
- ½ cup granulated sugar
- 2 cups all-purpose flour
- ¼ teaspoon table salt

**FOR THE FILLING**

- 1 ¾ cups granulated sugar
- Grated zest and juice of 3 lemons
- ¾ cup all-purpose flour
- 4 large eggs, at room temperature

These bars have a thick layer of buttery shortbread. Layered on top of that is a tart lemon filling. The top of the bars form a crust and the center is a soft, curd-like texture. Dust the bars with confectioners' sugar and serve them up on a warm summer day.

**TO MAKE THE CRUST**

1. Preheat the oven to 350°F. Line an 11-by-7-inch baking pan with aluminum foil and spray it with cooking spray.
2. In a large mixing bowl, using an electric mixer on medium speed or a wooden spoon, beat together the butter and sugar until light and creamy. This will take about 3 minutes if using an electric mixer or 5 to 6 minutes if creaming by hand. Add the flour and salt, and beat on low speed or by hand until the dough comes together, about 1 minute.
3. Press the crust dough evenly into the prepared pan, covering the bottom of the pan completely
4. Bake for 20 minutes.

**TO MAKE THE FILLING**

1. In a large bowl, whisk together the sugar, lemon zest, and flour until combined. Whisk in the lemon juice and eggs until thoroughly incorporated.
2. When the crust comes out of the oven, pour the filling over the top.
3. Bake for about 35 minutes, until the top is set.
4. Let cool to room temperature and then refrigerate for 2 to 3 hours to set. To serve, cut into 12 bars. Serve chilled.

Dust the top of the bars with confectioners' sugar for an extra-pretty bar.

# Milk and Cookie Bars

**MAKES 12 BARS**
Prep: 35 minutes
Bake: 35 to 38 minutes
Shelf Life: 4 to 5 days

**FOR THE COOKIE DOUGH**

Nonstick cooking spray

2¼ cups all-purpose flour

½ teaspoon baking soda

½ teaspoon baking powder

½ teaspoon table salt

½ cup (1 stick) unsalted butter, at room temperature

¾ cup packed light brown sugar

½ cup granulated sugar

1 large egg

2 teaspoons pure vanilla extract

12 chocolate sandwich cookies, crushed

**FOR THE CHEESECAKE FILLING**

8 ounces cream cheese, at room temperature

½ cup powdered milk

¼ cup granulated sugar

1 large egg

1 teaspoon pure vanilla extract

Cookies inside cookies? That's a thing! My husband didn't believe me at first until he got to try these bars. They're filled with a cheesecake center and bits of chocolate sandwich cookies in the cookie dough. That may sound crazy, but they're always a big hit! The cheesecake is made with powdered milk, which you can find in the baking aisle of your supermarket.

**TO MAKE THE COOKIE DOUGH**

1. Preheat the oven to 350°F. Line a 9-by-13-inch baking pan with aluminum foil and spray it with cooking spray.

2. In a medium mixing bowl, sift or whisk together the flour, baking soda, baking powder, and salt.

3. In a large mixing bowl, using an electric mixer on medium speed or a wooden spoon, beat together the butter and both sugars until light and creamy. This will take about 3 minutes if using an electric mixer or 5 to 6 minutes if creaming by hand. Add the egg and vanilla, and beat to combine. Add the dry ingredients and the crushed cookies and beat on low speed or by hand until the dough comes together, about 1 minute.

**TO MAKE THE CHEESECAKE BATTER**

1. In a large bowl, using an electric mixer on medium speed or a wooden spoon, beat together the cream cheese powdered milk, and sugar until light and creamy. This will take about 3 minutes if using an electric mixer or 5 to 6 minutes if creaming by hand. Add the egg and vanilla, and beat to combine.

2. Spread half of the cookie dough in an even layer in the bottom of the prepared pan. Spread the cheesecake batter on top of the cookie dough in the pan. Add the remaining cookie dough on top of the cheesecake batter by pinching off pieces of the dough and placing them on top of the cheesecake batter until all or most of the cheesecake is covered with the dough.

3. Bake for 35 to 38 minutes, until the top is golden and a skewer or toothpick comes out without batter on it.

4. Let cool to room temperature, then refrigerate for 1 to 2 hours to set. To serve, cut into 12 bars. Serve chilled.

Substitute another flavor of sandwich cookie for the chocolate sandwich cookies for a fun twist on these bars.

# No-Bake Rocky Road Bars

**MAKES 9 BARS**
Prep: 20 minutes
Chill: 1 hour
Shelf Life: 4 to 5 days

Nonstick cooking spray

1 ¾ cups chocolate sandwich cookie crumbs

5 tablespoons unsalted butter, melted

2 cups semisweet chocolate chips

3 tablespoons salted butter, melted

1 tablespoon vegetable oil

3 cups mini marshmallows

¾ cup chopped walnuts

Another ice cream inspiration coming right up! These bars have a thin chocolate cookie crust. On top of the crust are marshmallows and walnuts enrobed in a thin layer of semisweet chocolate. They have a great texture from the crunchy cookie base, fluffy marshmallows, and bits of walnut.

1. Line an 8-inch square baking pan with aluminum foil and spray it with cooking spray.
2. In a medium bowl, combine the chocolate cookie crumbs and unsalted butter. Stir until the butter has coated all the crumbs. Press the crumbs evenly into the bottom of the prepared pan.
3. Put the chocolate chips and salted butter in a large microwave-safe bowl and heat on 50 percent power in 30-second intervals, stirring in between, until melted and smooth. Stir the vegetable oil into the chocolate, which will loosen it up. Using a rubber spatula, fold in the marshmallows and walnuts until everything is coated with chocolate.
4. Pour the mixture on top of the chocolate cookie crust and spread it out evenly. Press the marshmallows to make the bars a little more compact. Refrigerate for at least 1 hour to set. To serve, cut into 9 bars. Serve chilled.

Not a fan of semisweet chocolate? Substitute milk chocolate chips for a sweeter bar.

# Frosted Sugar Cookie Bars

**MAKES 12 BARS**
Prep: 35 minutes
Bake: 40 to 45 minutes
Shelf Life: 4 to 5 days

**FOR THE COOKIE DOUGH**

Nonstick cooking spray
2 cups all-purpose flour
1 tablespoon cornstarch
½ teaspoon baking powder
½ teaspoon table salt
½ cup (1 stick) unsalted butter, room temperature
1 ¼ cups granulated sugar
1 large egg
½ cup sour cream
2 teaspoons pure vanilla extract

**FOR THE FROSTING**

¾ cup (1 ½ sticks) unsalted butter, at room temperature
3 cups confectioners' sugar
3 tablespoons milk
1 tablespoon pure vanilla extract
Gel paste food coloring (optional)

These bars are perfect when you don't have time to mess around with cut-outs or drop cookies. They are dense, but moist. I love that they are so much easier than regular sugar cookies, but taste just as delicious.

**TO MAKE THE COOKIE DOUGH**

1. Preheat the oven to 350°F. Line an 11-by-7-inch baking pan with aluminum foil and spray it with cooking spray.
2. In a medium mixing bowl, sift or whisk together the flour, cornstarch, baking powder, and salt.
3. In a large mixing bowl, using an electric mixer on medium speed or a wooden spoon, beat together the butter and sugar until light and creamy. This will take about 3 minutes if using an electric mixer or 5 to 6 minutes if creaming by hand. Add the egg, sour cream, and vanilla, and beat to combine. Add the dry ingredients and beat on low speed or by hand until the dough comes together, about 1 minute. Spread the cookie dough in the prepared pan in an even layer.
4. Bake for 40 to 45 minutes, until the top is golden and a skewer or toothpick inserted into the center comes out clean or with crumbs, but not batter.
5. Let the cookie layer cool completely to room temperature before adding the frosting.

**TO MAKE THE FROSTING**

1. In a large bowl, beat together the butter, confectioners' sugar, milk, and vanilla for about 1 minute, until light and fluffy. Add food coloring if you like.

2. Spread the frosting on the cooled sugar cookie layer. To serve, cut into 12 bars.

Finish these cookies off by using a spoon or your finger to make a repeated small circular pattern in the top of the frosting. Sprinkle festive sprinkles or rainbow sprinkles on top.

# Maple-Pecan Oatmeal Bars

**MAKES 15 BARS**
Prep: 20 minutes
Bake: 30 to 35 minutes
Shelf Life: 4 to 5 days

- Nonstick cooking spray
- 1 3/4 cups all-purpose flour
- 1 teaspoon baking powder
- 1/2 teaspoon baking soda
- 1/2 teaspoon table salt
- 1 cup (2 sticks) unsalted butter, at room temperature
- 1 cup packed light brown sugar
- 1/2 cup granulated sugar
- 2 large eggs
- 1 teaspoon maple extract
- 1 3/4 cups old-fashioned rolled oats
- 1 cup chopped pecans

These bars are dense and chewy and loaded with old-fashioned oats and bits of pecans. If I use pecans, you better believe maple is to follow. The maple flavor brings everything together to make this bar highly addicting. I recommend trying it with some vanilla ice cream.

1. Preheat the oven to 350°F. Line a 9-by-13-inch baking pan with aluminum foil and spray it with cooking spray.
2. In a medium mixing bowl, sift or whisk together the flour, baking powder, baking soda, and salt.
3. In a large mixing bowl, using an electric mixer on medium speed or a wooden spoon, beat together the butter and both sugars until light and creamy. This will take about 3 minutes if using an electric mixer or 5 to 6 minutes if creaming by hand. Add the eggs and maple extract, and beat to combine. Add the dry ingredients and the oats, and beat on low speed or by hand until the dough comes together, about 1 minute. Using a rubber spatula, fold in the pecans until incorporated.
4. Spread the cookie dough evenly in the prepared pan.
5. Bake for 30 to 35 minutes, until the top is golden brown.
6. Let cool to room temperature. To serve, cut into 15 bars.

Not a nut person? Omit the pecans in these bars.

# Piña Colada Bars

**MAKES 9 BARS**
Prep: 30 minutes
Chill: 1 hour
Bake: About 1 hour 5 minutes
Shelf Life: 4 to 5 days

**FOR THE CRUST**

Nonstick cooking spray

1 cup all-purpose flour

1 tablespoon cornstarch

¼ teaspoon table salt

½ cup (1 stick) unsalted butter, at room temperature

½ cup confectioners' sugar

1 teaspoon pure vanilla extract

**FOR THE FILLING**

3 large eggs

¼ cup granulated sugar

¾ cup sweetened condensed milk

2 tablespoons maraschino cherry juice

4 cups sweetened flaked coconut

1 cup crushed pineapple, drained

20 maraschino cherries, quartered

¼ cup all-purpose flour

These bars are similar to coconut macaroons, but they have sweetened coconut, crushed pineapple, and maraschino cherries and juice to flavor them. The bars have a light pink color from the cherry juice, which gives them a nice, summery feel. They hold together beautifully, too.

**TO MAKE THE CRUST**

1. Preheat the oven to 350°F. Line an 8-inch square baking pan with aluminum foil and it spray with cooking spray.

2. In a medium mixing bowl, sift or whisk together the flour, cornstarch, and salt.

3. In a large mixing bowl, using an electric mixer on medium speed or a wooden spoon, beat together the butter and sugar until light and creamy. This will take about 3 minutes if using an electric mixer or 5 to 6 minutes if creaming by hand. Add the vanilla and beat to combine. Add the dry ingredients and beat on low speed or by hand until the dough comes together, about 1 minute. Press the dough evenly into the prepared pan.

4. Bake for 15 minutes. Remove the pan from the oven and reduce the oven temperature to 325°F.

**TO MAKE THE FILLING**

1. In a large bowl, beat together the eggs, sugar, sweetened condensed milk, and maraschino cherry juice for about 1 minute, until frothy. Fold in the coconut, crushed pineapple, and maraschino cherries, and stir until everything is coated with the egg mixture. Sprinkle the flour on top of the mixture and fold it in until it is incorporated.

2. Pour the filling on top of the baked crust, spreading it out evenly.

3. Bake for about 50 minutes, until bits of coconut are golden brown and there's no liquid sitting on top of the bars.

4. Let cool to room temperature and refrigerate for 1 hour to set. To serve, cut into 9 bars. Serve chilled.

These are tall bars; to create a shorter bar, use an 11-by-7-inch baking pan.

# Strawberry Cheesecake Crumb Bars

**MAKES 12 BARS**
Prep: 35 minutes
Chill: 1 hour
Bake: 40 to 45 minutes
Shelf Life: 4 to 5 days

**FOR THE CHEESECAKE**

8 ounces cream cheese, at room temperature

⅓ cup granulated sugar

1 large egg

1 teaspoon pure vanilla extract

**FOR THE CRUST**

Nonstick cooking spray

1 cup (2 sticks) unsalted butter, at room temperature

1 cup confectioners' sugar

½ cup granulated sugar

2 teaspoons pure vanilla extract

2 cups flour

½ teaspoon table salt

¾ cup strawberry jam

I'm all about these buttery bars. The strawberry jam and cheesecake filling go perfectly together. In fact, I like it so much I would eat cream cheese and strawberry jam every day on a bagel if I could get away with it. The golden-brown crumb topping is pretty nice, too.

**TO MAKE THE CHEESECAKE**

In a large mixing bowl, using an electric mixer on medium speed or a wooden spoon, beat together the cream cheese and sugar until light and creamy. This will take about 3 minutes if using an electric mixer or 5 to 6 minutes if creaming by hand. Add the egg and vanilla, and beat to combine. Set aside.

**TO MAKE THE CRUST**

1. Preheat the oven to 350°F. Line an 11-by-7-inch baking pan with aluminum foil and spray it with cooking spray.

2. In a large mixing bowl, using an electric mixer on medium speed or a wooden spoon, beat together the butter and both sugars until light and creamy. This will take about 3 minutes if using an electric mixer or 5 to 6 minutes if creaming by hand. Add the vanilla and beat to combine. Add the flour and salt, and beat on low speed or by hand just until the flour is incorporated, about 1 minute.

3. Press three-quarters of the crust dough evenly into the bottom of the prepared pan.

4. Spread the cheesecake batter on top of the shortbread.

5. Drop the jam by the spoonful on top of the cheesecake. Use a butter knife or toothpick to swirl it through the cheesecake batter.

6. Add bits of the crust dough on top of the jam and cheesecake. The cheesecake and jam don't need to be completely covered.

7. Bake for 40 to 45 minutes, until the cheesecake is set. Gently shake the pan; if the batter jiggles slightly, it's done.

8. Let cool to room temperature and then refrigerate for 2 to 3 hours to set. To serve, cut into 12 bars. Serve chilled.

Strawberries and cream cheese taste amazing together, but you can substitute grape jam or any other flavor for the strawberry.

# Pumpkin Streusel Bars

**MAKES 9 BARS**
Prep: 25 minutes
Chill: 2 hours
Bake: 35 to 40 minutes
Shelf Life: 3 to 4 days

**FOR THE CRUST**

Nonstick cooking spray

1 cup all-purpose flour

1 tablespoon cornstarch

¼ teaspoon table salt

¼ teaspoon ground cinnamon

½ cup (1 stick) unsalted butter, at room temperature

¼ cup packed light brown sugar

¼ cup confectioners' sugar

1 teaspoon pure vanilla extract

**FOR THE CUSTARD**

1 cup packed light brown sugar

1 teaspoon cinnamon

½ teaspoon ground nutmeg

¼ teaspoon ground ginger

¼ teaspoon ground cloves

1 (15-ounce) can pumpkin purée (not pumpkin pie filling)

3 large eggs

1 teaspoon pure vanilla extract

¼ teaspoon maple extract

½ cup evaporated milk

I had to be on point with this recipe since my husband is a die-hard pumpkin pie fan. These bars have a sweet pumpkin pie custard and a brown sugar shortbread base. Add a dollop of whipped cream and I bet these bars could replace your next pumpkin pie!

**TO MAKE THE CRUST**

1. Preheat the oven to 350°F. Line an 8-inch square baking pan with aluminum foil and coat it with cooking spray.
2. In a medium mixing bowl, sift or whisk together the flour, cornstarch, salt, and cinnamon.
3. In a large mixing bowl, using an electric mixer on medium speed or a wooden spoon, beat together the butter and both sugars until light and creamy. This will take about 3 minutes if using an electric mixer or 5 to 6 minutes if creaming by hand. Add the vanilla and beat to combine. Add the dry ingredients and beat on low speed or by hand until the dough comes together, about 1 minute.
4. Press the cookie dough evenly into the prepared pan.
5. Bake for 15 minutes.

#### TO MAKE THE CUSTARD

1. In a large mixing bowl, whisk together the brown sugar, cinnamon, nutmeg, ginger, and cloves. Add the pumpkin and stir to incorporate. Whisk in the eggs, vanilla, and maple extract until incorporated. Whisk in the evaporated milk.
2. Pour the pumpkin pie custard on top of the shortbread.
3. Bake for 35 to 40 minutes, until the center is set. Gently shake the pan, and if the center jiggles, it's done.
4. Let cool to room temperature and then refrigerate for 2 hours to set. To serve, cut into 9 bars. Serve chilled.

Finish off these bars with a dollop of whipped cream. Whip up a batch by beating 1 cup heavy cream with 1 to 2 tablespoons confectioners' sugar until thick and puffy. It should stay firm on the beater when lifted out of the bowl.

# Peanut Butter Overload Bars

**MAKES 15 BARS**
Prep: 20 minutes
Bake: 40 to 45 minutes
Shelf Life: 4 to 5 days

- Nonstick cooking spray
- 2 ¼ cups all-purpose flour
- 1 teaspoon baking soda
- ½ teaspoon table salt
- 1 cup (2 sticks) unsalted butter, at room temperature
- 1 cup creamy peanut butter
- 1 ½ cups packed light brown sugar
- ½ cup granulated sugar
- 2 large eggs
- 2 teaspoons pure vanilla extract
- 2 ¼ cups all-purpose flour
- 1 teaspoon baking soda
- ½ teaspoon table salt
- ¾ cup peanut butter chips
- ¾ cup Reese's Pieces
- ¾ cup mini peanut butter cups

"Hey, let's throw everything peanut butter into a bar!" I have no regrets. This one is for my entire family since we are all crazy for peanut butter. It's a peanut butter cookie loaded with peanut butter chips, peanut butter cups, and peanut butter candies.

1. Preheat the oven to 350°F. Line a 9-by-13-inch baking pan with aluminum foil and spray with cooking spray.
2. In a medium mixing bowl, sift or whisk together the flour, baking soda, and salt.
3. In a large bowl, using an electric mixer on medium or a wooden spoon, beat together the butter, peanut butter, and both sugars until light and creamy. This will take about 3 minutes if using an electric mixer or 5 to 6 minutes if beating by hand. Add the eggs and vanilla, and beat to combine. Add the dry ingredients and beat on low speed or by hand just until incorporated, about 1 minute. Using a rubber spatula, fold in the peanut butter chips, Reese's Pieces, and peanut butter cups until incorporated.
4. Spread the dough in the prepared pan.
5. Bake for 40 to 45 minutes, until the top is golden and a skewer or toothpick inserted into the center comes out clean or with crumbs, but no batter.
6. Let cool completely in the pan and then cut into 15 bars.

Do you prefer peanut butter M&Ms? Substitute them for the Reese's Pieces. In fact, the peanut butter chips, Reese's Pieces, and mini peanut butter cups can all be switched out for your favorite peanut butter candy.

# Chocolate Granola Bars

**MAKES 12 BARS**
Prep: 20 minutes
Chill: 1 hour
Shelf Life: 4 to 5 days

- Nonstick cooking spray
- 2 cups rice cereal
- 2 ½ cups quick-cooking oats
- ¼ cup packed light brown sugar
- ¼ cup honey
- ½ cup (1 stick) unsalted butter
- ¼ teaspoon table salt
- 2 teaspoons pure vanilla extract
- 1 cup mini chocolate chips
- 1 cup semisweet chocolate chips

These bars have a nice crunch from the rice cereal and chew from the oats. They are best stored in the refrigerator to firm up and then cut into bars. The bottom is coated with chocolate for an over-the-top bar. Plus, it helps it hold together better!

1. Line a 9-by-13-inch baking pan with parchment paper. Coat the sides of the pan and the parchment paper with cooking spray.
2. In a large bowl, stir together the rice cereal and oats.
3. In a small saucepan, bring the brown sugar, honey, butter, and salt to a boil over medium heat. Let the mixture boil for 2 minutes while stirring often. Remove from the heat and stir in the vanilla. Pour the mixture into the bowl with the cereal and oats and stir to coat. Let the mixture cool for 5 minutes, then stir in the mini chocolate chips.
4. Press the granola mixture into the prepared pan. Use a piece of wax paper to press it down if the mixture is sticking to your spatula.
5. Refrigerate for at least 1 hour to set. Cut the granola into 3 rows of 4 bars.
6. Put the regular chocolate chips in a microwave-safe bowl that is long enough to fit the bars and heat on 50 percent power in 30-second intervals, stirring in between, until melted and smooth.
7. Dip just the bottoms of the chilled bars in the chocolate and place on a piece of wax paper to dry.

For extra crunch, after dipping the bottoms of the bars into chocolate, dip them into rice cereal and place them on the wax paper to dry. You will need 1 to 1½ cups more rice cereal.

# Chocolate Chip Cookie Dough Cheesecake Bars

**MAKES 12 BARS**
Prep: 35 minutes
Chill: 1 hour
Bake: 30 to 35 minutes
Shelf Life: 3 to 4 days

**FOR THE CRUST**

Nonstick cooking spray

1 ½ cups graham cracker crumbs

5 tablespoons unsalted butter, melted

1 tablespoon granulated sugar

**FOR THE CHEESECAKE**

12 ounces cream cheese, at room temperature

½ cup granulated sugar

1 large egg

¼ cup sour cream

1 teaspoon pure vanilla extract

These cheesecake bars with bits of cookie dough baked into them make the perfect chilled dessert. The family, especially kids, will go crazy for them. I love the idea of using a traditional graham cracker crust like the one you would find under a cheesecake.

**TO MAKE THE CRUST**

1. Preheat the oven to 350°F. Line an 11-by-7-inch baking pan with aluminum foil and spray it with cooking spray.

2. In a large mixing bowl, stir together the graham cracker crumbs, melted butter, and sugar until the mixture resembles wet sand. Press the mixture evenly into the prepared pan.

**TO MAKE THE CHEESECAKE**

1. In a large mixing bowl, using an electric mixer on medium speed or a wooden spoon, cream together the cream cheese and sugar until light and creamy. This will take about 3 minutes if using an electric mixer or 5 to 6 minutes if creaming by hand. Add the egg, sour cream, and vanilla, and beat to combine.

2. Pour the cheesecake mixture on top of the crust mixture in the baking pan.

### FOR THE COOKIE DOUGH

¼ cup (½ stick) unsalted butter, at room temperature

½ cup packed light brown sugar

2 tablespoons granulated sugar

2 tablespoons milk

1 teaspoon pure vanilla extract

1 cup all-purpose flour

¼ teaspoon table salt

½ cup mini chocolate chips

### TO MAKE THE COOKIE DOUGH

1. In a large mixing bowl, using an electric mixer on medium speed or a wooden spoon, beat together the butter and both sugars until light and creamy. This will take about 3 minutes if using an electric mixer or 5 to 6 minutes if creaming by hand. Add the milk and vanilla, and beat to combine. Add the flour and salt and beat on low speed or by hand just until incorporated, about 1 minute. With a rubber spatula, fold in the mini chocolate chips.

2. Pinch pieces of the cookie dough and scatter them on top of the cheesecake. The cheesecake should be peeking through.

3. Bake for 30 to 35 minutes until the center of the cheese-cake is set. Shake the pan gently, and if it jiggles, it's done.

4. Let cool completely to room temperature. Cover and refrigerate for 2 to 3 hours to set. To serve, cut into 12 bars. Serve chilled.

Turn the cheesecake into a chocolate cheesecake by beating 4 ounces of melted milk chocolate or baking chocolate in with the cream cheese and sugar.

APPENDIX A

# MEASUREMENT CONVERSIONS

## VOLUME EQUIVALENTS (LIQUID)

| US STANDARD | US STANDARD (OUNCES) | METRIC (APPROXIMATE) |
|---|---|---|
| 2 tablespoons | 1 fl. oz. | 30 mL |
| ¼ cup | 2 fl. oz. | 60 mL |
| ½ cup | 4 fl. oz. | 120 mL |
| 1 cup | 8 fl. oz. | 240 mL |
| 1½ cups | 12 fl. oz. | 355 mL |
| 2 cups or 1 pint | 16 fl. oz. | 475 mL |
| 4 cups or 1 quart | 32 fl. oz. | 1 L |
| 1 gallon | 128 fl. oz. | 4 L |

## OVEN TEMPERATURES

| FAHRENHEIT | CELSIUS (APPROXIMATE) |
|---|---|
| 250°F | 120°C |
| 300°F | 150°C |
| 325°F | 165°C |
| 350°F | 180°C |
| 375°F | 190°C |
| 400°F | 200°C |
| 425°F | 220°C |
| 450°F | 230°C |

## VOLUME EQUIVALENTS (DRY)

| US STANDARD | METRIC (APPROXIMATE) |
|---|---|
| ⅛ teaspoon | 0.5 mL |
| ¼ teaspoon | 1 mL |
| ½ teaspoon | 2 mL |
| ¾ teaspoon | 4 mL |
| 1 teaspoon | 5 mL |
| 1 tablespoon | 15 mL |
| ¼ cup | 59 mL |
| ⅓ cup | 79 mL |
| ½ cup | 118 mL |
| ⅔ cup | 156 mL |
| ¾ cup | 177 mL |
| 1 cup | 235 mL |
| 2 cups or 1 pint | 475 mL |
| 3 cups | 700 mL |
| 4 cups or 1 quart | 1 L |

## WEIGHT EQUIVALENTS

| US STANDARD | METRIC (APPROXIMATE) |
|---|---|
| ½ ounce | 15 g |
| 1 ounce | 30 g |
| 2 ounces | 60 g |
| 4 ounces | 115 g |
| 8 ounces | 225 g |
| 12 ounces | 340 g |
| 16 ounces or 1 pound | 455 g |

APPENDIX B

# WEIGHT CONVERSION CHART

| | 1 CUP | 1 TABLESPOON | 1 TEASPOON |
|---|---|---|---|
| ALL-PURPOSE FLOUR | 120g | 8g | 3g |
| CAKE FLOUR | 120g | 8g | 3g |
| SIFTED CAKE FLOUR | 100g | 7g | 2g |
| SUGAR (GRANULATED, BROWN, SUPERFINE) | 200g | 13g | 4g |
| POWDERED SUGAR | 120g | 8g | 3g |
| COCOA POWDER | 80g | 5g | 2g |
| CHOCOLATE, CHOPPED | 168g | 11g | 4g |
| BUTTER | 224g | 14g | 5g |

28 grams = 1 ounce

For a more comprehensive list, visit the USDA Food Composition Database
https://ndb.nal.usda.gov

# RECIPE INDEX

# INDEX

## C

## G



## H



## I



## J



## L

## P



## Q



## R

# ACKNOWLEDGMENTS

To my husband, who has always been incredibly supportive of me and picked up the slack while I worked on this book, thank you! You are an amazing man.

To my dad, who thinks I can do anything, and my mom, who helped make me the baker I am—I'm lucky to call you two my parents.

Lastly, I owe a *huge* thanks to the Roefs family, who critiqued every recipe with me. Sorry about the weight gain!

# ABOUT THE AUTHOR

**MIRANDA COUSE** is the baker and photographer behind the dessert blog *Cookie Dough and Oven Mitt*, where her main focus is sweets and baked treats. She's been featured in *Redbook*, *Country Living*, *Parade* magazine, and *Buzzfeed*. Miranda lives in upstate New York.

CPSIA information can be obtained
at www.ICGtesting.com
Printed in the USA
BVOW05s2223121017
496653BV00002BA/2/P